Making V

David Robb (2nd Mate) and me on *Dentonia Park*

Making Waves

A mariner's tale, 1939-48
Paddle steamer to liner …
Portuguese coaster to Norwegian tanker

Charles Aitchison

Maritime Heritage
from
The NOSTALGIA *Collection*

© Charles Aitchison 2010

All rights reserved. No part of this publication may be reproduced, stored in a retrieval system or transmitted, in any form or by any means, electronic, mechanical, photocopying, recording or otherwise, without prior permission in writing from Silver Link Publishing Ltd.

First published in 2010

British Library Cataloguing in Publication Data

A catalogue record for this book is available from the British Library.

ISBN 978 1 85794 327 6

Printed and bound in the Czech Republic

Some photographs remain uncredited – the author has tried in every case to discover the copyright holder, but it has proved impossible.

SLP

Silver Link Publishing Ltd

The Trundle Ringstead Road Great Addington
Kettering Northants NN14 4BW

Tel/Fax: 01536 330588
email: sales@nostalgiacollection.com
Website: www.nostalgiacollection.com

Contents

1	My First Ship	6
2	Life on board a liner	19
3	Life on a tramp steamer	37
4	Under a foreign flag	57
5	More foreign flags	64
6	Two more tankers and a liner	83
7	On a convoy Rescue Ship	102
8	My last days on the lower deck	122
9	A short spell ashore	138
10	A new lifestyle	146
11	On a Glasgow tramp	162
12	The *Masunda*	173
13	The 'run job'	187
14	My last ship: part 1	196
15	My last ship: part 2	208
16	My last ship: part 3	221
17	My last ship: part 4	231

Appendix:

   Background to ships and the sea   244

Index   249

1

My first ship

'At Banavie we see RMS *Gondolier* – red funnel, white superstructure and shimmering brass.' Thus did MacBrayne's advertise their steamer that was to take passengers through Loch Lochy, Loch Oich, Loch Ness and the Caledonian Canal between Banavie and Inverness.

Alas, I was the one that had to do most of the shimmering. As 1st class pantry boy I had to polish all the portholes from the paddles to the stern, while the 3rd class pantry boy was limited to those from the paddles to the bow – a less daunting task.

Since she was a paddle steamer, she could have been referred to as PS *Gondolier*, but as she carried the odd bag of mail, her owners preferred the grander title of Royal Mail Steamer.

It was all part of a luxury two-day trip between Glasgow and Inverness. The *Gondolier* took passengers from Inverness to Banavie, where they boarded a train for the short journey to Fort William. This was to avoid a lengthy negotiation of the eight locks (called Neptune's Staircase) that formed the 62-foot drop from the canal to Loch Linnhe. They then boarded the *Loch Fyne* and sailed to Oban to spend the night there.

On the following day they went by bus to Ardrishaig where the *Saint Columba* picked them up and took them to Glasgow. Next day was the reverse. So on Mondays, Wednesdays and Fridays the *Gondolier* sailed south and on Tuesdays, Thursdays and Saturdays we went north. Obviously the trip could have been done by train in one day at a great deal less expense, so we had many passengers that were pretty affluent, and the catering reflected this. Since Queen Victoria had sailed up the Great Glen in 1873, that part of journey from Banavie to Inverness came to be known as the Royal Route.

For the technically minded the *Gondolier* was built in 1866, had a double-expansion steam engine, a haystack boiler and was reputed to be the first ship to have oscillating cylinders.

*

My first ship

But let us go back a bit. I had left school in 1939 and was looking for some interesting activity before taking up the serious business of training to be a civil engineer. My father's relations had a place in Fort Augustus called the Richmond House Hotel, although calling it an hotel was stretching things a bit. It boasted three public rooms, six bedrooms, and a room for a maid.

While there on holiday as a lad, I had often seen *Gondolier* passing through the five locks there. She fairly towered above her surroundings and was clearly the highlight of the day, both for the locals and the tourists. I was most impressed and this gave me a somewhat romantic view of the steamer.

As she ran for only the months of June, July, August and the first half of September, this seemed the answer to my search for a summer diversion. My father's cousin was her Purser, so it was a simple matter of asking him to put forward my name for a job.

I was offered pantry boy or chocolate boy. Chocolate boy did not seem to me to be a real job, so I chose pantry boy. Well, instead of being a diversion it turned out to be the hardest work I had ever done.

At Inverness I rose at 6.30am and my first task was to make up the beds of the Purser, the Checker (assistant Purser) and my own. We had no cabins and slept in the 1st class lounge after the passengers had departed. This meant that all my worldly goods were in a suitcase in a locker under the cushions in this lounge, and I had to look out what I needed for each day as I could hardly ask a 1st class voyager to rise while I delved into my locker.

The milk and bread had then to be taken on board and stored. The ladder leading down to the saloon was scrubbed and the brass boiler for making tea had to be polished. Next I tackled the job of making 16 dishes of butterballs, and by the time I had finished all my tasks it was 8.30am, the ship had cast off, and the passengers were appearing for breakfast. This consisted of a choice of cereal or porridge, followed by fried fish, then bacon, eggs and toast. It was certainly a good start to their day.

After this, the Officers arrived for their breakfast, and by the time we had finished with them and cleaned up we had our own meal at 10am. I had been working since 6.30am and all I had had in that time was a cup of tea and a biscuit. Scarcely was our meal over when the passengers that had breakfasted were now descending on us for their morning coffee.

My main job was to take whatever was necessary from the galley (ship's kitchen) to the pantry and to wash up all the dishes, glasses and cutlery. The sink was filled with cold water and heated by a steam pipe that entered at the bottom of the sink. A bar of soap was placed in an old tin that was riddled with holes, and this was held over the pipe until the water was very hot and soapy. It was so hot that my hands (we were not permitted to use cloths) could be in the water for only 2 seconds at a time. Glasses were washed first, cutlery next and dishes last. The drying was done with what was termed a pantry cloth, which would be about 4 feet long and 2 feet wide. We usually lifted and dried about five plates at a time.

The saloon-steward, Andy Haxton, took in hand my training. First of all he demonstrated how to make a sailor's bed. Then he showed me how to make up the butterballs and how to dry dishes and cutlery at speed. MacBrayne's cups looked as if they had been specially designed for Andy's methods, for they could be picked up by the right hand and held firmly in the cloth while the left hand inserted the other part of the cloth into its interior. A short sharp twist in opposite directions by both hands finished with the thumbs meeting inside the handle and resulted in the cup being completely dry – and this meant even the handle.

Andy had been a steward on trains and certainly knew his stuff. He regularly carried five plates of soup from the pantry out to the dining saloon. Two were clutched in his left hand, while the other three were balanced on his left arm, leaving his right hand free to do any steadying required. He claimed that, if pushed, he could manage seven plates at a time. I found this hard to believe so, to dispel my doubts, he filled seven soup plates with water and gave me an exhibition of his ability.

We stocked Lea & Perrins Worcester Sauce, and one day Andy said to me, 'Put a drop or two of that in your soup lad, and you'll think every day is your birthday.'

However, when taking his advice the 2nd steward told me to watch while he put some of this sauce on a piece of cloth and dragged it across the copper boiler. It produced a bright shimmering swathe across the dull copper-coloured surface. 'That's what Lea & Perrins does to your stomach,' said he.

They were both having fun at my inexperience, for I did not then appreciate that there were acids in my stomach much stronger than any that the firm of Lea & Perrins could concoct.

I did not object to hard work, or even long hours, but I had a feeling that conditions were unhealthy. Most of the day I was working in the pantry where there was very little ventilation. The porthole in the pantry could not be opened while sailing as it was aft of the paddles and would allow water to come cascading in. The heat was so intense that I was usually compelled to discard all clothing save for trousers and white jacket.

My first ship

For breakfast and high tea the stewards wore a conventional dark blue single-breasted jacket with maroon silk lapels on which was embroidered in gold the famous MacBrayne's crest. However, for lunch they had a posh white tunic fastened diagonally down the front with silver buttons. It also had two silver buttons on each shoulder, ornamented with twisted blue silk cord between each button. It was most impressive.

MacBrayne's had many ships in their fleet and these sailed all over the west of Scotland. This occasioned the four-line stanza:

> 'The earth belongeth to the Lord,
> And all that it contains;
> Except the Western Isles for they
> Belongeth to MacBraynes.'

On any day of the week, every ship in the MacBrayne's fleet had exactly the same menu. This was to ensure that any traveller going from one of their vessels to another would not have to face the same fare again. For instance, on Mondays the sweet would be whole rice, on Tuesdays it was ground rice, Wednesdays provided rice custard, next day semolina, then sago and finally on Saturdays it was plum duff.

Lunch was a five-course affair and cost 3s 6d, a sum that would then take three hours for a working man to earn. The soup was followed by fresh salmon and salad, then there was a choice of joint or entrée. After this came the dessert (quite a selection of puddings, jellies and fruit) and finally biscuits and a variety of cheeses with coffee.

The 3rd class passengers dined in the fore-cabin and their lunch cost only 2s 6d, as they were not given the salmon and salad, or the cheese and coffee. Actually this 2s 6d – or 'half-crown' – lunch was available to any of the 1st class tourists if they were to choose it. I recollect that when the chief steward was carving up the joint in the pantry he would ask the serving steward if the recipient was a 'half crooner' – if so he did not give out as good a cut as the others got.

Lunch landed me with about 300 dishes, and there were two sittings, at 12 noon and 1pm. Add to this the fact that the 3rd class saloon rang a bell for their lunch at 12.30pm and quite a few of them finished by mistake with us. As they were all potential tippers the stewards did not turn them away if there was any room.

The stewards came to the hatch in the front of the pantry and asked for whatever was required. I distinctly recall that the gender of the diner was always specified. For example, the steward might say,

'Three gents' roast beef and two ladies' roast beefs'; the ladies always got a much smaller portion.

Years later, when I was about to be married and my fiancée and I were looking at bedroom furniture, we were shown two wardrobes, one considerably larger that the other. Being so conditioned by my experiences on the *Gondolier* I remarked to the salesman that the big one would probably be mine.

With a horrified look on his face he replied, 'Oh no sir – that's the lady's.' I then found out that in many ways the lady was now to come off better.

Back to the *Gondolier*. After the second sitting the officers came for lunch. By the time it was served and we had finished cleaning up after them, it was after 2.45pm before we had ours. There was no meal hour or anything like it; the longer I took, the more dishes were piling up for my return. By this time the passengers that had taken the first lunch were coming at us for their afternoon tea! This consisted of toast, scones and cakes.

Our food was outstandingly good. I do not suppose that it was MacBrayne's intention to see that we all enjoyed such excellent cuisine; rather, I fancy, it would have been uneconomic to have had to provide two different lots of grub. Naturally at lunch we did not get the salmon and salad – or the cheese and coffee course.

None of the steam pipes leading to the pantry were lagged and, when scrubbing the deck, I often had the misfortune to let my arm come in contact with one and the result was a nasty burn. These were dressed by the Checker, who was a second-year medical student.

'It's a good job we have someone like you here to do this sort of thing,' I remarked.

'Why?' asked he.

'Well,' I replied, 'you must have had plenty of practice, seeing that you are studying medicine.'

'Oh, no,' he countered, 'all I've done so far is to cut up dead bodies. I learned to bandage in the Boy Scouts.'

We arrived at Banavie about 3.40pm and the passengers left. The vessel was only 4 or 5 yards short of the width of the canal so the galley boy and the two pantry boys had to turn out on deck to help the bosun and four deckhands cant the ship so that she was facing north for the return voyage.

As soon as this was accomplished I had to go to the post office to collect any mail. I then joined the other pantry boy and the galley boy on the quay, where they were peeling two large sacks of potatoes for the following day.

While we were doing this, the deckhands were coaling the ship.

My first ship

It was quite a primitive method of pushing barrows loaded from a truck (in the railway siding above the pier) and wheeling them on to the ship. After this they washed her down with fresh water and she was always remarkably clean.

On the way north I did not have to rise until 7am as we did not sail until 11.30am, having to wait until the *Loch Fyne* had delivered our passengers. It was before this that all the outside polishing had to be done. We were given Brasso to do this work but were constantly reminded how lucky we were as, until recently, the job had been done using oil and something called 'bath brick'.

This time we had no voyagers for breakfast but we had them for high tea about 5pm when the ship was near Foyers, on Loch Ness. If a flag was hoisted on the pier at Foyers we went alongside to pick up a few more passengers, otherwise we kept sailing for Inverness.

One day, when heading up Loch Ness, the skipper sighted an odd object on the surface of the loch, and all on board were agog at the possibility of seeing the monster. Excitement was intense until we drew near and discovered that it was one of the spheres used by drift-net fishermen to buoy their nets.

On the subject of the monster, my father's uncle Tom (father of the Purser) and my cousin Ian both claimed to have seen it. As Tom was returning from a funeral at the time of the incident, he was greatly disbelieved. Many folk from the south fancy that Highlanders allege to have seen it in order to enjoy the publicity. I found the reverse much more likely. Certainly there are people who may well have seen something but are disinclined to go public for fear of being ridiculed.

We usually arrived at Inverness at 6.30pm. I stocked up on biscuits, butter and other stores from MacBrayne's warehouse for the next day, then, when I had laid out three beds in the saloon, I could go off for the evening.

In the middle of the season, on Tuesday evenings, we ran a cruise from Inverness to Urquhart Castle and back. By the time we were tied up and the trippers (including drunks) were off, it was nearly midnight. No overtime was paid for this due to some legal quirk that no one quite understood.

We were paid on the Saturday afternoon and the cash for this was brought on board by my father's uncle Jack (from the hotel in Fort Augustus). I had swallowed the tale that he was strictly teetotal, but soon discovered that he had this veneer only when his sister Maggie was present. I could not believe my eyes when, on being asked if he would like 'a refreshment', he downed a generous glass of whisky.

On the subject of whisky, a bottle then cost 12s 6d, but when poured out as glasses it brought in £1 2s 6d. It was a common practice for a steward to buy a bottle, secrete it somewhere in the saloon; then, if a passenger should ask for a glass when the chief steward was absent, he would pour from this bottle and pocket the cash. Thus each bottle sold in this way could mean a gain of 10 shillings for the steward, or, to put it another way, about 80% profit! Of course MacBrayne's, who were buying their liquor at wholesale prices, were making more than that.

After six weeks the *Loch Fyne* had engine trouble and the *Loch Eil* took her place. Unfortunately she was about half a knot slower so that we now got away from Banavie half an hour later and did not reach Inverness till 7pm. But there was worse than that – the Tuesday cruise on Loch Ness now did not finish until 12.30am!

The total crew was 24: Master, Mate, bosun and four deckhands made up the deck squad, while the Chief Engineer (there was only one), donkeyman and fireman were the engine room staff. In the catering department we had the chief steward, 2nd steward, fore-cabin steward (to look after the 3rd class passengers), deck steward, saloon steward, cook, galley boy, pantry man and two pantry boys. To complete the picture there were the Purser, Checker, stewardess and chocolate boy.

To give some idea of the wages, the purser was paid £5 a week, a fairly good wage in those days and (discounting his free food) about 40% more than a tradesman. The cook received £3 and the stewards (who relied a lot on tips) got only £1 17s 6d. The pantry man got £1 and each of the pantry boys was paid 14s 6d. The chocolate boy was given 10 shillings, but his job was a sinecure. He looked after a small shop selling sweets, books and postcards. Twice each voyage he took a tray of his wares round the ship, and on top of this he got tips. To be fair to him he was so bored that he often helped me with the drying of the dishes.

Deckhands received £2 15s, but had to find their own grub. Of my 14s 6d, I sent home a 10 shilling note every week and lived on the remaining 4s 6d. I sent my clothes home to be laundered, but had to keep myself in haircuts, shoe leather and bus fares to and from Banavie and Fort William.

One day, when I was told to throw overboard some biscuits that were broken and thus unsuitable for our high-class diners, I chanced to see one of the deckhands nearby coiling a rope.

'Could you use these?' I asked him, thinking that it would be a shame to waste them on seagulls.

He grabbed the paper bag and made off at speed. The second time I did this Andy Haxton was close by.

'What the devil do you think you are doing?' he demanded.

I explained that I thought the sailors would appreciate them.

'Just let the chief steward catch you at that game and you'll get the sack.'

At that age I was a trifle ingenuous and did not think anything through. To the pure, all things are pure, and I did not realise that the chief steward might think the deckhands were paying me for the favours – and indeed, that I might not be above seeing to it that a few extra biscuits were broken if the supply fell short of the demand!

The head lockkeeper at Muirton Wharf (our berth when at Inverness) had five daughters and I began dating the middle one, Cathie, who was 15. We were doing fine until the youngest sister began to attach herself to us everywhere we went. I do not know whether this was individual initiative or parental scheming, but it became very irksome.

Since she was on a bicycle, we tried to make her pursuit as difficult as possible by choosing routes with plenty of steps – but she could not be deterred. I put it to her that if she persisted in stalking us I would let the air out of her tyres. She still refused so I carried out the deflation.

The minx continued to dog us and ride the bike, claiming that if the wheels were damaged her parents would send me the bill. Then followed an uneasy week until it dawned on me that, damaged or not, the parents were not going to make an issue of it.

As far as food was concerned, the ship's officers were a bunch of fads. The Purser insisted on having all his solids before being served with any beverages; the Mate did not want gravy; the skipper's tea had to be stewed for half an hour before he came to table otherwise he said it was too weak (maidens' water, I recall, was his favourite term); and the Chief Engineer had to have his fried egg turned in the pan while being fried.

One morning, as the engineer was impatiently tapping his eating utensils on the table waiting for his breakfast, it arrived with his egg 'sunny side up', as the saying then had it. No one quite knew what to do and it was too late to take it back to the galley. Recognising that this was a *Gondolier* version of the Gordian knot, I at once turned the egg upside down on his plate and sent it out to him. He ate it with relish and did not notice the difference.

The highlight of my day on the trip south was a visit and a cup of tea at my relations' hotel at Fort Augustus. We arrived at the bottom of the five locks at 11.20am, and did not leave the top lock until 11.55am.

The sluices were at that time opened by hand, as were the lock gates. The opening of the gates was done by capstans into which were inserted stout poles that were pushed by the lockkeepers and some of the deckhands. The skipper – always keen to knock a minute or two off the time of the passage – used his charm to persuade tourists on the banks of the canal that manning the capstans was a romantic activity, and the best possible way to spend half an hour. The locks are now fully electrified and it takes twice the time to go through them. This is termed progress!

Our deck steward, Alec Beaton, was very religious and, as well as church attendance on Sunday, he went to a prayer meeting every Thursday evening. One Thursday we put a knot at the foot of his pyjama trousers and played tug o' war with them to make the knot really firm. As we all slept in the lounge we got into our beds and waited for the fun to begin. Alec came in about 11.00pm and, as was his custom, sat for 10 minutes perusing his testament by means of a small torch while we all pretended to be sound asleep. Then came the moment for which we had been eagerly waiting. Alec tried in vain to get his legs into the trousers and, since we had no lights in the saloon then, it took him some time before he twigged what had happened.

When at last it dawned on him, he shouted, 'Out, out, boys!' and proceeded to use the pyjama trousers to lash out at all of the younger members in turn. As there was the knot to be considered, Alec got some satisfaction in hearing our yells but, all in all, it was worth it. Alec had a very red nose but, in my innocence, and bearing in mind his religious proclivity, I drew no conclusions from this.

I became friendly with the Checker, David Watt, and one warm evening at the Banavie end we swam together about half a mile up the canal.

'Do you fancy a swim across Loch Linnhe?' he enquired.

This took me aback – especially as I had only learned to swim just a few months earlier. He explained that every year there was a race across the loch from the west bank to Fort William.

I did not relish the notion but he said, 'Oh, come on. I'm sure you can do it and you'll be company for me.'

He added that although there was a gold medal and a silver cup for the winner, the next five (regardless of time taken) would all get silver medals.

So, on a very cold evening in August I lined up with the Checker and two local lads; another four entrants had wisely called off. I had no idea what was involved and did not even have any grease with me. Someone gave me a little Vaseline and I made the most of it.

I tried to find out what was the state of the tide, but opinions were mostly conflicting and I just had to head for the other side of the loch and hope for the best.

My first ship 15

When I was little more than half way across I heard a muffled cheer from the other bank. This turned out to be the Checker winning the race. I plodded on for a while accompanied by a boat containing two men and a boy. They kept me abreast of events and some time later let me know that the other competitors had given up. About 60 yards from the shore I felt really bad as my limbs had seized up and I was making little progress. The thought that I might be doing myself permanent injury occurred to me so I gave the distress signal to those in the boat. Since I was so close to the shore, and thought I would get a silver medal for finishing regardless of my time, I had a horrible feeling that they would try to persuade me to continue. Not so. They immediately hauled me into the boat and, while the boy rowed, the two men began using me as a punch bag. I could feel nothing.

They carried me up to MacBrayne's shed on the beach and gave me first a brandy (which tasted like water), then put me near a fire. Just as I was beginning to feel a bit warmer they decided that I had had enough of the fire, took me away from it and resumed the pummelling. Then I was given hot coffee and more punching. After a quarter of an hour feeling began to return to my body and I was none the worse for the experience.

Later I realised that I never would have been awarded a medal, as one of the conditions was that that the swimmer would leave the water and walk up to McBrayne's shed. This I could not have done.

The episode was reported in the Highland edition of the *Daily Record* newspaper, much to the astonishment of my father, who knew how little I could swim.

As already stated we were a luxury trip and had a fair share of celebrities. One day I remember seeing this distinguished-looking gentleman and heard the Chief Engineer remark that he thought it was Montague Norman – at that time Manager of the Bank of England. Now, pantry boys do not argue with engineers but I thought he was wrong and plucked up courage to ask the gentleman in question.

'Are you Sir Thomas Beecham?' I enquired.

'I am,' was the reply.

Now, Beecham was one of the greatest orchestral conductors that this country had ever produced and, although I had never before asked anyone for an autograph, I decided to make an exception. I had to wait until the voyagers were disembarking before I could approach him. It was a Tuesday, the day of the cruise down Loch Ness, and scores of passengers were crowding on to the ship as others were leaving.

'May I have your autograph?' asked I diffidently.

'Certainly,' said the great man, and signed away quite unconcerned while scores of people were jostling him to get on board for the evening cruise.

'Anything else?' he enquired.

'Please could I have one for my pal, the Checker?'

'By all means.'

Accompanying him was a youngish blonde, Betty Humby, a concert pianist who was about to become his third wife.

One passenger that never paid a fare was a little terrier that came on board nearly every week at Fort Augustus, jumping on to the paddle-box, and getting off at Laggan. The dog returned by the same method a day or two later.

A pigeon with a broken wing landed on deck one day. The Checker made a splint for it and looked after it until the wing healed. After that, the bird used to fly astern of us.

The steering on the ship was direct; in other words there was no engine to help move the rudder as one found on larger vessels. So it was quite hard work turning the wheel and in the tortuous sections of the canal both the Mate and the bosun were required for this.

On one of the quieter days on Loch Ness I learned to steer the ship and can still remember that the course was north-east-by-east a quarter east. In those days most compasses showed points rather than degrees.

I also asked one of the deckhands to show me how to make various knots and how to splice rope, as I was more interested in seamanship than in catering. After showing me how to make a bowline and some other knots, he demonstrated the way to make a back splice, an eye splice and a short splice by taking a piece of rope and handing me a similar piece, with instructions to follow exactly what he was doing. Learning all the stuff he taught me was not difficult, but I did not realise at the time that he was left-handed. Years later, when I was a deep-sea sailor, every time I was splicing someone was sure to ask me if I was left-handed. It was then I grasped what had happened.

Does the splice weaken the rope? The deckhand that taught me swore that, as the splice was twice as thick as the rope, it would never give way. Another deckhand said the opposite and was adamant that the splice would break. Wanting a working majority I asked the Mate for his opinion. He wriggled out of commitment by saying that if the rope was perfect the splice would break but, since every rope had a flaw, that was where the break would occur.

Later I realised that all three were wrong. In a big rope the splice weakens the rope because the 'fid' (a conical piece of wood used for

My first ship

opening up the strands of the rope) breaks up the lay, widening it a great deal to get an opening for the strands to be inserted. This is the reason, apart from neatness, why sailors halve the yarns in the final two tucks to lessen this disturbance of the lay. It is at this point that a rope will break.

As war loomed, the number of passengers fell away and I had mercifully less work to do. Andy Haxton quit the ship because of a dispute with the 2nd steward and the deck steward. These stewards had two tables apiece, each with eight seats, at the front of the dining room. As the ship tapered towards the stern Andy had four smaller tables, each provided with six seats. When we were fully loaded with passengers there was no trouble, but now that their numbers had fallen drastically the dining room would be scarcely a quarter full and Andy, being at the stern, came off badly.

To make matters worse, the other two stewards would slyly put a hand on one of their chairs as the first passengers arrived. This gesture, however slight, was looked on as an invitation to sit at that table and Andy would be left with four or five diners. I had a great deal of sympathy for him, as stewards depended a lot on gratuities and he was really the victim of sharp practice.

The day war was declared was a Sunday and I remember Chamberlain's voice on the radio giving us the fateful news. Also it was later announced that all pigeons had to be reported to the Government. This was quite amusing, as ours was still with the ship.

Although we had still two weeks of our season to run, it was not worthwhile carrying on and we were discharged. I had to pay my fare back to Glasgow (as I had had to do on the way up) because MacBrayne's were exceptionally tight-fisted. They even made the other pantry boy and me go to a doctor in Fort Augustus and get him to examine us and give MacBrayne's certificates to state that we were equal to all the hard work they were requiring of us. For this, the doctor let us off with 2 shillings each.

So I came home that day on a train loaded with soldiers. One of them was busy telling his friends that the war would not last long as the Poles were putting up a good show. Whether this was to calm their fears, or whether he really believed it, I shall never know. Many of the troops were from Highland regiments and wearing kilts. Over the kilts were khaki garments of waterproof material – I was seeing for the first time trench aprons.

On this train was the former flyweight world boxing champion Benny Lynch of Glasgow. He had fallen on hard times mainly due to his love of drink, and had been reduced to fighting in booths. I recall him continually calling on the steward for more beer. When eventually the beer ran out, he immediately demanded lager.

I arrived at the Central station to find Glasgow a city of darkness. There was a 'blackout' and all windows had to be provided with some means of stopping the light getting out. This was rigidly enforced by the ARP (Air Raid Precautions), whose wardens were extremely zealous. I recollect that the tramcar that took me home from the station had only two lamps in place of the customary 12 or so – and even these two were coated in dark blue paint.

Next day half of the blue paint had been scraped away by irate conductors who, on the following morning, had found their bags to be nearly half full of assorted coins from all over the world.

2

LIFE ON BOARD A LINER

Towards the end of 1940 I tried to become a cadet or apprentice, but was just too old. The skipper of the *Gondolier* had given me a coasting discharge so, armed with this, I went to the shipping office in Glasgow to seek employment afloat. As this discharge showed me to have worked in the catering department, I was immediately offered work as a steward at £16 a month all found. I was not attracted to catering and wanted to go on deck, but all that I could get was a job as deck boy at £6 15s a month. This I accepted and was sent to a liner *Reina del Pacifico* (*Queen of the Pacific*) lying in the Clyde estuary.

After taking the train down to the Tail of the Bank I stood looking out at the many ships congregated there, feeling uncertain about my future.

'Which one is the *Reina del Pacifico*?' I asked a man who was standing near the jetty.

'It's that big black one over there,' said he, pointing to a large vessel with two funnels. 'I believe the crew call her the black bastard.'

Her battleship-grey paint was darker than usual and, with the sun almost behind her, she was more or less silhouetted, giving her this black look. Now I realise that the man recognised me as an utter greenhorn and was having fun discomfiting me.

A boat took me out to where she was anchored and I climbed up her accommodation ladder and was greeted by a sailor who took me down to the quarters where the four deck boys lived. This was a small cabin about 5 yards long and little more than 2 yards wide, with two bottom bunks and two above. The cabin was rather untidy and this did nothing to dispel my concern.

There seemed to be no hurry to sign me on and I stayed on her two days and nights before she sailed up to Glasgow and docked. It was a Sunday as I recall, and I arrived home to find my parents attending a meeting of the residents in our air-raid shelter.

This was certainly an anti-climax. After an emotional send-off here was I returning two days later, and the only sailing I had done was up the River Clyde. On Monday 22 February 1941 I signed on as deck boy, but it was not for another three weeks that we set off for the Bristol Channel.

Reina del Pacifico was built in 1930 and at that time was the largest and fastest motor liner in the world. She must have looked smart in her peacetime garb: white hull, white superstructure, two squat yellow funnels and green boot-topping (the narrow strip at the waterline, usually painted red). She was owned by the Pacific Steam Navigation Company (PSNC) and her regular trade had been to Valparaiso and the west coast of South America. The PSNC was joked about by the crew, who maintained that the letters stood for 'passengers should never complain', or 'poxy sailors never cured'.

I had no clear idea what to expect, so everything was completely new to me. One deck boy looked after the chief petty officers (bosun, carpenter and carpenter's mate) and one looked after the other POs (three bosun's mates, six quartermasters and a lamp-trimmer). This left the other deck boy and me to look after about 20 sailors and three ordinary seamen.

Each morning I scrubbed out the mess-room and the room where one of the watches lived, while the other deck boy scrubbed out the WCs and the rooms where the other two watches lived. This arrangement was changed round from week to week.

Each watch consisted of a bosun's mate, six sailors and one ordinary seaman, and there were two sailors always on day work. We took their food down from the galley in metal containers known as kits, served their meals and cleaned up afterwards.

When at sea there was always roughly a third of the deck crew on watch, and the other two-thirds could have their meals in the mess-room in relative comfort. So, rather than make the mess-rooms large enough to accommodate all the seamen that would need to use it when in port, ship owners had their ships designed with smaller mess-rooms to save space. This meant that, in port, a third of the crew had to take their food into their sleeping quarters and eat it there, which did not help in matters of tidiness or cleanliness. We did not wash their plates but provided them with pails of hot soapy water into which they dipped their plates between courses.

Our type of work – serving sailors, cleaning up after them and keeping their quarters tidy – was looked upon as women's work and named 'peggying'. Consequently we were more often called 'peggies' rather than deck boys. This kind of occupation did not appeal to me, but if performing it was necessary to get my foot on the first rung of a ladder leading to AB, I would just have to put up with it.

In addition to the merchant crew there were two naval gunners. These were known as DEMS (defensively equipped merchant ships) gunners and were sometimes from the Army, or occasionally Marines. Fortunately we had nothing to do with attending to them, for they looked after themselves.

When at sea we began early in the morning and were given most of the afternoon off. This arrangement was, I understood, to compensate us for having to serve and wash up after sailors who were on watch from 4pm to 8pm and had no meal break. The cook put their food in the oven at 6pm (when he finished his work for the day) and this was known as the 'black pan'. We served it up when they came off watch, washed up and tidied the mess-room afterwards.

In due course *Reina del Pacifico* sailed into Avonmouth, and we stayed there for eight days loading provisions for the 2,000 troops and 300 nurses we were to carry. This was all a new experience to one who had never been out of Scotland, but I was settling down and making the best of it.

As if I had not had enough new events to cope with, we had three air raids on successive nights. I recall, during one of these raids, coming back to the ship late in the evening when bombs were falling everywhere and fires were springing up all over the quays. It was obviously an attempt to destroy ships and docks.

There was no use just watching what was happening. I decided to pitch in and found myself on the roof of a small dock shed helping a policeman to pour buckets of water on to one of the fires. Other seamen were helping in different ways and this was typical of the camaraderie that was generated by the war. After the fire was put out and the steady signal of the 'all clear' sounded, I went back to the ship.

I tried to leave the ship at Avonmouth, or at least go home for a few days, but I was not allowed. I was hoping to leave for good, as I was getting no experience in seamanship, and I was not enamoured of our food and quarters. Some air raids near Glasgow had just taken place and I was relieved to hear that none of my relations or friends had been affected.

About this time the Germans began to use magnetic mines against merchant shipping, and these would have been a deadly threat had not the British boffins come up very quickly with equipment called degaussing gear. The so-called degaussing girdle was an electric cable rigged all round the hull of the ship and was switched on as soon as we entered dangerous waters to neutralise the magnetic attraction of the ship.

The *Orontes*, lying next to us, was also full of soldiers, and together we left for the Clyde with a sub-chaser. We had just cleared the Bristol Channel when there was a terrific crash and the ship swayed dangerously first one way then the other. The engines stopped, then restarted, but with a horrible grinding sound, then stopped again.

Most of us rushed on deck to find out what had happened. It was typical of merchant ships (as I was later to find out) that all sorts of tales started to go the rounds. Some said it was an unexploded mine; others were sure we had run aground. Whatever it was, there was no shortage of rumours.

Finally we went on our way at a much-reduced speed and eventually reached the Tail of the Bank, where a host of troop-laden liners was ready to sail. Next morning the other liners had gone and a diver was inspecting our damage. It seems we had hit a submerged wreck, had lost one of our propellers and were now unfit for sea.

Again there were rumours. Some said we were going to Belfast; others said Glasgow, but two days later we were in Gladstone Graving Dock (dry dock) in Liverpool for repairs.

The blitz was in full swing, and as this area had many big ships it was thus singled out for special attention. During one attack three bombs landed in our dock but did not explode. Two hours after the 'all clear' the ship was partly lifted out of the water by one of these bombs. Luckily the dock had been flooded the previous day or the consequences could have been serious.

Gladstone Dock and the other docks where we berthed were at the end of a long line of docks stretching about 7 miles along the side of the River Mersey. There was an overhead railway line along the full length of the docks but, because of the constant bombing of Liverpool, one could never travel the full distance as there was always some part of the line under repair.

While our damage was being patched up, joiners came on board and did conversion work on the troops' accommodation. Being a trifle naïve I supposed that this was to give the soldiers more comfort, but soon discovered it was to cram a few hundred more into an already crowded ship.

The dockers at Avonmouth used to pilfer the stores while loading the ship with provisions, but what went on at Liverpool was wholesale robbery. They would not content themselves with food, but took shirts, socks, books, etc, intended for the troops. Their philosophy seemed to be that anything taken off a ship was not stealing; whether it was out of the hold or out of sailors' cabins.

Later I was told that when goods were sent overseas to the NAAFI (the institution that offered goods to the Navy, Army and RAF at reduced prices) they counted it lucky if 25% reached their destinations. So serious was this plundering that the Government at one stage resorted to the practice of using two ships for sending out a consignment of shoes; one vessel was given all the left shoes and the

Life on board a Liner

other all the right ones. This shows how desperate affairs were, for if one of these ships was sunk the other would reach port carrying a cargo of unusable goods.

The soldiers meantime were at camp supremely unaware of such dirty dealings. I had stuff stolen from our cabin and learned to lock up everything before going ashore.

The day before departing, the troops and nurses came back. Apart from the Queen Alexandra nurses, we had a hundred or two from the Royal Horse Artillery, but most of the soldiers were New Zealanders.

All shore leave was cancelled for us. We were very disappointed by this, but I hit on a plan to get ashore. Taking the other three deck boys into the scheme, we rigged up dummies in our beds using life jackets and other clothing so that it would appear to any chance passer-by that the occupants of the cabin were fast asleep. We were in the habit of emptying buckets of refuse on the quay so, armed with a pail of muck each and wearing an old coat over our going-ashore garb, we walked down the gangway and never a word was said to us. Once on the dockside we discarded our buckets and the coats, and brought them back on board after the night's escapade.

When we got back we did not take the dummies out immediately but sat chuckling at the success of the plan. In walked the bosun. He was a tall, angular Irishman who spoke with a heavy brogue and had a peculiar squint – one eye looking straight ahead while the other was pointing not only outwards but also upwards. This made talking to him an ordeal and acutely embarrassing, as one was never sure where to look.

Being rather taken aback, he looked first at the beds and then at us (or perhaps it was at the same time, one eye on us and the other on the beds); however, he must have had some sense of humour for he laughed, muttered something that sounded like 'young scamps', and was gone.

After a stay of three and a half weeks we left Liverpool on a fine warm morning and the last sound we heard, while sailing down the Mersey, was the mournful wailing of the air-raid siren. Joining us were *Empress of Asia*, *Empress of Russia*, *Highland Chieftain* and *Dominion Monarch*. Three destroyers escorted us to the Firth of Clyde.

It was 9pm on a Saturday night, two days later, when we finally departed from the UK. As twilight approached, 11 destroyers stealthily slid out past the boom. It was a splendid sight. Our Commodore ship, *Strathaird* (a P&O liner), was next to follow, then came the other liners. By the time *Reina del Pacifico* left, darkness had descended and the only distinct lights were those of the small boats picking up the pilots as they were dropped. I stayed on deck watching the haze of light that was Scotland fade into the night, then went below.

Next day was quite warm for April, and I was able to see more of the convoy, which included quite near us a Polish liner, *Sobieski*. I could make out *Stirling Castle*, *Stratheden* and several others with the battle cruiser *Repulse* plump in the middle of the convoy together with an armed merchant cruiser. These armed merchantmen were fast liners that had their decks reinforced to enable them to carry 6-inch guns.

I took the opportunity to expose my skin to the sun to prepare it for what was to follow. We were still in the dark as to our destination but, as the troops had been issued with tropical kits, we guessed it to be somewhere in Africa.

Strangely I had a feeling that something did not seem quite right – or, at least, not what I expected. I thought about it a lot, but it took a day or two before I knew exactly what it was. When on holiday at a seaside resort, people always talk about the smell of the sea. There was absolutely no smell here. I became conscious of the fact that what these folk called the smell of the sea was really the smell of the seashore, with the seaweed and all the other stuff to be found on beaches.

There are always those that are ready to take advantage of any situation and, after the first day out, two of the New Zealand soldiers set up a daily sweepstake. Anyone who cared could enter by paying the appropriate fee and hazarding a guess as to how many miles the ship would sail that day. If more than one person hit on the right mileage, then the prize was shared – after the New Zealanders had deducted 10% for their efforts.

The *Reina del Pacifico* had a crow's-nest but I cannot remember it being much used. I recall conversing with an AB while he was keeping lookout on the fo'c'sle head, but there may have been another sailor in the crow's-nest as well. Certainly if the visibility were poor the lookout would be up for'ard on the fo'c'sle head.

After the First World War the Treaty of Versailles limited the size of warships that Germany could build. However, early on Hitler found a way round the prohibition by building three ships known in Germany as heavy cruisers but termed 'pocket battleships' by the British. They were named *Deutschland*, *Admiral Graf Spee* and *Admiral Sheer*. They were about 10,000 gross tons (which is extremely small for battleships), but were heavily armed with six 280mm (11-inch) guns and had powerful diesel engines to give them a speed of about 28½ knots.

One of their captains boasted that his guns had a greater range

Life on board a Liner

than any British cruiser, and although our battleships could outgun him they had not the speed to catch up with him. This meant that he feared only three warships in the entire Royal Navy, *Hood*, *Renown* and *Repulse*, which were battle cruisers, could match his speed and had bigger guns. The *Graf Spee* had been engaged by three of our cruisers and, in a most daring encounter, they severely damaged her and forced her into Montevideo, where she was eventually scuttled on Hitler's orders. If either the *Graf Spee*, *Admiral Scheer* or *Deutschland* (later renamed *Lützow*, as Hitler was concerned with the blow to prestige if a ship bearing that name were to be sunk) met up with any convoy, the situation would be grim. This was obviously why we had the *Repulse* with us.

The fine weather prevailed for a week, then it became very warm. Many flying fish were to be seen; they were bluish in colour, and darted out of the water with their diaphanous fins rigid like wings while they glided above the surface for quite a time. I was told that they left the water only when being chased by dolphins or bonitos. As the predators were waiting for them to return to the sea, nearly every flight was a flight of death. Later, when I was in deeply laden cargo ships, sailors would put a lamp on top of the hatch at night and the flying fish would land there. They made a tasty meal.

Another noticeable feature of sailing in the tropics was that the ship's wake took on a milky blue phosphorescent appearance – as did the fish that used to sport about near the bow. Also the sky changed quite a bit, and we could now see the Southern Cross and a star named Canopus, which is the second-brightest star in the sky but cannot be seen in northern latitudes.

I had been well warned about the dangers of sunburn and took precautions. On the first day of the hot weather I exposed my body for only 5 minutes, on the second day 10 minutes, the third day 15 minutes, the fourth day 20 minutes, and on the fifth day half an hour. After that I could stay in the sun as long as I chose without fear of damage.

Others were not so cautious and no sympathy could be expected if one had a dose of sunburn. Often someone would say 'Hello there' or offer some such greeting while giving the unfortunate a slap on the back in mock friendliness. One of the young assistant butchers actually fell asleep while sunbathing and had a very sore back for a considerable time.

At various parts of the ship there were pairs of bollards (sometimes called bitts), which were used for securing a mooring rope by putting it around them in a figure-of-eight fashion. They were made of iron and the first-trippers were so used to having a seat on them in the cooler climate that they got a nasty surprise when trying to do the same in the really hot weather. One could have almost fried an egg on them, and you can picture what happened when someone, wearing thin trousers, put his posterior on one.

There were two monkeys with us. I do not know how they came to be on board but some joker among the troops on a previous voyage had decked them out in khaki uniforms, making the larger of the two a sergeant by sewing three stripes on to the sleeves of both arms. They hung around the galley for scraps of food, but their favourite spot was the petty officers' mess. We all took their presence as a bit of fun, but one of the bosun's mates was violently opposed to them and would lash out at them with a wet cloth whenever they came near. They hovered around this mess at meal times and if anyone took his eyes off his plate for a second an arm would lift food off the plate at great speed. Strangely enough, it was this bosun's mate that was nearly always their victim.

The Commodore ship had, in addition to its own captain, a Commodore who was in charge of all merchant ships and the running of the convoy. He frequently sent out flag signals to the other vessels. The naval escorts had an SOE (senior officer of the escort), and he would most likely have been on board the *Repulse*, which was the largest vessel in the escort.

Sailors had a limited variety of work on a liner. The quartermasters did all the steering and the lamp trimmer would do what little splicing was required. If an eye was needed in a wire hawser and there was not time to make a splice, the end was bent back and the eye made using bulldog grips. This was disparagingly referred to as an 'American splice'.

Sailors looked after the paintwork by a method known as 'soogee'. In this process one sailor went ahead with a bucket of warm water containing plenty of washing soda and possibly a little soft soap. He applied this to the painted surfaces and a few minutes later a second sailor came along with fresh water and cleaned it off. The result was quite striking.

One of the other tasks was holystoning the wooden decks. The bigger holystones were mounted on a swivelled bracket at the end of a pole. The deck was wetted and some sand thrown over it, then the sailor with the holystone came along and pushed this huge stone back and forth over the deck. It certainly made the deck look very clean. There were also smaller holystones that were held in the hand and used for cleaning wooden rails and the like. Both tasks were disliked as being monotonous jobs.

Sailors also washed down the decks frequently. The bosun's mate

Life on board a Liner

operated the hose and the sailors scrubbed the deck with brooms while the ordinary seamen followed behind the bosun's mate, helping to move the hose about and to stop it from kinking.

Many of the troops were inclined to spit all over the decks. Various suggestions were put to them, but to no avail. One bright spark put up a notice saying 'If you spit on the floor at home please spit on the deck here, because we want you to feel at home'. That did the trick.

Washing clothes – or doing your dhobi (an Indian word), as it was always called at sea – was something new to me. I put some in a bucket of soapy water and put this on the galley fire to boil them. Unfortunately I had a vest and pants in the same bucket as a coloured jersey and finished with pink underwear for the rest of the trip.

Apart from the six quartermasters who steered the ship and were kitted out in naval caps, bell-bottoms, etc, the other deck ratings usually wore dungarees. These were not the type then worn by shore workers, where the trousers extended upwards forming a bib at the neck, but just trousers made of similar material and saxe-blue in colour. I later found out that they were very popular in the USA, where they were called 'jeans', but in Britain they were sold only in special shops near the docks. As well as dungaree trousers there were jackets made of the same cloth, and together this was the standard dress of the deck ratings – although one might occasionally see someone in a boiler suit. However, I have no doubt that in peacetime (with passengers on board) all deck hands on liners would be kitted out like the quartermasters.

The general method of washing dungarees was to lay them on a board and scrub them with a scrubbing brush. Perhaps they did not enjoy a long life by this method, but it was quicker and easier. Some sailors tied them to a heaving line and dragged them behind the ship for two or three hundred miles; they then had to have considerable soaking to get the salt out of them. I believe some engineers put theirs in a large drum of soapy water and put a mop into the bucket. They then connected the mop to some piece of machinery that caused the mob to plunge up and down in the bucket – a primitive washing machine.

Another item that all sailors wore, for obvious reasons, was a knife and, being anxious to look the part, I hurriedly bought one before leaving Glasgow. It was the type commonly associated with Boy Scouts and did nothing to enhance my nautical image. The regulars had a brand of knife known as 'Green River', which was exceptionally sharp and certainly looked nothing like a scout's knife. Often the bosun's mates had a double sheathe to accommodate the knife and also a small marline spike; as well as being used for splicing wire, the spike was handy for tightening and slackening shackles that joined chains together.

I managed to get hold of a piece of canvas and one of the ABs instructed me in the making of a kitbag. He lent me a palm – a gadget that fits on to the palm of the hand with a piece of metal above the ball of the thumb allowing the blunt end of the needle to be pushed down through the canvas – a sailmaker's needle and also some sail-making twine, which I treated with beeswax (this not only helped to preserve the twine against rotting but also made it easier to push it through the canvas). The finished article was not an object of beauty, but it gave me my first taste of using palm and needle and offered extra space when taking home the food I intended to buy.

The heat became intense. We had no fans but, while at sea, metal air-chutes were fixed to the portholes, which drew in a current of air caused by the ship's motion. They were like large flour scoops and, since no lights could be shown in convoy, they had a baffle next to the porthole to allow air in but prevent light getting out.

Many of the crew now began sleeping on deck and I joined them. It was a new and wonderful experience to breathe in fresh air all night long. I relished it and thereafter, any time I was on a ship in tropical waters, I was among the first to forsake sleeping indoors, and one of the last to return to inside quarters.

It was so humid that I am sure I was taking about eight showers every day, and still feeling a bit sticky. Naturally all showering was done with salt water; the fresh drinking water was under lock and key and opened for only half an hour each day. There were no detergents in these days and we used what was termed 'salt water soap'; it did not give much of a lather but was better than nothing.

Early in the voyage we were given lime juice every day. Without giving it much thought I assumed it was being issued to give us vitamin C for the prevention of scurvy. One day, when chatting to an army medical orderly, the subject came up and he laughed at my naive supposition.

'It's got nothing to do with scurvy,' he declared. 'We have plenty of fruit and vegetables in the refrigerators.'

'Well, why are they giving it to us?' I wanted to know.

'To keep your natural desires at bay,' was his reply.

'If that's true, why are the soldiers not getting any,' I said, still unconvinced.

'We doctor their tea with bromide,' he responded.

After about three weeks our convoy split up. At the start it had consisted of a dozen troop-carrying liners, seven fast cargo vessels, one armed merchant cruiser, 11 destroyers and lastly the battle cruiser *Repulse*. The cargo ships left us, and nearly all the escort, but we were now out of range of aircraft.

We sighted land on a Friday morning, and at 8am dropped anchor in Freetown, Sierra Leone. I was later told that Sierra Leone meant 'lion-like mountains' and that Freetown got its name because it started off as a settlement for freed slaves. At any rate, I was looking forward to our stay with much excitement.

As soon as we arrived, out came narrow canoes resembling skiffs; the occupant had a spear-shaped paddle that was wielded with some dexterity. There was another paddle, somewhat like a shovel in appearance, and, apart from assisting the first paddle, it was used to bail out the water that was constantly accumulating in the boat.

Later the bumboats appeared, which were larger and carried two or more natives. Each boat had a line, a weight and a basket and, before long, we were all busily engaged in trading. They offered sandals, small baskets, limes, bananas, pineapples and a new fruit I had never seen before – mangoes.

The troops were so keen to get at the food that they would give anything for it. Prices rose rapidly since we were not allowed ashore and bananas cost as much as a shilling a dozen. The natives would accept cash but much preferred clothing, etc, and I think the PSNC would miss a few blankets at the end of the trip. If you did not keep your wits about you, you were liable to see your shirt disappear over the ship's side in some other person's basket!

The heat was stifling and everyone was now sleeping on deck. During our six-day stay the convoy was bunkered and watered. We were disappointed to find Freetown blacked out, but next day the reason was found to be the short distance from Dakar. A German Junkers plane flew over the convoy, but one ship opened fire and it disappeared. I was not sorry to see the last of Freetown, for the ship was in a mess with fruit skins, etc, and their accompanying smells.

Our food was always steaming hot except for Sunday's tea. Complaints were made by the crew but nothing was done about it. It was fine if you were a nurse or an Army officer as you had salads and a dessert of ice cream.

At one time in Glasgow we had neighbours called MacQuarrie, and the man of the house, Donald, came from Mull. On the *Reina del Pacifico* the second baker spoke with exactly the same accent and his name happened to be Lachie MacQuarrie. I asked him whether he had relations in Glasgow but he, thinking that some of the crew had put me up to it, was highly suspicious and would not be drawn. Later I gave him more details of our erstwhile neighbours and, when he knew that my enquiries were genuine, he revealed that Donald was his brother.

This was an unexpected blessing. The second baker on a liner is the real boss of the work (the chief baker doing mostly administration) and I received many extra titbits. The bakers were also classed as confectioners and handled all the desserts, including ice cream. Many a time Lachie would slip me an ice cream, and he also gave me rolls to which only petty officers and above were entitled.

There was the question of hair-cutting – no one wanted long hair in the hot climate. One of our firemen had the equipment and skill and offered to cut hair as often as required for the sum of 2s 6d, to be paid at the end of the voyage. This was indeed a bargain and he made a very good job of the cutting. He did all right, too, because there is plenty of spare time on a ship with nowhere to go, and at the end of the trip he would be collecting at least £9.

The further south we travelled, the cooler it became and the open-air sleeping gradually stopped. It was hastened somewhat when one night a sudden heavy shower disturbed the slumberers, and the poor unfortunates were thoroughly soaked.

The convoy zigzagged frequently, and it was done with precision. Each vessel had an accurate clock with a brass ring round its circumference. Attached to this ring were several brass studs at various distances along the ring, and projecting about half an inch from the ring. The minute hand of the clock had a small flexible strip at its tip and each time it contacted one of the studs a bell rang, giving the signal for all vessels in the convoy to alter course at the same time.

The studs could be anything from 4 minutes to 10 minutes apart, and the details of their spacing were set out on special cards. There might be a dozen or more of these cards, with different combinations of the placing of these studs, and you might be using a card for barely 10 minutes when a flag signal from the Commodore ship would instruct you to change from perhaps card three to card nine at a set time.

Since the *Repulse* and the destroyers had left some time before reaching Freetown, we now had a cruiser in the centre of the convoy.

Going round the Cape of Good Hope the weather became really rough and the wind blew so violently that it turned the surface of the water white like snow, and thin spray arose from it, giving the whole an appearance of a hot seething mass. Shining through the spray, the sun produced rainbow-coloured forms scurrying over the face of the water. One moment the sea towered above us like some great hill, and the next moment it was far below us resembling a large valley. Ocean liners were tossed about like corks and the convoy made little speed.

Life on board a Liner

We afterwards learned that a Brazilian liner had been lost in the same storm.

The deck boys' cabin was at the stern. *Reina del Pacifico* had four propellers, and in stormy conditions the ship's stern would rise out of the sea, causing the blades of the propellers to race; this created a loud noise and made sleep impossible.

Once round the Cape the weather became better. The morning of our arrival in Durban presented the most beautiful sunrise I had ever seen. The sky was royal blue, while golden-coloured clouds shaped like cotton wool dotted the sky, and just above the horizon it assumed a lovely light green-blue colour.

Durban at that time was the chief port in the Union of South Africa. Its harbour was a bay with a narrow entrance and we anchored there for a few hours before going in to dock. The convoy was intact save for *Highland Chieftain*, which had rammed a ship one dark night and had to remain in Freetown. We passed our time at the anchorage watching huge sharks with their pilot fish leading them.

Durban at once impressed me with its cleanliness. It was very modern and most enterprising. The Seaman's Mission, Service Canteens, etc, were much superior to those at home and provided free books, magazines, concerts and a cinema show every night. The general layout of the town suggested plenty of *lebensraum* and the only blot on the pleasant life there was the very decided colour bar: cinemas, buses, seats and so on were labelled European and Non-European (obviously euphemisms, for Australians were deemed European), the former always being the much better of the two and suggesting that it was degradation rather than segregation.

One of the ABs decided to make a one-man protest against this. He hired a rickshaw and had the man pull him quite close to the town centre. Thereupon he ordered the man (who was a trifle unwilling) to sit in the rickshaw and he then pulled the vehicle right through the centre of Durban. The locals were furious but, at that time, seemed to be unable to do anything about it.

Censorship was very strict and everywhere there were posters saying 'Careless talk costs lives' and 'Loose lips sink ships'. Our letters were read and censored, but I wanted to give my parents some idea of where I was. Anyway, by the time my letters reached home my past whereabouts would be of little interest to anyone. So my father and I concocted a method whereby I could let them know where I was. This involved spelling out the word by using the first letter of the first word, the first letter of the fifth word, the second letter of the 12th word, the first letter of the 19th word, the first letter of the 25th word, the third letter of the 29th word, and so on. Below is the beginning of a letter that used this method to indicate that I was in Durban. I have emphasised the relevant letters.

Reina del Pacifico
26th May 1941

Dear Pop,
    During this voyage and **U**ntil I get home again no letters o**R** parcels can reach us; so I **B**etter send this off to you **A**s fast as I ca**N**.

As long as the letter sounded natural and not contrived, I cannot see how anyone could possibly have spotted what was going on. We changed the code for each trip.

All the other liners left with their troops to go to Suez, but we discharged ours and turned back to Port Elizabeth. At the time I did not understand why, but later I realised that ours were probably being sent to fight the Vichy French in Madagascar.

Port Elizabeth was much smaller than Durban but just as clean. The docks were a very short distance from the town, which seemed to be formed around one main street, which was lit by mercury vapour lamps. We loaded dried fruit, maize and onions and, at 12 noon on a Saturday, left for Cape Town, where we arrived at 9am on the following Monday.

This town is about 30 miles north of the Cape of Good Hope. Below it is Table Bay and behind it is the flat-topped Table Mountain, which is roughly 3,500 feet high and consists of a horizontal top about 2 miles long. Sometimes south-east winds cause a cloud to hang over the summit and this is known as the 'table cloth'.

Approaching the town at dawn it was a most imposing sight as it was lit up in the semi-darkness and we could easily discern the rugged black outline of its surrounding mountains. Here we took on board oranges and copper ingots during a three-day stay.

Earlier on I had made friends with a steward, Robert Cromb, from Partick in Glasgow. He had registered as a conscientious objector and had been in prison several times. The authorities were playing the 'cat and mouse' game that years before they had used on suffragettes – putting them in and out of prison. Cromb had had enough and slipped off to sea.

Stewards lived in quarters that went by the name of 'glory holes', and had no food after their evening meal. On the other hand, we had our own supplies and could go back for more, if the tea or sugar ran short. It was not handed out willingly, or without some grumbling,

Life on board a Liner 33

but we were usually given enough to see us through until the next issue of rations.

One evening about 9pm I decided to make a pot of tea with bread and butter and share it with Cromb, who was waiting up on the boat deck. I was standing in the galley wearing only bathing trunks and had just put boiling water in the pot when the cook and his mate arrived with a huge dish of eggs for the next day's breakfast. Guessing that there would be about 40 eggs in the dish, I planned to acquire a couple.

It was the work of a second to pop two eggs into the teapot when the cooks were otherwise engaged. As I did not want to arouse suspicion I was in no hurry to leave and chatted with them for 2 minutes while the eggs were in the boiling water, then slipped off to join Cromb on the boat deck.

Cromb thoroughly enjoyed the repast and it was amusing when I went back to the galley later and found the cooks debating what had happened to the missing eggs. They had both counted all the eggs twice and it was a complete mystery to them how two had vanished into thin air. As I had been standing in the galley only in trunks with no pockets of any kind I was never under suspicion. It never occurred to them that the objects were being cooked under their very eyes in a teapot quite close to them. I knew that they would get more eggs without question, but watching their puzzled faces was really amusing. I would not have fancied being found out, as the second cook was a large red-headed man who was reputed to have once been a champion boxer in the Indian Army.

The people of Cape Town were very obliging and most hospitable. It seemed that they could not do enough for us, and went out of their way to make us feel at home. I spent all three evenings in private homes where I was made most welcome. One of these was a friend of a friend in Glasgow, and lived in a beautiful little town, Muzenberg, some miles south of Cape Town.

Despite this, there were others with Nazi sympathies. Some time later a harbour master divulged to the Germans the departure times of seven liners, which resulted in six of them being sunk. The one that escaped sinking was the *Nea Hellis* (*New Greece*), which was the old Anchor liner *Tuscania* that we had sold to the Greeks. She was bought back from the Greeks, but it was decided not to bother changing her name again. She survived the war and had many narrow escapes that made her name a legend.

On the way home we had some trouble with the bosun. As I previously explained we stayed up to look after the 4 to 8 watch and give them their 'black pan', and for this we were given time off in the afternoon. The bosun objected to our going ashore to shop and, when in Cape Town, he had us holystoning and chipping rust in the afternoon and continued working us every afternoon on the road home. I put it to him that, taking into account the black pan, we were now working overtime and should be paid for it. This he refused to countenance, so I said that we would not henceforth do the black pan.

At 8pm the next evening we lay in our bunks waiting for the storm of abuse that would certainly follow from our absence in the mess. Sure enough the sailors came to us and expressed their disapproval vehemently. We steadfastly refused to serve them and gave them our reasons, which, at the time, they found unacceptable. However, a few days later many of them came to us, said that under the same circumstances they would have done the same, and wished us well. The bosun dug his heels in and overtime was not paid; we likewise remained intransigent and had to work in the afternoons.

The voyage home to Liverpool was without convoy. We went at full speed and did various zigzagging. As we approached the danger area for U-boats there was mild concern, but we were fast and unlikely to be a victim.

It was only now, when sailing alone, that the vastness of the ocean became evident. Day after day after day this lonely ship was pushing along, but with nothing to see from horizon to horizon it did not seem to be going anywhere. You look at an atlas and see the great expanse of blue on it, and you know how many miles you have to sail, and how long it will take. However, it is only when you are actually in the middle of the ocean that it strikes you so forcefully.

I requested permission to be allowed to steer the ship under the quartermaster's guidance. This was granted and I had several hours at the wheel. It was a great deal easier than I had expected as she had telemotor steering to turn her huge rudder and was doing 19 knots most of the time – a fast ship is much easier to steer than a slow one.

As we were approaching the UK many of the crew got quite excited at the prospect of going home, and this state of mind was always referred to as 'having the channels'.

*

My first trip had thus been a great disappointment. We deck boys, apart from chipping rust and holystoning, did nothing but attend to the needs of sailors. However, each time we cast off, tied up or anchored I went on deck with the sailors and helped (unpaid) with the ropes, so at least I did learn something. As I was the only one of the deck boys who could splice and do all the required knots, I asked the

Life on board a Liner

bosun if I could come back as an ordinary seaman. He would have me again as deck boy but refused me promotion, so I left.

At the time I was most annoyed with the bosun. However, on reflection, I realised that if the three ordinary seamen all wanted to stay on the ship he could hardly get rid of one of them to suit me.

Lachie MacQuarrie offered to take me on as an assistant baker at £17 12s 6d a month – the same wage as an AB – and I was sorely tempted because I would be learning a trade. However, I decided against it and made up my mind to try for an ordinary seaman's berth at £12 15s a month.

I was now given a seaman's discharge book. This contained details of the ship's name, gross tonnage, net tonnage, the port where I was signed on and the place where I was discharged. Also given were reports on my character (a) for ability and (b) for general conduct. Unless one's character was distinctly poor, 'VG' (very good) was entered for both – otherwise 'DR' was used ('declined to report').

As I prepared to leave the docks I noticed onions (which at the time were in exceedingly short supply) all over the ground as some slings had burst. I slipped three into my pocket and made for the dock gate.

I knew that there would be a policeman at the gate and decided, rather than try to sneak past him, to go straight up to him and ask him some question about where one caught a train for Glasgow. It was perhaps good enough psychology, but the policeman probably had plenty of experience of amateur psychologists and asked what was in my pocket. When I produced the three onions he merely smiled and waved me through.

While in Durban I had bought as much food as possible to take home. To stop seamen dealing in the black market, each was limited to 25lb and not more than 5lb of any rationed product. Thus you could take 5lb of tea and 20lb of onions because onions were not rationed – just unobtainable. I brought home 5lb each of tea, sugar, butter, bacon and tinned meat, and gave this to my parents, who were overjoyed.

The Waterguard (uniformed members of the Customs) were responsible for controlling this, and some were ridiculously overzealous, carrying out their duties to the letter of the law rather than the spirit. One galley boy shopped where tea was sold only in 2lb packets. When the Waterguard found him with 6lb, they took a 2lb packet from him.

When the Customs were making their usual search they discovered 3,000 cigarettes hidden in the dummy funnel. Their concession was that each seaman was allowed 200 cigarettes (or the equivalent weight in cigars or tobacco) free of duty. Since it was difficult to judge the time of arrival exactly when ordering tobacco, we tended to overestimate rather than be left with fewer than the 200 concession. The stupid part of this Customs regulation meant that if you arrived with 250 cigarettes (and were foolish enough to declare them) you were charged with duty on the whole 250, not just the extra 50. The price on ship was 1s 3d for 50, while the folk ashore were paying 5 shillings, hence the tremendous incentive to smuggle.

On 22 June 1941, shortly after we had sailed from Cape Town, Germany attacked the USSR. The Soviets had moved into Poland at the time of Hitler's invasion (presumably to stop the Germans coming any closer to them) and the Poles were still technically at war with them. Accordingly many Poles refused to take any further part in the conflict.

A deal of hypocrisy was taking place. Early in the conflict Stalin had declared that it was a capitalist war and he had no intention of 'pulling their chestnuts out of the fire'. Nevertheless, when the USSR was attacked they immediately changed their terminology and declared the war to be 'a glorious crusade against fascism'.

The duplicity was not one-sided. On Sunday evenings, about 9pm, the BBC broadcast a programme called 'Our Allies'. During this they played the national anthems of Britain, France, Belgium, Holland, Norway, Czechoslovakia, Denmark and those of all the British Empire countries. When the USSR was attacked this programme was immediately stopped. No reason was given, but I suspect that they just could not stomach the playing of the *Internationale*. For a time the USSR was not considered to be an ally but – with fine semantic distinction – was referred to as a 'co-belligerent'.

I was ready for my ten days' leave and on 9 July was paid off the ship, after all deductions for money asked for in port, etc, with £4 4s 6d, which was not at all bad when you consider that I had an allotment note for £3 sent to my mother every month.

The Appendix at the end of the book explains some of the nautical terms and gives a background to life at sea as it was then. Those who already know, or those not interested, can just skip this Appendix.

3

LIFE ON A TRAMP STEAMER

After my leave was over, on 25 July 1941 I reported to the shipping offices and landed a job as ordinary seaman, at £12 15s a month, on an old tramp, the *Newton Pine*, belonging to a Cardiff shipping company and built in 1925. The company's ships were all named after trees – *Newton Ash*, *Newton Beech*, *Newton Elm*, etc. She was lying at anchor up the Holy Loch (a sea loch in the Clyde estuary) discharging demerara sugar into barges.

This was altogether a different life. There were five ABs, two ordinary seamen and two apprentices, plus of course a bosun and carpenter. Two watches would have two ABs and one OS, and the remaining one would have one AB and the two apprentices. There being no deck boys, the ordinary seamen would do all the 'peggying'.

Conditions were very much worse than on liners. Seven of us had to sleep in a very small fo'c'sle and, like the *Reina del Pacifico*, our messroom could not take all of us at the same time when in port.

Unlike liners, where proper mattresses were supplied, we were given palliasses – nicknamed 'donkeys' breakfasts' – to sleep on. These had three main periods in their life. The first was the most uncomfortable, when the straw was fresh and inclined to be prickly, and the last stage was when the straw had been lain on for a prolonged period and was as hard as concrete. The middle one was passable. No linen was provided and the food was the minimum of the Board of Trade allowance, which the company set as their maximum.

There was no running water and to get a drink or a wash you had to go to a pump in the well deck and pump up the water. This pump was not completely reliable and many times had to be primed before use. In a rough sea it could be hazardous trying to dodge a wave while pumping.

Her lifeboats were not like those on the *Reina del Pacifico*, which were inboard mounted on a slanting metal frame from which they could quickly be launched by gravity. Instead, those on the *Newton Pine* were not kept on deck but swung over the side of the ship and lashed to a boom, all ready for a quick launch. When at sea we did not take off all our clothes when bedding down, but doffed our footwear and kept on most of our clothes ready for a quick dash on deck.

Some sailors asked for money when signing on articles, and a sum based on their wages was given on an 'advance note'. This note had to be cashed by someone ashore and, since it was not unknown for a seaman to fail to sail on the vessel, a commission of 10% or so was deducted from the sum paid. If the sailor did not turn up, the payer of the advance note got only 10% of its face value, but the shipping company suffered no financial loss whatever.

Our sailors consisted of a New Zealander, a Scot who had lived for many years in Canada, a chap from Surrey, one from the Midlands and finally Jack Rosa, who had been a training-ship boy. The other ordinary seaman hailed from Greenock.

I remember that half way through the first morning the bosun shouted to me 'smoko', and this appeared to be the signal to knock off work for a smoke. Naturally everyone stopped their tasks for a cup of tea, whether or not they smoked.

Of the two apprentices, one of them had been on another of the company's vessels, the *Newton Beech*, which had been sunk south-east of Ascension Island by the pocket battleship *Admiral Graf Spee*, which later transferred him to the notorious *Altmark*, which was a prison ship. I recall asking him what the food was like on the *Graf Spee* and he replied that it was a lot better than we were now getting!

Before the convoy system was started up the 'pocket battleships' took the merchant crews on board before sinking their vessels, but now that we had convoys they would just run riot and sink as many as possible while the convoy was dispersing. They were more to be feared than either aircraft or U-boats.

The firemen were all Indians. Unlike the lascars manning the P&O and similar lines, they were resident in Britain and were paid the full wages for firemen, greasers, etc. In fact, a fireman received more than an AB as traditionally he was paid about 10 shillings extra a month. I believe this had its origin in the firemen having to have a thorough wash after each watch, and this would cost a fair sum for soap.

Firemen (referred to by people ashore as stokers) attended to the ship's furnaces. The pattern for doing this was to pitch, slice and rake. Pitching required them to shovel coal into the fire; slicing meant that they picked up a large metal pole called a slice and thrust this into the fire, then leaned heavily on it to lift up the coal and let air in, just as one would do at home with a poker; and raking involved using a rake to pull the burning coal and spread it over the surface of the furnace.

The coal they used was in the bunkers, and transferring it to the firemen ready for stoking was the work of the trimmer. The greaser, as the name implies, looked after the lubrication of the bearings, while the donkeyman, among other things, looked after the donkey engine, an auxiliary engine used mostly in port when the main one would be shut down.

There was brown sugar all over the decks and I mentioned to an AB that I could perhaps skim a pound or two of the dirty stuff off the top and take some clean stuff back home.

'Don't bother doing that,' said he. 'Get a pillowcase and go down the hold for some and I'll help you.'

We went into the hold and got the sugar. Climbing up the rope ladder to get back up on deck I did it the same way as I would have done if I was coming up a ladder on the side of a ship. But the ladder was hanging in the air unsupported, and this was an entirely different matter. I was greatly amazed when it shook violently at each step. After taking a considerable time to reach the deck, I looked back to see the AB coming up the ladder very quickly by an entirely different method. He held on to one rope only and faced the side of the ladder, putting one foot inside and the other outside the rungs. Even to this day I see very few people who know how to do this.

I put the pillowslip into my kitbag and went off on the launch with the dockers. Arriving home I thought I would have a bit of fun and said to my mother, 'I could have brought you a pound or two of sugar, but it was brown and I thought you preferred white.'

Mother indicated that she could have used brown sugar, whereupon I plonked the pillowcase down on the table saying, 'That's brown sugar.'

She turned white as a sheet, and rushed to the window expecting to see a posse of the Glasgow constabulary in hot pursuit, but my father, being of a practical frame of mind, pulled out a spring balance and weighed it. It was 33lb. That kept them going for quite a time, as the weekly ration was just an ounce or two.

We took a few days to finish discharging the sugar, then went alongside at the James Watt dock in Greenock for an hour or two. There we had rubble dumped on the hatches to act as ballast, then we sailed.

What a difference from the last convoy, where next day we were well out at sea – on this one we were still in the Clyde estuary. I was now getting my first experience of a slow convoy in the North Atlantic.

Churchill knew the importance of these convoys and said, 'Battles might be won or lost, but our power to fight to keep ourselves alive rests on the outcome of the struggle for control of the Atlantic.'

Also different from the last convoy, we were doing scarcely 7 knots, and the total escort to look after 70 or so ships was one corvette and an armed trawler! The term corvette had been used in Nelson's time, but had been dropped; it was now used to apply to a new type of vessel that owed much to the design of the whalers. They were smaller than either destroyers or frigates and had nothing like their speed, but I suppose they could be built quickly and cheaply. They were about 900 tons and had a speed of around 16 knots.

At first, convoys were normally escorted only a certain distance either east or west into the Atlantic, after which they dispersed and proceeded independently to their destinations. Only relatively slow ships were put in convoy; the rest sailed independently.

Churchill had decided to arm 1,000 merchant ships with 12-pounder guns from a stockpile dating from the First World War. Once the Germans knew of this, it was taken as an invitation to attack any armed ship. Some ship-owners were against this idea, in the belief that it actually encouraged U-boats to torpedo their ships.

Early in the war the U-boats (like the 'pocket battleships'), meeting a lone merchant vessel, signalled for her crew to take to the boats, gave them about 15 minutes to abandon ship, then used shells to sink her. Torpedoes were highly sophisticated and costly weapons and, in these circumstances, their use was neither necessary nor desirable. Once merchantmen were in convoys – particularly after they were armed – it was a different matter entirely, and torpedoes were then fired without warning.

I recall one of my mates telling me that, early in the war, his ship was given 15 minutes' warning for its crew to take to the boats before being sunk. The submarine then contacted them and asked if they were all right for food. As they had managed to gather some up before leaving their vessel, they said that they had enough. Whereupon the U-boat towed all four lifeboats for several hours before casting them adrift because they were now in sight of land and to carry on towing would be dangerous.

Another important point was that prior to the fall of France the German submarines had to leave Germany and go round the north of Scotland to reach the Atlantic. Now they housed their U-boats in bomb-proof shelters in Lorient, and the Admiralty reckoned that this saved the subs 450 miles in travel.

Merchant vessels were classed as non-combatant and any gun of use against a submarine had to be at the stern so that there was no question of being able to chase a submarine. The only guns allowed to be at the front of the vessel were anti-aircraft ones, as there was even less likelihood of chasing an aircraft! Strangely enough, a few U-boats were sunk by merchant ships, usually by catching the submarines unawares and ramming them. Two ships in a company called Ropner

Life on a Tramp Steamer

had sunk submarines in this manner and were jokingly described as 'Ropner's Navy'. After the war I learned that, earlier in the conflict, the *Newton Pine* had sunk a U-boat by her 4-inch gun, which was quite an achievement!

At the start of the convoy system, the Royal Navy appeared to have set ideas on how to deal with U-boats. It seemed to go against the grain for them to be waiting to be attacked. It was considered far better to go out and find them and sink them. This 'attack is the best means of defence' policy was all very stimulating in theory but not really efficient. There was simply too much ocean and too few ships, and the U-boats experienced little difficulty in keeping clear of the destroyers.

I always thought it odd to have destroyers racing around after submarines. If Hitler had 1,000 U-boats in the Atlantic, they were doing him no good unless they were sinking merchant ships. If the destroyers had accompanied the convoy they would have plenty of opportunities to sink U-boats. All through the war I blamed the Royal Navy for this attitude, but I was totally wrong. After the war was over it appeared that it was really Churchill's idea. The RN's expert on convoys was a Captain Talbot, who was in favour of destroyers escorting the convoys.

Every convoy was led by a Commodore whose ship always headed a centre column. This Commodore was responsible for marshalling the convoy, and seeing that the merchantmen, of all shapes, sizes and speeds, kept in formation. At night, in fog, and in high seas, this could be a difficult and unenviable task.

'Wolf packs' (groups of German submarines) usually attacked from the surface by night, and submerged by day. Ideally U-boats used their great surface speed to get ahead of the convoy and, when it came into range, attacked it at periscope depth. Surface raids were made at night because then the U-boats, slim and low in the water, were hard to see. Their commanders preferred to attack when surfaced, for they could then dominate most situations with speeds of close to 20 knots, which was faster than most of the escorts!

A common practice was for one U-boat to go ahead to look for convoys. When it found one, it reported the position to the U-boat Command and this sub would be ordered to shadow the convoy. The U-boat Command was then able to direct the rest of the pack to home in on the contact sub. The pack would then stay ahead of the convoy all day and, when dark, would dive in front of it, then surface inside it.

Whenever possible they would strike from the windward side; this was the most awkward side for a convoy's lookouts to check, and the submarine's bow waves would be at a minimum.

A convoy like this one could stretch 7 miles wide and deep, and thus covered quite a large area. One of the weaknesses of the convoy system was the fact that coal-burning vessels could produce a lot of smoke.

I was put on the 4 to 8 watch and took the wheel from 4pm to 6pm. It was a bit different from the *Reina del Pacifico* as the steering engine was not as powerful and did not work as quickly as the telemotor. This made the steering a bit sluggish. Fortunately the weather was fairly calm and I had a chance to get used to it.

For some strange reason we did not steer using the wheel in the wheelhouse. Instead we used an extra wheel fitted up on 'monkey island' (the deck above the wheelhouse) and this was an appalling practice. The man on the fo'c'sle head, when keeping lookout, can march up and down to keep his feet warm, but on 'monkey island' there was little the helmsman could do but stamp his feet. In really cold weather 2 hours at the wheel was an ordeal.

Steering a vessel is not like driving a land vehicle. The ship is in a fluid and, if changing course, you cannot just wait until the new course is reached, then turn back the wheel – the ship will just keep going in the new direction. It is necessary to check the turning by putting the wheel back before the new course is reached.

On the *Reina del Pacifico* each watch had a bosun's mate, six sailors and an ordinary seaman. They were 4 hours on watch then 8 hours off. In the old days of sail it was 4 on and 4 off, known as 'watch and watch', and must have been really hard going. I think every country in the world except Britain and Greece changed over from 'watch and watch' to the more civilised 4 on 8 off. For some cargo ships Britain did not completely change over, but had a compromise of roughly 4 on 8 off, followed by 4 on 4 off.

The table below should make things clear, and I have called the watches A, B and C. It meant that every morning (0800 to 1200) there would be two watches on deck, the normal one on steering, lookout, etc, and the other with all the hands doing general work. The system was known as working 'field days', and the second watch (in the diagram) was the 'field day' watch.

	Sun	Mon	Tue	Wed	Thur	Fri	Sat
0000-0400	A	A	B	C	A	B	C
0400-0800	B	B	C	A	B	C	A
0800-1200	C	CA	AB	BC	CA	AB	BC
1200-1600	A	B	C	A	B	C	A
1600-2000	B	C	A	B	C	A	B
2000-2400	C	A	B	C	A	B	C

Life on a Tramp Steamer

This resulted in the shipping company getting 72 extra unpaid hours each week from the crew, and each deck worker doing 64 hours a week without overtime! I have yet to find out how and why this iniquitous system came into being.

At the stern of the ship was a propeller-like object called the log. It was spinning round and was attached to a line that was connected to a mechanism for measuring the distance travelled. At the end of every watch (and sometimes more often if necessary) its reading was noted by the officer of the watch. If the officer on the bridge wanted anything done he blew a whistle for the standby man to do what was required. As often the reading of the log was what was wanted, it would not have been sensible to blow for the man, then to tell him to read the log. Accordingly, the officer gave one blast for general work and two blasts so that the man could read the log then report to the bridge.

The food was very poor and not anything like as good as liner standards. We ate off enamel plates and, since our only source of water was the pump out on the well deck (where you stood a good chance of being drenched by a wave), we cleaned them in between courses by using bits of bread. We each had a bucket and kept the plates there.

I developed a taste for tinned corned beef, mainly because all the cook had to do was to slice it – the meat was already cooked. There was always some left over after a meal and I used to keep this so that next day, if the meat was poor, I could always use it together with the potatoes and vegetables.

Cockroaches seemed to proliferate anywhere there was food. Each week we were issued with a tin of condensed milk. The standard practice was to pierce two holes in it, one to let the milk out, and the other to let air in. These holes had to be kept firmly closed by using wadding of some sort otherwise the cockroaches would crawl in and help themselves.

From time to time we were given a 7lb tin of jam. Unfortunately it was never from a single fruit, but always mixed with apple – no doubt for reasons of economy. Thus it could be 'raspberry and apple' or 'rhubarb and apple', but always apple had to be there.

It was now that I learned that the skipper was usually referred to as the Old Man, regardless of his age. Our Old Man was named Fowler and the bosun called him Captain Reilly-Fowler (pronounced 'really fowler') after a current newspaper comic cartoon strip. He had no idea of Morse code and every message had to be translated for him. We were nearly always falling back out of our station and being reprimanded by the Commodore vessel, which finally decided to press ahead and leave us to catch up as best we could.

'He's leaving the convoy behind,' cried he on seeing this (one ship doing barely 7 knots being his idea of the convoy), and asked the 2nd Mate to signal him and ask if he would slow down. When the reply came it was so rude that it was fortunate that he could not read Morse, and the 2nd Mate had to water it down considerably.

Apart from the heavier bombers, the real threat was the dive-bomber, notably the Junkers. When firing at a plane you do not aim at the aircraft but at the spot where the plane will be by the time the shell reaches it. This is known as 'aim off'. Likewise, the aeroplane has to make a similar allowance when dropping a bomb, as the missile takes the direction and speed of the aircraft as it drops, and the shell will hit its target when the plane is directly above.

With the dive-bomber, little calculation needed to be made. The plane pointed straight at the target, the missile was released and the aircraft then pulled out of its dive. Later, when I was on a gunnery course, we were instructed on a battery-type projector that launched about 20 rockets at the plane, and was said to be guaranteed to hit the bomber. The big snag was that by the time you released the missiles the bomber had already released hers!

As a protection against these, several vessels in the convoy would be fitted with barrage balloons similar to those ashore in the towns but about a quarter of the size. The only answer the Germans had to this was to try, if the convoy was within fighter range, to shoot down the balloons.

Although I was not enjoying the life and conditions on a tramp, I was starting to learn some seamanship and this was a consolation. On the first week out I helped one of the ABs to make a new rope ladder and picked up a few tips at the same time.

The weather was very cold during this crossing of the Atlantic, but as we approached the USA it warmed up considerably. A distance from the USA that was reckoned to be safe from submarines was arranged for our rendezvous and all ships reached it safely. We then split up to our various destinations and, since the sea was reasonably calm, we started shovelling the ballast overboard.

Approaching New York we encountered a tremendous thunderstorm, and the flashes of lightening followed in such quick succession that the night was almost turned into day. It was a splendid sight but it was not until morning that the real sight appeared. We had anchored in the Hudson River and, shortly after sunrise, a low-hanging mist rose and revealed Manhattan in all its glory – like a dream city built on air.

However, such visions do not last and before long we saw New York in its true form, the summer sun beating down mercilessly on

Life on a Tramp Steamer

a large crowded city – people hurrying here and there in confusion, and all sorts of small craft buzzing up and down the river, blowing horns and contributing to the general hubbub. I noticed immediately that the USA tugs had large fenders padding their bows and pushed their charges in the required direction, rather than towing them with hawsers as is done in Britain.

After being fingerprinted and questioned by the meticulous immigration officials, we were allowed ashore. They were concerned about seamen leaving the vessel illegally, what was known as 'jumping ship'. Since most sailors could not bear to pass by a public house, they were soon drunk and easily picked up by the authorities.

For anyone to visit the USA for the first time and land in New York is quite thrilling. Everything was so different: the towering buildings, the gigantic ferry-boats, the wonderful neon signs on Broadway, right down to the humble drug stores, soda fountains and hot-dog stands.

I had drawn $15 from the ship and set off from Brooklyn, where we were berthed, walking across to Manhattan. For the past two years food had been severely restricted and I now was presented with chocolates, fruit, soda drinks, hamburgers and other temptations. I regret to say that I sampled them all and next day was feeling queasy.

Uptown in Manhattan were the big stores. As I made to enter one there were crowds of people parading outside with boards marked 'Gimbels unfair to employees'. This was picketing and something I had never seen before. I preferred these big stores as their prices were clearly marked and I felt that some of the smaller shops (with unmarked goods) might take advantage of me when they heard my accent.

On subway, bus or tram, there was only one fare for the journey. Usually 5 cents in the form of a nickel coin was put into a turnstile, which then allowed one to enter. Very few had conductors and, when they did, he sat halfway along the vehicle in a little box. You could pay the fare and immediately pass to the front of the tram, or wait until you were about to get off and pay him then. So all the folk at the front of the vehicle had paid and those at the rear had still to pay. I thought that these were excellent ideas that could be applied in Britain. Later I realised that if you had to get change to pay into a turnstile, this held up passengers and caused delays. Also, the idea of putting a nickel in the slot of the turnstile was not for efficiency; rather it was to make matters simple for some of the out-of-town hillbillies who could not have coped with Glasgow's one stage for ½d, two stages for 1d, four stages for 1½d and so on.

Talking to Americans could be quite revealing. I would be asked how I thought the war was going and tried to be as optimistic as the situation would allow. Almost invariably the conversation would turn to what would happen were we defeated. The burning issue was, would we scuttle the Royal Navy to prevent its falling into German hands? I began to appreciate that they had no real interest in whether or not Britain survived, as long as the USA was safe.

It was astonishing to me how clean New York was. American sailors wearing their tropical whites would sit down on a bench in a public thoroughfare, confident that they would rise from it without fear of dirtying their uniforms.

The dockers wore denims (they called them jeans) when working at the quays and changed into clean clothes when going home, so that it was impossible to tell from his appearance what a man worked at. Moreover, they had the jeans washed frequently. I could not help contrasting this with Britain, where our dockers wore dungarees over their clothing and travelled home in public transport in this condition. I do not think they ever had their dungarees laundered and just threw them away when they were past redemption.

We were to load maize and this required all the holds to be thoroughly cleaned. Normally each hold had wooden battens to keep the cargo away from the metal sides, which were liable to be damp. These battens, of course, had to be removed.

When carried in bulk, grain is very liable to shift, the angle of repose of a pile of grain being about 25 degrees, so that the rolling of a ship at sea is capable of setting it in motion. To prevent this, a temporary wooden bulkhead composed of planks was constructed, extending from the front end to the after end of each hold and stretching from the bottom up to the deck. These were known as shifting boards. The grain was pumped into the vessel through a wide canvas hose until the hold was full. When the ship went to sea the grain would settle down due to the motion of the ship, so a box-shaped feeder had to be built in the hatchway and filled with grain so that it fed the hold below.

Shore workers came on board to carry out this work while we did the cleaning of the holds. Unfortunately 'we' turned out to be the other ordinary seaman and me, as all the sailors did not return to the ship and were ashore drinking. It was hard going with the temperature rising to 95°F. The sailors began to drift back as their funds ran low, and demanded more money. The skipper said that no cash would be offered until the holds were completely clean. Grudgingly they joined us.

We battled away getting the holds cleaned for the grain cargo and, since the temperature was still fairly high, we developed intense

Life on a Tramp Steamer

thirsts. One of the ABs suggested sending for some beer. Now I was brought up to view all forms of alcohol with deep suspicion and to regard public houses as the upper echelons of hell. I had no notion for beer, but the need was desperate for something to cure my parched throat, and I agreed to try it. I remember it being a brand called Pabst beer, and I found it cool, palatable and very refreshing. This was the first time I had tasted an alcoholic beverage.

After five days in Brooklyn the job was completed and we sailed to Weehawken in the state of New Jersey, across the Hudson River, to load the grain.

I was looking forward to getting another $15, but the Old Man limited each seaman to $5 on account of the behaviour of the drinkers. This was most unfair and clearly he had not taken into account the two that had worked every day. He apologised, but by that time it was too late to rectify the situation.

As with most US cities, it is very easy to find one's way around New York. There are various avenues running north to south and they all are numbered. All the main streets are likewise numbered and run east to west. So if someone asks where a certain small street is, he could be told that it ran off Third Avenue between 16th and 17th Streets, and would have no trouble finding it.

Weehawken was just across the river from the famous 42nd Street and, there being a regular ferry, it was handy for shore leave. There was a triangle where one of the avenues and 42nd Street were cut diagonally by Broadway. This was the heart of New York and was a wonderful sight.

On one of the walls of the buildings in this triangle the latest news was flashed around in lights. There was also a very large area about 10 yards by 8 yards on the side of one building lit by electric bulbs. This was before the days of computers, and yet they managed to black out several of these lamps to form silhouettes of a lady in evening dress and man in top hat and tails. Not only that, but they kept switching the lights on and off so that the two silhouettes appeared to be dancing. I was most impressed.

Sailing away from Weehawken, down the Hudson River, we passed the French liner *Normandie* tied up in Manhattan. There was also the spectacle of the Empire State Building, which at that time was the tallest building in the world. Apparently the rents in this building were exceptionally high, resulting in many parts being unoccupied and giving rise to the joke that it should be renamed the Empty State Building! Anyway, all this presented a fascinating picture as we said farewell to New York.

Within three days we were safely at anchor at the port of Sydney

Cape Breton, enjoying the closing days of a Canadian summer. After a further three days waiting for convoy, we set out on our return voyage in company with 40 other merchant ships, four corvettes and a destroyer.

During both crossings we zigzagged, but in a very different way from the liner convoys, where all the vessels turned together at the same time. This method was impracticable due to the variety of ships. If a convoy had seven columns, each of seven vessels, the leaders of each column altered course together when instructed to do so by the Commodore ship. The second ships in line did not follow them but maintained their course and speed until they reached the spot where the leaders turned. They then turned while the third-in-line ships continued up to the same spot. The precise spot was not difficult to find as each ship ahead, at that point, would be seen end-on by the vessel that was to follow it.

Convoys crossing the Atlantic tried to make difficulties for U-boats by sailing on a very northern route. However, three days out from Canada we were some distance south of Cape Farewell in Greenland when trouble started. At 4.30pm submarines were reported to be in the vicinity. The destroyer and a corvette left us to give chase. Everything was peaceful until 8pm when the Northern Lights appeared in the sky. The magnificent spectacle was not fully appreciated, for two sharp explosions announced the beginning of an encounter with U-boats. We rushed on deck but all we could see after a few minutes were some lifeboats signalling with lamps. Twenty minutes later a third ship was torpedoed, so we took the hint and looked out our articles of value.

Fifteen minutes afterwards a fourth ship was hit. She was a petrol tanker carrying her full load and, within a short time, was an inferno with flames rising more than 100 feet into the sky – a ghastly spectacle. The Northern Lights became brighter, the tanker burned more fiercely and soon the darkness was almost like daylight.

Three more explosions occurred in quick succession and three more ships sank. As more explosions followed we had orders to scatter, with *Newton Pine* ploughing along on her own at less than 7½ knots and hoping for the best.

The practice was for the Commodore ship to give out each day the latitude and longitude of a rendezvous in case the ships are forced to scatter. The *Newton Pine* arrived at the prescribed meeting place two days later. Unfortunately a dense fog prevailed, and it was not until a further three days had passed that what was left of the convoy had reassembled. Ten ships were missing.

Three days from home we met with some dirty weather and the

Life on a Tramp Steamer

decks were constantly awash. In these sorts of conditions it was the practice to rig up a rope all along the sides of the well deck so that you had something to hold on to as the ship rolled all over the place; this was known as a lifeline for obvious reasons. In the galley there were metal bars fitted up round the cooking pots to prevent them from crashing on to the deck, and when eating we put wet cloths on the tables to stop the plates from moving about.

It was during this rough spell that I was almost washed overboard. I was on the weather side drawing water from the pump. One very big wave struck the after deck, lifting myself and the bucket over to the rail. It was only by luck I managed to hold on to a bollard and to stay on board.

Looking back at these periods of really rough weather, there was always some joker who would say, 'Pity the poor sailors on a night like this.' And there was also always someone to give the stock answer, 'Yes. The poor sailors in the Sailor's Home at Cardiff.'

Avonmouth was our next haven and our two days there were free of air raids. We discharged our cargo and, after the unpleasant task of cleaning the bilges, we dry-docked across the Bristol Channel in Cardiff. Before arriving, I had a mental picture of Cardiff as a coal-begrimed bunkering port in the Bristol Channel. I was therefore pleasantly surprised to find a very clean modern city with many attractive suburbs and beautiful parks.

We had signed six-month articles and not, as with the *Reina del Pacifico*, for one voyage only. This meant that, as we had been on the vessel for less than six months, we should have to do another trip on her. The other ordinary seaman began acting strangely as we approached port. Now, as said before, this was a common occurrence and was known as 'having the channels', meaning getting over-excited at the prospect of going home. However, his behaviour became grotesque and he was paid off as being mad.

Jack Rosa threw a brick into a jeweller's window and was 'detained at His Majesty's pleasure'. The AB from Surrey managed to get discharged, but the most ingenious trick was pulled by the Midlands AB. He put a crystal of potassium permanganate on to his glans penis and kept it in place with a wet bandage. After a few days it created a swelling similar to that produced by a gonorrhoea infection. He then read up all about the signs and symptoms of this disease and presented himself to the federation doctor, who was taken in completely and pronounced him unfit for sea.

We dry-docked in Cardiff and this was a new experience. No one could use the ship's toilets and had to go to the shore ones and share with dockers, etc. These were most unattractive and you may well imagine what it would be like to be caught short in the middle of the night. It was here that I learned that the term 'crabs' was used to denote pubic lice. In one of the cubicles was a notice stating 'Sailor stand not on this seat. These bloody crabs can jump six feet!'

After leaving the *Reina del Pacifico* I had found walking uncomfortable because of a pain in my foot. My family doctor claimed that it was a verruca, advised me to keep paring it with a razor, and gave me an ointment to put on it. However, after much paring, many applications of the ointment and a voyage on *Newton Pine*, it was no better and, if anything, slightly worse. I asked the Chief Mate for treatment for the foot, and he sent me to the Shipping Federation doctor.

This doctor was an ill-tempered man who kept prodding the sole of my foot and, when I understandably moved it, yelled at me to keep it still. It would have been a simple matter to have provided a stool on which to rest the foot, but he expected me to keep it still in mid-air! After the prodding was over he announced that I was fit to go to sea.

Now, I did not know that the Federation doctor did not offer any cure for ailments, but was merely there to certify whether or not a seaman could return to sea. The Chief Mate had assumed that I was using my foot as an excuse to get off the ship and had sent me to the wrong doctor.

When I asked what I could do to alleviate the pain, he shouted, 'Get out of here, you cheeky bugger, or I'll throw you out!' I maintained a calm front and informed him that I had come in good faith for medication, not to listen to his intemperate language and, if I were to leave, I would most certainly do so under my own steam, for I seriously doubted if he could have knocked the dew off a daisy!

I went to the Seamen's Union and complained, and later the Chief Mate apologised and sent me to a Cardiff hospital where I was given attention, courtesy and treated as a human being. There I was told that I had a welt, and a few days of proper care would cure it. Unfortunately the vessel was leaving the next day, so I had to go with the ship and take the welt with me.

We had a different captain for our second voyage, and quite a few new members in our crew, notably our ordinary seaman. I completely forget what his name was for he was always called 'Happy' on account of his sunny disposition. He used to do the craziest things and laugh them off with a smile, and was not above telling us stories about his past indiscretions.

One I remember well was when he was leaving the wheel in the middle of the watch, and there was a pilot on the bridge with the skipper.

'Do you fancy a cup of tea, pilot?' asked the captain.

'That would be fine,' replied the pilot.

'Bring the pilot up a cup of tea,' said the skipper to the departing ordinary seaman.

By the time Happy arrived back on the bridge the Old Man was peering through binoculars and the pilot was in the toilet.

'Where's the pilot?' asked Happy, and the skipper, still looking through the binoculars, indicated by his elbow that he was in the toilet.

It would be expected that Happy would leave the cup of tea outside the toilet and inform the pilot of this. But Happy, being Happy, opened the door of the toilet and handed the cup and saucer to the pilot, who was seated on the throne with his trousers down at his ankles!

On another occasion he was asked to empty the 'rosie' (a large bucket containing all the scraps of food and refuse from the galley) when his ship was riding at anchor. Now, he had enough sense to wet his finger to find out which was the lee side of the ship and thus avoid rubbish being blown back on him. However, he did not bother to look over the side of the ship and no sooner had the muck been disposed of when there was a long and horrendous yell from over the side. Apparently the garbage had descended on a launch full of captains going to attend a convoy conference – and all attired in their No.1 uniforms!

Talking about masters attending convoy conferences, one of the main objects of these meetings was to ascertain the speeds of the various vessels. Now, skippers are notoriously proud of their commands and do not like to admit that they are in charge of old rust-buckets that are as slow as cart-horses. If one captain says his ship can do 8 knots, the skipper sitting next to him is indeed loath to admit that his can barely do 7½ knots, and there is a strong temptation for what at best could be described as exaggeration. As the war went on this was recognised as a hazard and it was determined that the Chief Engineers should accompany the masters to these conferences. They knew that however much the skipper wanted to impress, the engineer would tell the truth for he was the person who had to make the captain's wishful thinking a reality.

After loading coal we set off for Canada. Carrying coal can be quite tricky and poses the risk of fire or explosion. After it is loaded it emits a flammable gas that can explode on contact with a naked flame – or even a spark. Accordingly maximum ventilation was needed during the early part of the voyage, and often the corner hatch boards were removed to increase ventilation. However, too much ventilation could cause oxygen to be absorbed by the cargo, and this might give rise to spontaneous combustion. So we trod a dangerous line between insufficient ventilation, causing a possible explosion, and too much, risking a fire.

We had a very rough crossing but no mishaps. Outward-bound we discovered that little had been done while in dry dock. The ship had a bad leak and this was not discovered until we were at sea. So, as well as having to contend with U-boats, aircraft surface raiders and possibly mines, there were the added risks of sailing on a ship that would not have been deemed fit for sea in peacetime.

Nevertheless the leak was fixed and we arrived safely at Halifax in Nova Scotia with 1,000 tons of coal in our holds. We were sent up to Montreal for another grain cargo; this time it was to be wheat. It was a three-day sail up the St Lawrence River, during which time the derricks were raised, the hatches opened and the ship got ready to discharge the coal.

The dockers worked three days and nights and, in that time, the coal was discharged, the holds swept clean and 8,000 tons of wheat loaded. As the ship was also bunkered and provisioned, it was quite fast work.

I was chosen to be night-watchman for the three days. This meant that I was on duty from 7pm until 7am the next morning. The main job was to attend to the gangway and mooring ropes and to adjust these with the rise and fall of the tide. Also, there were two fires in each galley and one was let out every night. It was expected that the watchman would clean out this fireplace, relight it from the other fire and have a large pot of boiling water all ready when he called the cook at 6am.

In consideration of this he would receive bacon and egg to cook a meal for himself. This was a treat, as normally bacon and egg meals on tramp ships occurred only on Thursday and Sunday mornings.

The downside to this job was that it was difficult to get sufficient sleep. No consideration was given to this, and the crew might well be chipping rust off the decks just outside the watchman's sleeping quarters.

Still, I had plenty of time to do some shopping and load the 25lb of food to take home. Also, I bought a fur hat with little earflaps that could be either tied up over the hat, or worn down over the ears to keep them warm.

My aunt had knitted me a hollow navy-blue scarf about 6 feet long. The idea was to put one's head into the hollow at one end, and wrap the rest of the material twice round the face, covering all but the eyes. It was a godsend in really cold weather and kept one amazingly warm. Nevertheless, the fur hat was much more convenient when going ashore on a cold day.

I complained again about my foot and was sent to the Montreal General Hospital together with the 2nd Mate, who also had a foot complaint. There was no having to hold the foot in mid-air; a neat little gadget was brought in on which to rest the foot. The young doctor took one look at the foot and said that he thought that there was a foreign body in it. A few seconds later, with the aid of a scalpel, he showed me a piece of steel just under a quarter of an inch long. Obviously this had been caused by walking about on the steel parts of *Reina del Pacifico*'s deck in my bare feet. He said he could speed up the healing process if I came back in a day or two, but, as was now usual, the ship had to sail.

We left Montreal and went down the St Lawrence River to Sydney Cape Breton where we had to join the convoy. Our crossing was attended by intense cold, bad storms and the continual dropping of depth-charges.

A submerged U-boat loses its surface speed and becomes unaware of what was happening above; it was therefore vulnerable to depth-charge attacks. The most effective attacks by the escort vessels were when they worked in tandem. One would maintain contact with the sub by means of Asdic (a device for detecting a submerged submarine by bouncing a sound wave off its hull). It would then radio the U-boat's position and depth to the second vessel, which would speed to the spot and drop depth-charges set to go off at the level of the sub, as shown on the Asdic.

These were dropped four at a time. They could be thrown out from the stern or from either side near the stern. As the vessel was moving the standard practice was to project one from the stern, then one from both sides near the stern simultaneously, and again another from the stern. This meant that the depth-charges formed a diamond pattern with the estimated position of the U-boat at its centre.

When encountering surface raiders, a convoy would be ordered to scatter (by the senior naval officer present) only as a last resort if the attacking force was overwhelmingly strong. Thereafter, each merchantman had to keep radio silence and make for its destination without protection.

The signal 'scatter fanwise and proceed at your utmost speed' entailed a simple and well-understood procedure. The centre column (or when there was an even number of columns, the right-hand column of the centre two) continued ahead. The columns on either side turned away 10° port or starboard. The next columns turned outwards 20° (10° more than their neighbours) and so on to the wings of the convoy. In this way a compact convoy dispersed in a slowly expanding fan; marauders would attack some of the vessels, but this manoeuvre usually secured the safety of most. Convoys of 40 to 50 ships occupied many square miles, and they would consist of several columns of ships some distance apart.

Churchill had authorised generous insurance cover for ship owners to encourage them to send to sea every vessel capable of carrying cargo. The obvious result of this benevolence was that many ships in poor condition were now being pressed into service. This time there were some unusual ships in the convoy, exceptionally narrow in the beam with the bridge almost at the bow and the engine room and after superstructure close to the stern. In between there were many holds and I was told that these were boats specially built for transporting grain round the Great Lakes and were about 1,800 gross tons. I was very glad that I was not sailing on them.

The narrower a ship's beam, the more she is inclined to ship seas. Just imagine putting the lid of a barrel into a tank of water and agitating the surface of the water. The lid will remain fairly dry. Now picture a plank, 6 inches wide and an inch thick, weighted at one side with lead and floating edge uppermost. If the water is now stirred up the surface of the plank will quickly become very wet. These vessels were not made for the North Atlantic and it shows how desperate for shipping space we were, when they were pressed into service.

Each merchant ship had a senior and two junior radio officers, generally known as 'sparks'. In the early part of the war they kept their watches on the bridge and, when necessary, used an Aldis lamp to flash messages in Morse code. Our 3rd Radio Officer was just 16 years old and the Mate was inclined to be very indulgent with him. On the 4 to 8 watch he would do any necessary signalling himself and let the boy stay in his bunk until 6am.

One particular day I had just been steering the ship from 4am and was about to go below to do standby from 6am to 7am.

'Give the 3rd sparks a shake when you're on your way for'ard,' requested the Mate as I was departing.

I accordingly obliged and saw the young lad on his way to the bridge. As I had to pass through the saloon from his cabin I paused and realised this was a heaven-sent opportunity to get some extra sugar to augment our meagre allowance. I was wearing the scarf that my aunt had knitted for me and, as described earlier, it was wound twice round my face.

When in the saloon and just opening a drawer to get at this sugar, all of a sudden I had a sixth sense that I was not alone. Turning round, I was confronted by the 2nd Mate who had the midnight to

4am watch and should have been fast asleep in his bunk at this hour.

As he said nothing, I felt constrained to offer some explanation for my presence, and said the first thing that came into my head: 'I'm looking for the 3rd sparks.'

'Well,' said he with an expressionless face, 'you won't find him in that drawer.'

I was grateful for my aunt's scarf, which covered my embarrassment.

About two-thirds of the way across, the shifting boards in one hold gave way and the grain moved from port to starboard. With the list becoming increasingly worse, we had to go down into the hold and carry wheat in sacks (each weighing about half a hundredweight) from one side of the shifting boards to the other. This was not an easy task as we were walking on top of grain while carrying this load on our backs and our feet were sinking into the wheat at every step. It was several hours before we had the vessel straightened up.

This work was done when we were off watch, and when we had finished we still had to continue on our 64-hour week! Moreover, we would not be paid a penny in overtime as it specified in the articles that, if the captain declared the work to be for the 'safety of ship', no extra payment would be made.

It is worth pausing to ponder this question of 'safety of ship'. It was considered that in emergencies, when sailors could be required to man the pumps to save a vessel from sinking, it was not right that they should be paid extra money when their own lives were at stake. This premise is debatable and 'left-handed' logic. If the sailors were helping to save their own lives they were also helping to save the ship and possibly its cargo, and could be paid at least a percentage of normal overtime rates.

The system was open to malpractice by unscrupulous masters – and they were nearly all unscrupulous. Suppose a ship is lying well offshore and at anchor, waiting to go to the quay to discharge cargo. The skipper sees another vessel leaving an anchorage nearer the dock and decides it would be a good idea to take the place of this ship. He calls out the bosun, carpenter and two sailors and they weigh anchor and go to the new anchorage. If any of the seamen asks for overtime they are told that the captain had decided that the old anchorage was not safe – and who can argue with the skipper's opinion?

On the subject of swindling seamen there was another abuse. Ships' articles stated that on days of arrival and days of sailing seamen would be required to work 10 hours before any overtime was paid. So, on weekdays, the seaman was diddled out of 2 hours' overtime, but on Sundays he could be cheated out of 10 hours.

During my first-aid lessons I had learned that cold water should never be applied to a burn. At the beginning of the 20th century the treatment was carron oil, then tannic acid jelly, then a variety of remedies, but always the overriding *caveat* that water should never be used.

One day our carpenter was burning paint off one of the lifeboats with a blowlamp when he accidentally gave himself a severe burn. He rushed to the pump with me, the ordinary seaman (with the ink scarcely dry on my first-aid certificate) running after him to tell him that on no account should he put water on the burn.

'Who says so?' the carpenter demanded to know.

'The British Medical Association,' I replied, airing my new-found knowledge.

He then told me – in a manner distinctly his own – what he thought of the British Medical Association, as he proceeded to pump cold water all over the wound. Writing this, more than 60 years later, it appears that the carpenter was right, and the British Medical Association has since done a 180° turn.

But despite the thoroughly miserable crossing, we arrived safely at Loch Ewe with our pump and two winches out of order and the stove in our quarters wrecked. We sailed down to the south part of this loch and anchored off the town of Poolewe. It was here that we learned that the Japanese had attacked the USA fleet in Pearl Harbor.

From Loch Ewe we proceeded to Methyl, and from there to the River Tyne. It was not until we were in the river that we learned that we were to discharge at Dunstan, a few miles from Newcastle.

Newcastle-upon-Tyne was quite a strange place where, at the railway station, the newsvendors were selling condoms together with their newspapers!

These two voyages had lasted from 25 July until 8 December 1941 and, since our articles were for a period of six months or more, we could have been forced to do another trip on the *Newton Pine*. No one wanted to do this and our new skipper was decent enough not to insist on it.

Next year the *Newton Pine* was in Convoy ONS 136 bound for Halifax. During a storm she became separated from the convoy and was sunk by U-136 on 15 September 1942.

4

Under a Foreign Flag

Only now did I learn that there had been plans to prevent the Germans landing soldiers in Scottish lochs. It sounds hard to believe, but there were certainly four launches stationed on Loch Lomond with this object in mind. They were actually manned by naval and military personnel, and fitted with Lewis guns, and were expected to give a warm reception to any seaplanes attempting to land enemy troops in Loch Lomond.

I paid off the *Newton Pine* on 8 December 1941 with ten days' leave due to me. This took me up to 18 December, and I did not want to ship out so near Christmas so I volunteered to go on a gunnery course that was to last two weeks and would safely take me into the New Year. This took place at a naval building in Govan on the outskirt of Glasgow.

We were given instruction on all types of guns from the 12-pounders (for use against subs) to the various anti-aircraft guns such as the Bofors, Oerlikon, Browning, Hotchkiss, Lewis, etc. We were also instructed on using the Holman Projector, which was a crude form of mortar and used steam under pressure to launch hand grenades at low-flying aircraft.

The big guns required a gunlayer, who was in charge of the gun and determined the range to be used by raising or lowering its elevation, a gun trainer, who was responsible for the gun's sideways movements, and about four other members to load, ram and so on.

We had two DEMS gunners on board *Newton Pine* but, if the gun had to be operated by two instead of six, its rate of fire would hardly be more than two shells a minute, so the course I embarked on was to provide extra gunners from the normal crew. Those signed on as 'merchant gunners' would be paid sixpence a day on top of their wages, but, true to their skinflint ideals, only two of them on each vessel would be paid.

At sea at that time there were fast liners that had had their decks reinforced to accommodate 6-inch guns. They were termed 'armed merchant cruisers', flew the white ensign and had personnel that were part merchant and part naval. There were also large sea-going rescue tugs that were run on similar lines. Their articles (T124) were for a period of six months and, desperate to be afloat again, I went to the St Enoch Hotel to be interviewed by a Lieutenant-Commander Parker RN with a view to sampling life in the Royal Navy.

He seemed to like the cut of my jib, as the nautical saying goes, and asked me many questions. Now, at that time the Navy was proposing to add an 'X' to the cruiser articles and a 'T' to the tug articles, and this would make the signing-on for the duration of hostilities. I asked the Lieutenant-Commander if the articles were T124 for six months, or T124X for the duration. When I found out that the Navy wanted me for a lengthy period I declined their offer.

The Navy was intent on plundering the merchant navy in many ways. There was the Royal Naval Reserves (RNR), in which merchant seamen signed up for a one-month period of naval training each year and, in time of war, were called to the colours. There was a deal of snobbery in some passenger companies, and if they had a certain number of their officers and ratings in the RNR they were permitted to fly the blue ensign instead of the red. Also, many good merchant navy cooks were drafted into the Royal Navy and were replaced by six-month trainees.

There was also the RNVR (Royal Navy Volunteer Reserves), whose members were roughly the equivalent of the Territorial Army. The RN officers had straight gold bands denoting rank, the RNR had chain bands, and the RNVR had large wavy bands – hence their nickname of the 'Wavy Navy'. There was an old joke that the RN was gentlemen trying to be sailors, the RNR was sailors trying to be gentlemen, and the RNVR was neither, trying to be both!

In addition to pilfering sailors for merchant cruisers and rescue tugs, the RN indulged in a very sharp practice to get radio officers. Many young lads aspiring to be radio officers in the merchant navy went to a college and paid fees over a period of six months to get the necessary tuition and certificate. They were not the equivalent of the Chief Radio Officers but had an adequate knowledge of radio and were proficient in sending and receiving Morse signals – both visual and audio. When they passed out they joined the firm of Marconi (or in fewer cases Siemens) and were sent to a merchant ship, but paid by Marconi (or Siemens). The Royal Navy learned of this and waited until the boys had their certificates, then called them up for service in the RN. They were given the amount of the fees that they had incurred, but the RN now had a fully trained rating ready to go to sea.

One of my friends was treated in this cavalier way and I met him later in Halifax. Had he been allowed to join the merchant navy he would have had officer status, but in the RN he was a wearer of bell-bottoms and sported on his sleeve a pair of red wings with a thunderbolt through them. As he was a very intelligent lad, with four good Highers to his credit, I asked if there was any chance that he could be promoted to officer. He said that he was sure he could have had a commission in any other branch of the RN but, in his area, a BSc degree in electrical engineering would have been required.

During this spell ashore I applied for a scholarship for the Nautical College of the University of Southampton and was awarded one. It was a four-year correspondence course for a 2nd Mate's certificate, and I was supposed to send in a paper every month where this was possible. The studies were certainly very comprehensive and, at times, I thought they were tutoring me for an Extra Master's ticket!

There did not seem to be many jobs going for ordinary seamen and, desperate to get back to sea, I applied for a post on the *Loch Garry*, a steamer owned by MacBrayne's. It would be coasting, but it would be a change. Some hitch occurred – I forget just what was the matter – but I lost the job. This was just as well, as she sank on 21 January 1942 and more than 20 of her crew drowned. Oddly enough it was not due to enemy action – she was shipwrecked on Rathlin Island in foggy weather.

After this long time ashore I became restless and volunteered for convoy duty. This meant standing by in readiness for any immediate need of men when a convoy was putting out to sea. I was only half an hour in the shipping office when a sailor was required for the *Gaizka*, a Panamanian vessel. Now Panamanian ships were generally reckoned to be comfortable and the crews well looked after, so I accepted and dashed home for a hasty meal before going back to the shipping office. My father was a bit apprehensive, but I was steeped in euphoria.

I was taken by taxi to Gourock where I made what was termed a 'pierhead jump'. The *Gaizka* was lying at anchor some way out and, in company with several others who were obviously being shanghaied to different ships, I boarded a launch that took me to the vessel. On being told to board her, I was greatly taken aback. True, she was a Panamanian – the flag was fluttering in the evening breeze and a painted version of their colours on the hull was lit up on either side amidships – but she was only about 300 gross tons, and overloaded with coal.

Her crew numbered 13 and we would have sailed that night had not one of her members disappeared. Seemingly he had asked for a sub to buy a pair of boots. They must have been seven-league boots, for he departed and was never seen again. As it was, we stayed at anchor for two days, then sailed out one member short.

The *Gaizka*'s skipper was a Basque, her Chief Engineer and Mate were Spanish and the rest were Portuguese, with the exception of a young Newfoundland AB and myself.

Before signing on I was shown the articles. It seemed that the *Gaizka* was owned by a Compañia Naviera Urto Zara of Lisbon and was sailing under what was usually described as a 'flag of convenience'. She was on a regular triangular mission: coal taken from Britain to Lisbon; the coal discharged and the ship loaded with wine for Dublin; then across to Britain for more coal.

The wages were £35 a month, which was roughly twice what a British AB was receiving. Furthermore, there were generous bonuses. If you went on a voyage in convoy you were entitled to half a month's extra wages for the voyage, but, if without convoy, a full month's wages would be paid.

I could scarcely believe it. At a minimum, one triangular trip a month with convoy would bring in £87 10s, while, at a maximum, two without convoy would net £245! This was real money then and, although cash was never my main concern, if someone was throwing large chunks of at it at you, it did not seem sensible to duck and let it fly over your head. So I signed on.

I was at the wheel when she left the Clyde and it was an ordeal. Steering by landmarks, I managed to take the ship through the boom, but when I had to resort to the compass the real fun began. The binnacle was lit by two very small paraffin lamps that repeatedly went out, leaving me to steer with one hand and hold an electric torch in the other. The wheel being stiff, this was very tiring.

Once out of the Clyde, the navigation lights were lit and a strong beam shone on the painted Panamanian colours on her sides as we settled down to a five-day voyage to Lisbon without convoy. We were short of one deck rating, so had to make do with three instead of four. It was arranged that we would do 2 hours steering and 4 hours work or standby. This meant 8 hours a day at the wheel – but worse was to follow. Our room was very much too small and we also had to eat as well as sleep there, as there was no mess-room. It was practically devoid of ventilation and the dirt was caked on the deck.

After two days at sea a stiff breeze sprang up and the *Gaizka* began to roll violently and ship seas. That night found us battling with a real storm and our speed reduced to 1½ knots. In the middle of the night one of the falls on a lifeboat parted, leaving the boat dragging in the water. After a weary 2 hours' work we brought it back on board again, with the assistance of two firemen, the cook and several hurricane lamps. We hardly moved that night and lay with all lights on, fair game for any raider.

Daylight saw the glass still falling and the swell increasing. The *Gaizka* now proceeded to give an exhibition of unbelievable acrobatics. She pitched, tossed, rolled, corkscrewed and did everything but turn over. The galley was wrecked and surrounded by water. The cook was inside and unable to get out, while we were outside and unable to get in.

I felt distinctly queasy and had a horror of being seasick. This feeling was reinforced when I brought up my breakfast. Fortunately it was not actually seasickness and, as long as I did not eat anything, I did not retch, whereas with real seasickness it is a deal worse on an empty stomach.

The Mate decided to put Fernando, the third deckhand, below with the firemen to see if we could increase our speed. This left the Newfoundlander and me to work the ship. We arranged to do 3 hours steering and 3 hours standby, a daily total of 12 hours at the wheel!

The 3 hours when we were not steering were never really free time, as there was always something coming adrift and requiring to be secured. As we were bothered with fleas I recall that, when steering, I was too tired too scratch myself and merely rubbed my chest up and down one of the spokes on the wheel.

Going to read the log was an ordeal. You had to clamber on top of the after hatch, cling on to its derrick and wait for a suitable break in the waves that were lashing over the poop. It could take considerable time and effort.

Our room flooded, leaving the Newfoundlander and me to shake down on the deck of the chart room. The galley was still in a state of siege, so we lived on bread and biscuits. Our day consisted of 12 hours steering, 5 hours work and odd snatches of sleep in between in our wet clothes. We were supposed to reach Portugal in five days, but after six days we put in to Queenstown, in the south of Ireland, having given up all hope of reaching Lisbon.

At first I had thought of doing maybe two or three trips on her, then decided that one was enough – now I just wanted off as soon as possible. The Old Man gave up any ideas of reaching Lisbon and announced that we would go to Cardiff.

Arriving at Cardiff, I was at the wheel when we picked up the pilot. He started giving the helm orders in Spanish and was greatly surprised to find that I was British. He told me that I should get off the ship right away and that, if I had any trouble, he would help, stressing that he was an Extra Master in sail, and knew what he was talking about. He then informed me that she was not fit for sea, and had been obliged to change her name twice to get new crews.

We had this notion about her lack of seaworthiness ourselves and, at Queenstown, cherished the idea that, if the skipper would not pay us off, we would lower a lifeboat, row ashore at night and make for the British Consul. However, the captain promised to release us at Cardiff, thus saving us from committing an illegal act.

So short-handed were we that the skipper took over the wheel, leaving me to help with the mooring. The Mate and Fernando were for'ard and the Newfoundlander and I were aft. On entering the docks we singled up the ship with wire hawsers, I being at the capstan. The wire, unfortunately, had jagged pieces of metal protruding from the strands and, before we tied up, my hands were cut beyond description.

In case you wonder why I did not wear gloves for this task, let me assure you that I should have done so had I considered it to be safe. The risk with putting on gloves was that if these jagged ends of wire caught in the glove, the hand could be quickly pulled into the capstan and the fingers mangled – better to have cut palms.

Once the ship was moored I got ready to pack but found that 200 cigarettes had disappeared from my case. Further investigation revealed that my going-ashore trousers were also missing. I went to the skipper and demanded a search of the ship. He became irate and began pushing me and, being thoroughly annoyed, I pushed back. For a moment it seemed that there would be a real furore when, all of a sudden, a voice broke in with, 'Let's not have any unpleasantness – perhaps I can help.'

Turning round I became aware of the chaplain of the Flying Angel Mission to Seamen, complete with dog-collar. It ended up with my going to the mission that evening, and the minister giving me an old pair of his clerical-grey trousers to see me home.

Since we had not completed the voyage and had spent a total of 13 days on board, I received only £13 10s for my work. I regarded myself as being cheaply rid of a very bad ship. I arrived home looking a bit the worse for wear and with only a few tins of fruit that I had managed to get someone to buy for me in Queenstown.

I took the little leave I was due and registered at the Pool. This was like a labour exchange for seafarers and you were paid £3 a week while waiting for a ship. Now I could easily have accepted the £3 and lived on it and taken part-time employment, as there was plenty of it around, but such is the impetuosity of youth that I was bursting to get back to sea.

Food shortages were worsening and there seemed to be queues everywhere. It was policy to join any queue in the expectation of getting something extra. I had little to do when on leave so every time I saw a queue at a fishmonger's shop I joined it. I recall paying for three pieces of lemon sole but, on arriving home, finding two of them to be doubtful specimens. I returned to the shop and complained that I had not been given three lemon soles.

'Are you an expert in fish?' was the impudent enquiry.

'No,' said I, 'but I know that there are two different kinds of fish in this package. If this one is a lemon sole, the other two are not, and if they are lemon soles, this one is not.'

He claimed that the ones I had doubts about were actually better.

'Right, I said, 'if these are better, give me three of the ones that you reckon are not so good.'

It finished up with my money being refunded. This practice of the fishmonger was known as a conditional sale, and was against the law. The others in the queue knew that to get a piece of lemon sole they would have to accept two inferior fish, but did not see fit to protest. The sale of women's hose was subjected to similar abuse. To get a decent pair of stockings they would have to buy a substandard pair in the same purchase.

5

More foreign flags

After a few weeks ashore and no sign of work, someone advised me to try the Norwegian Consul for a job. The Norwegians ran their own lines at a profit and, if any of their vessels were sunk, they bought a new one with the insurance money. However, the Norwegian seamen could not be replaced, and they had to accept other nationalities.

After some two weeks pestering the Consul I signed on the cargo ship *Norvarg* as an ordinary seaman – or, in Norwegian, a 'lettmatros'. Actually, a 'lettmatros' (literally 'little sailor') was counted a bit better than an ordinary seaman and this was reflected in the wages. I was to receive £18 a month, which was slightly more than a British AB. On the subject of wages, before Greece was forced into the war it chartered ships to the UK. They paid their ABs about £50 a month, showing how much profit British ship-owners were pocketing!

The *Norvarg* was everything that the *Gaizka* was not. We were housed two to a cabin, and each cabin was fitted with mirrors, adaptable tables, big lockers, radiators and bed-lamps. Our messroom was amidships and a messboy ('messgut') was provided to look after our needs. Her lower deck complement consisted of a bosun, a carpenter ('tommerman'), four ABs ('matros'), five OSs ('lettmatros') and a deck boy ('decksgut').

The food was excellent and there were no field days, as they worked a straight 4 hours on and 8 off. Also, unlike British ships, where the eating quarters were intentionally designed to accommodate only two-thirds of the crew, we had ample space for messing when the ship was in port.

Another definite plus for the Norwegians was their lifesaving outfits. On British ships all we had was a life jacket, connected to which was a light operated by battery. The Norwegians had something that started like a pair of rubber sea boots and continued with the same material upwards until it reached the neck, where there were strings to seal the equipment; also attached was a bright yellow rubber covering for the head. Therefore you could put on a lifejacket and cover it with this gear and you were then totally enclosed, waterproof, warm and buoyant.

We were a few days berthed at Rothesay Dock in Clydebank and I stayed at home and travelled down to work each day. There was no such thing as 'peggying' on this Norwegian ship. A mess boy had the job of serving our food and tidying up afterwards, and even our deck boy only did work of a seamanship kind.

What I especially liked on the Norwegian ships was the way they kept their vessels scrupulously clean. When taking rust off the decks of a British ship you were never quite sure how to proceed. One bosun would tell you that you had missed a bit, while on another ship you would be taken to task for being too long on the job and being over-careful. With the Norwegians you started off with a large hammer, pounding all the deck plates. Then you went on to a small chipping hammer, a metal scraper and finally a wire brush, until every speck of rust was removed.

I was asked to join the Norsk Sjømannsforbund (the Norwegian Seamen's Union) and readily complied. It was much better than our National Seamen's Union, for its delegate was actually one of the crew, and we could consult him about any matter, and at any time during the voyage. The badge we wore is pictured.

Our trip across the Western Ocean (the sailor's term for the North Atlantic) in convoy had a few days of bad fog but was otherwise uneventful, and we arrived safely at Cape Cod.

The war was not going at all well. The Yanks were more concerned with the war in the Pacific and did not take the Atlantic conflict seriously. They just had not considered the possibility of someone attacking them on their own shores. None of their businesses were prepared to dim their lights and, with ships silhouetted against this, it was like a shooting gallery.

We learned after the war was over that, on 13 January 1942, the U-123 had inched its way into New York Bay and was astonished to find bright lights everywhere. Ships were sailing along with navigation and masthead lights on and cars could be seen driving along the coast roads with full headlights.

This submarine waited until ships left New York and followed them until they were in about 20 fathoms of water, then sank them.

Her commander only wished that there had been more U-boats in this area, for the results would then have been utterly awesome.

In the first four months after America entered the war, 50 tankers had been sunk on its eastern coastline and in the Caribbean. For a time after this, all tanker traffic was stopped. The US reply to this was to send aeroplanes out to bomb subs, and many of these planes returned stating that they had sunk U-boats. Despite these claims, no German U-boats were sunk in the first three months after the USA entered the war, and the US Navy was unable to protect shipping in its own waters.

Admiral Dönitz, the German U-boat commander, sent all the subs he could get together to US waters. They could now meet off the US coast and be supplied by giant underwater tankers. This meant that they could double the length of their patrols.

A wave of U-boats enjoyed rich pickings in the next two months off the eastern coast of the USA. Figures showed that, in February alone, more than 430,000 tons of shipping was sent to the bottom of the sea. All this caused the Germans to boast about 'The American Turkey Shoot'. There was also stinging criticism from the Admiralty that the USA had not introduced a convoy system, and in the month of June 173 ships were sunk!

Since we were bound for Philadelphia it was thought safer if we went through the Cape Cod Canal, then sailed down the East River (between Long Island and Manhattan) to New York, thus taking us away from the open sea. It was delightful to sail on a canal for a change. It certainly turned out to be safer because the other part of the convoy was attacked by U-boats and badly mauled.

I was at the wheel when we sailed down the East River and the pilot engaged me in conversation.

'How's the war going, bud?' he asked.

'Not too well,' I replied.

'Well, you've nothing to worry about now.'

'How's that?'

'We're in it now and we've an army here that can lick the world – never mind Germany.'

'Beating Germany will do for a start,' I responded, amazed at his overweening confidence. It was obvious that he had no idea what the Germans were like.

On berthing at Philadelphia my heart sank when I was told I had to be a night watchman. Naturally I envisaged the British custom of 7pm till 7am every day with little chance to enjoy life ashore. But there was a pleasant surprise in store. They had two watchmen, one from 4pm until midnight and one from midnight until 8am. I was put on the midnight to 8am spell. This meant that I could enjoy an evening ashore, and the other watchman said I could come back late if I let him know in advance. Moreover, this spell at night gave me the opportunity to catch up on my correspondence course with Southampton University.

This was the first time I had been in the USA since the attack on Pearl Harbor, and it was quite a revelation. Walking down a street I noticed that the window in one house had its top part covered by a cloth banner on which was a gold star above the words 'Our son in the US Army'. In the next street another window was similarly decked out, but this time it was two stars and the words 'Our two sons in the US Marines'. And on it went: 'Our son in the US Navy', 'Our daughter in the WAVES', and so on.

We were there for 19 days loading steel ingots and baled cotton. One evening, when I was ashore, there was trouble on board ship. Apparently bales of cotton are liable to spontaneous combustion, and one of them caught fire. The deck boy, with commendable resourcefulness, quickly rigged up a hose and quenched the flames.

I was impressed with this city and learned more of American life. I visited the Pennsylvania State Museum, which was then unfinished because the citizens refused to pay more rates to fund the work, but I missed seeing the planetarium. This was a disappointment as there were, at that time, only four of them in the world.

Philadelphia is Greek for 'brotherly love', but some of my shipmates did not see much justification for the term. The ship's officers warned them against frequenting taverns in the vicinity of the docks but, as is usual, sailors cannot wait to get at the booze, so did not heed this advice. They paid dearly for their folly. A common practice ashore was to slip a small pill – a 'Mickey Finn' – into the drink of any likely customer, which rendered the victim helpless in a short time, after which the casualty was robbed of all cash and any articles of value.

By 5am a dozen or so of the crew had arrived back in dreadful condition. One was still missing, a fireman from Stornoway, who had sensibly bought himself several items of clothing before going on a binge. He was to fare even worse than the rest. At 7am, just as it was light, I spied a figure that looked to be walking in a peculiar manner along the ashes on the dockside. He had been given a 'Mickey Finn' and robbed of all cash and clothing. They took even his new shoes, hence the odd gait caused by his having to walk over the ashes with only stockings on his feet.

It was quite astonishing how many people were on our ship during the night. There were three detectives on board: one at the bow, one at the gangway and one aft at the gun and, in addition, two US coastguards. With one of our DEMS gunners and me, it made a total of seven. They were not taking any chances with sabotage.

I felt that we were a bit overstaffed and one night, when I was a bit tired, one of the detectives proposed that I go to my cabin and have a lie down, adding that he would cover for me if anyone asked where I was. As I was a bit sleepy on account of the crew keeping me awake by chipping rust outside my cabin during the day, I welcomed his suggestion. Unfortunately I dozed off. Seemingly the Mate had wanted to know where I was and the detective tried stalling by saying that he had seen me a few minutes ago.

Next thing the Mate was in the cabin saying, 'Is this the vay you keep a vatch? Do you think I have a vatchman for fun?'

This was obviously a rhetorical question.

The Mate did nothing further about the affair, but I decided not to take any chances. In future, on the only other occasion I felt the need of sleep, I led a thin rope from the detective's seat, through a ventilator down to the centre castle where I lay down, after having fastened the other end of the rope round my ankle. All the detective had to do was give the rope a tug.

These detectives were very interesting to chat to. One had been involved in bootlegging during the Prohibition period and regaled me with tales of how matters were conducted in the shebeens. In the smaller dens they kept the bottles in the sink so that, was a raid to take place, they could be broken and all the evidence destroyed. Of course, from time to time they had to send out for more bottles from their depot and, each time they did so, a second man was despatched to see that the first one was not being followed.

Prohibition was a disastrous mistake. As it continued for many years it drew masses of people into its folds: bricklayers who had been lucky to earn $80 a week were soon receiving $800 for unskilled work, with more to come as business grew.

When at last the Government realised the mistake and repealed the Act, it would be expecting too much for the bricklayers to adopt a philosophical attitude and say, 'Well, it was good while it lasted, but tomorrow we go back to bricklaying at $80 a week.' Having tasted the delights of making big money, they were to find other avenues that provided high returns; usually it would be some form of illicit gambling.

The coastguards were changed each night and I began to be able to place the different US accents when conversing with them. In Britain one's accent is a product of environment, education and social class. To some degree it is similar in the USA, but with the region being the dominant factor. Thus you could have a New York senator speaking very poorly and a street sweeper from Iowa or Nebraska talking beautiful English.

For my second sub from the captain, there must have been some misunderstanding for I was given $70, which was more than I had intended to draw. Rather than decline it I went out to buy some new clothes.

My first thought was to purchase a lounge suit, but on finding that they did not have turn-ups (the Yanks called them cuffs) on the trousers, I decided against it as I could get a similar suit at home with them, and British tailoring was much superior – so much so that the better tailors in Philadelphia used to advertise their products as 'English tailoring'. In prewar times all trousers in Britain – unless they were uniforms – had turn-ups or cuffs.

While I was deliberating, an American chap came in and kicked up a fuss because he could not get these cuffs on his suit while women could buy slacks with cuffs on them. This solved the predicament: I would buy a sports jacket and get a pair of trousers to go with them.

The jacket was made of beautiful green-blue tweed material but was a trifle long. They were all like that, what the Yanks called coats. What we called coats, they described as overcoats. The trousers proved to be the problem. First I was offered a pair of cream-coloured slacks with a half-inch dark-brown stripe running down them. I tried to be as tactful as possible, knowing that the salesman would not have any idea what was acceptable in Britain. Next I was shown a pair that were bright brick-coloured. Finally I settled for trousers that were a lighter blue than I wanted but were the best I could hope for.

Life ashore was very pleasant. The Merchant Navy Club arranged dances and other functions and insisted that any girl who wanted to attend them had to have two character references. At one of these I met a charming girl named Anne Richards. Before I could date her, I was invited out to her house for dinner and to meet her parents. This was quite understandable, but I seemed to have passed the test with flying colours for I was invited back and allowed to date the girl. I showed them photographs of my two nephews in their kilts and they said the usual 'How sweet!' and 'Aren't they cute?'

Anne could not have been any more than 17 and on the small side. So when she offered to run me back to the ship – a distance of 12 miles – I was at first nervy when she took the wheel of a monstrously large car. After 10 minutes I felt that she was competent enough, so I relaxed and enjoyed the run.

When we drew money from the ship, for every $4 issued £1 was deducted from our account of wages. Now, at the beginning of hostilities the rate of exchange was $4 to the pound, but Britain was not now financially strong because of the immense spending on the war, and I find this rate not easy to understand. I fancy the USA must have pegged the four-to-one rate of exchange for British seamen as a friendly gesture as, after all, it would not have been a great drain on their resources.

My theory was strengthened by the fact that when our seamen ran short of funds and gave pound notes to the owners of dockland taverns, they received $2 for each one. These proprietors really did not want pound notes, even at this low rate, and did the favour hoping that the sailor would spend the dollars on booze (most likely in their pub) and would later redeem the sterling when the skipper gave out more cash.

Alas, very few ever reclaimed the pounds, and the recipients of them would have to go to the banks where they certainly would not get anything like the ship's rate of exchange. If I had been a bit more worldly or astute, I could have visited these hostelries and doubled my money by buying back the sterling, but I was never that way inclined.

Apart from giving up pounds in exchange for dollars there was another avenue open to impoverished sailors. In Britain people gave blood on a regular basis to help the hospitals that needed it for transfusions, and the donors were thanked and given a cup of tea and a biscuit for their trouble. However, in the USA the hospitals were willing to pay blood donors. They did not seem to have an efficient system to check up on the frequency of the donors' visits, and as a consequence many sailors returned to sea positively anaemic.

In the UK, picture houses had three rates of admittance. The dearest seats were in the balcony, next were the back stalls and the cheapest were the front stalls. These prices were higher in the evening than in the afternoons and there were no morning performances. In the USA there was only one price for any performance and it was a case of first come, best served. However, the prices varied considerably during the course of the day. A really top-class cinema in the centre of the town would cost between $1.50 and $1.75 for an evening show, but only 50 cents in the afternoons and a mere 10 cents in the morning! Smoking was only permitted in the balcony.

We stayed almost three weeks. I enjoyed the watchman's job with its usual perks, but late one evening my cabin-mate, a Canadian, came back a bit tipsy and tried to do a juggling act in the galley, using some of the ship's crockery. The steward, also a bit inebriated, said that he would lock the galley in future so that there would be no more variety acts. I set no store by this statement and was confident that it was the ramblings of a drunken man who would see things in a different light when he sobered up.

Not so. Thereafter he locked the galley every night, despite my protests. Possibly I should have gone to the Mate and complained at the steward's irrational behaviour but, after the incident when he had caught me out in the cabin, I felt that, as Shakespeare would have put it, my credit 'stood on slippery ground'.

It called for action on my part. I thought that I could lift the skylight above the galley and climb down into it on a rope. This was a formidable task, as this immense skylight must have weighed nearly 1,000lb. There was a lifeboat near the skylight and it had the usual arrangement of ropes going through two three-sheaved blocks, top and bottom. I took one of the falls off the lifeboat and secured its hook to the skylight and pulled. It was no use.

Determination set in as I resolved not to be beaten by a steward. I got hold of what was termed a 'handy billy', a small block and tackle giving a threefold purchase. I connected this gadget to the falls of the lifeboat and, by the combined efforts of the two purchases, managed to lift the skylight about 4 inches. I had to secure this and go through the operation again. After five or six efforts the skylight was far enough open for me to get into the galley and help myself to whatever I fancied – and I fancied bacon, two eggs, fried potatoes and anything else that was capable of being fried. After the feast, I cleaned up, left the galley as I had found it and put back the lifting gear in its proper place. I did this every night for the remaining four nights in port, and the steward looked puzzled but could not figure out what had happened.

The American drug stores were really big cafés. One noticeable difference from Britain was that whereas we made ice cream on the premises but brought in all our aerated waters, the Yanks purchased all their ice cream from manufacturers but – with the exceptions of Coca-Cola, Pepsi-Cola and Seven Up – all their fizzy drinks were made while you waited.

On a warm day the attendant would present you with a glass of ice-cold water before taking your order. Asking for a cheese sandwich and a glass of milk was quite different from back home. You would be asked what kind of bread you wanted, whether you wanted it plain or toasted, what sort of cheese and butter (brazil nut, peanut, etc) you wished, and whether you wanted the milk warm or cold.

American public houses all had free toasted peanuts on their counters – presumably to promote thirst among their clientele – and also hard-boiled eggs at a modest price. If you stood at the bar, instead of sitting down at a table, every so often you would get a free round of whatever you were drinking. This could be every fifth or sixth time you ordered a drink, but one bar in Staten Island offered this bonus every third round.

When I was visiting an American family in a nearby New Jersey town I mentioned that my cabin mate was Canadian.

'Oh,' exclaimed my host, 'a French Canadian.'

'No,' I replied, 'he's not French.'

'Well, we call them all French Canadians,' was the response.

Later we were talking about the Germans, whom he described as Dutch.

'No,' I protested, 'they really are Germans.'

'Well, we always call them Dutch.'

'What then do you call the folk that live in the Netherlands?' I was most anxious to know.

'We call them Holland Dutch,' I was told.

This reminded me of the playwright George Bernard Shaw saying that England and the USA were two countries divided by a common language!

One real bonus was that all the time we were in port we had fresh milk every day, and this was much preferable to the tinned condensed milk we had at sea. Moreover, they managed to provide this milk for the first five or six days after leaving port.

We took six weeks to get to Wales due to time wasted waiting for convoys. On the way home we stopped at New York, Cape Cod, Halifax, Sydney Cape Breton and even at Belfast. Unfortunately we were not allowed ashore at any of these places.

If I remember correctly, this was the first time I saw a CAM ship. I was told that the initials meant Carrying Aircraft Merchantmen, but was later informed that it was Catapult Armed Merchantmen. They were envisaged by the Admiralty as the solution to the problem of long-range enemy bombers, such as the Focke-Wolfe Kondors, which were cooperating with U-boats in the Atlantic. For this purpose a makeshift system was devised whereby merchant ships were fitted with catapults from which a single fighter (either a Fulmar or Sea Hurricane) could be launched along a structure of girders with rocket assistance. The snag was that the pilots (the first were volunteers from the Fleet Air Arm) had to ditch the plane and bail out after making the interception.

Some merchant skippers resented the presence of the casual young aviators and their maintenance crews. Quite apart from the disruption they caused in the normal smooth running of the ship, they could be viewed as yet another danger in an increasingly unsafe profession. Any U-boat commander, sizing up a convoy and spotting a CAM ship in the ranks, would spend little time selecting his target. Quite serious also was the effect of spray and salt on the Sea Hurricanes, poised high on the catapults. The conditions necessitated far more work on the aircraft than was the case on airfields, but routine inspections could be dangerous for the crews.

Other disadvantages were that the aircraft were surplus old planes from the Battle of Britain and needed a deal of maintenance. The crews doing this job were used to working from firm ground and not scrambling about like monkeys over a structure slimy with oil, and heaving about if the seas were rough.

The CAM ship fighter pilots (usually two to a ship, working 12-hour shifts) were given remarkably little training in the difficult business of bringing their aircraft safely down in the sea. The reason was simple: there was no one to teach them. It was, in fact, more a matter of luck than good guidance.

Thirty-five merchantmen became CAM ships. They proved moderately successful, shooting down seven Kondors, with dozens more being scared away.

I enjoyed my stay on the *Norvarg* and liked the Norwegians. I developed a taste for their strong cheese made from goats' milk, and I liked their coffee, which was made each time from freshly ground beans. Twice a week we had a 'sweet soup' made from currants, raisins and prunes, and I amused the Norwegians by taking this with the dessert.

The only thing I found distasteful about some of the Norwegians was their intense dislike of the Swedes. Any time we were berthed near a Swedish ship they would hurl insults at the Swedish crew and accuse them of being Nazis. I considered this to be most unfair. After all, the Norwegians were in the conflict purely because the Germans had invaded their country. This left Sweden cut off from the rest of Europe and there was little they could have done to aid the Norwegians. Also, as well as some Swedish vessels sailing in our convoys, Sweden had offered 60% of her cargo fleet outside the Baltic to be chartered by Britain. I suppose some of the ill-feeling was due to the Norwegians getting their independence from Sweden only at the beginning of the 20th century. Still, it was good to have the Norwegians as allies, as they had the biggest tanker fleet in the world.

Because the *Norvarg* had no home port I could have paid off anywhere after my six months was up. I had a notion to pay off in the USA and offer my services to the Americans, who had very good wages and exceptionally fine conditions. Also, they had a windjammer running between San Francisco and Aukland and I was just immature enough to try a trip on her.

Unfortunately the grass is always greener on the other side of the fence. Some of the Norwegians who were leaving the ship reckoned that the *Norvarg* was poor by Norwegian standards, and painted glowing pictures of other vessels (especially tankers), which seemed to be like a paradise on earth. Sadly, I listened to their counsels and asked the Old Man to pay me off.

Before leaving the Bristol Channel I put 50lb of food into a kitbag and sent it home. This was twice the amount allowed but, in a ship where Britons were in the minority, I had no difficulty getting a Norwegian seaman to take it through as his own. The kitbag was fitted with a stout lock and I insured its contents for £20.

I arrived a day before the kitbag and was looking forward to handing out food and silk stockings to my folks. However, as I was delving into the bag I had an odd feeling that some stuff was missing and, sure enough, somebody had picked out the stitching at the bottom of the bag and stolen a considerable amount of grub. Thinking back to carrying the stuff on my shoulder in Philadelphia for over half a mile with the temperature about 90°F, my temper snapped and I hit my fist against the wall in a fit of fury.

Ten days later the swelling had not gone down and I was now afraid that the metacarpal bone of my right hand had been broken. This was confirmed by X-ray at Glasgow Royal Infirmary, who said that the only course of action was to break it again and set it afresh. They could not guarantee that it would go back to its original state, but assured me that it would be a great improvement.

They were as good as their word, but it now meant that I would have another six weeks at home before the hand was fit for hard work. My parents were delighted, but I was less than pleased.

Ships were being sunk faster than replacements could be built, and the nation was slowly but surely bleeding to death. Back as far as September 1940 President Roosevelt of the USA agreed to build 60 merchant ships to help Britain survive. An antiquated type was chosen because it was quick to build. The USA then decided to replace its reserve obsolete merchant ships by adopting a modified version of the British design.

They made a model and presented it to Roosevelt, who chuckled and said that it was an 'ugly duckling', but would get the job done. The name was to stick, although the official term was Liberty Ship – 27 September 1941 was declared Liberty Day, with 14 new ships launched across the nation.

In less than three months the USA was at war and shipbuilding was a top priority. A man named Kaiser who had turned his talents to shipbuilding led this project. What Ford did for automobiles, Kaiser did for ships. His idea was to prefabricate in industrial units, then

More foreign flags

assemble superstructures, hull sections and so on in shipyards. This revolution was brought about by welding instead of riveting; but there was a price to pay.

By the start of 1942 America was geared to construct the largest merchant fleet in history. These ships would have to be built by an unskilled labour force – most had no experience of building ships and a quarter of them had never seen the sea! Full-sized wooden templates were made and used to mark out the steel sheets to be cut out by oxyacetylene torches. The hull was fitted together by just over 40 miles of welding.

Eventually the USA would produce more than 2,700 of them. To construct one took 48 days from laying the keel to launching. This was cut to 15 days and on it went until finally one was launched in 4 days 15 hours 29 minutes after keel-laying.

Another point that no one is willing to mention is the fact that America just could not produce enough trained seamen to man these vessels. It started off in the late 1930s with a small merchant fleet manned almost entirely by naturalised Norwegians, Danes, Swedes and Finns. Now America was confronted with the task of finding seamen for the ever-increasing number of vessels it was turning out. It was one thing to make a ship in five days, but a totally different matter to provide a crew for it.

You just cannot make a sailor in a hurry. Other trades could furnish journeymen quicker if they really wanted to. I am reminded of a painter once saying to me (with a hint of pride in his voice) that an apprentice painter had to serve a year of his time before he was allowed to handle a brush. When I asked what he was doing for this first year, I was told that he ran messages, made the tea and mixed paint. I imagine other trades had similar attitudes.

If they were to set out to train a boy, things could be very different. Instead of doing routine jobs over and over again, the lad could be shown a new skill as soon as he had mastered one of the old ones. I am certain that this kind of schooling could lead to tradesmen being turned out after six months, or at the very most a year.

One cannot do this for a sailor. He serves three years to be an AB, and it is hoped that during this time a mast will have to be lowered to enable the ship to go under a bridge; steering gear will have broken down and need repairing; a mast will have become damaged and a jury mast will have to be rigged, and so on – and the sailor will learn how these jobs are tackled. The only way to make an AB in a year or less is to fly him from ship to ship (as necessity arises) in a helicopter to get experience of all the emergencies he is likely to encounter.

Nevertheless, however ungainly these Liberty Ships looked, and however raw and inexperienced their crews, there is no doubt that they made a major contribution to winning the Battle of the Atlantic.

During the war all buildings had to have firewatchers on duty at night. One of my friends, who was in his second year at university, together with other students, was fire-watching in the Sheriff Courts. They were more than keen for someone to take their places so they could have some nights off. I made some money at this to augment the £3 a week from the Pool. Disrobing on the first night, I was about to divest myself of my underwear, which had been purchased in the USA and comprised underpants made from a striped material, when one of the students asked if my mother had made them out of old curtains!

I enjoyed this extended leave but, as soon as I was fit, I signed on another Norwegian ship named *Acasta*. She had been built in 1918 and was lying off Gourock.

Now, tankers normally have the engine room at the stern. The reasoning behind this is that they often carry cargoes that are highly combustible and the engine room poses a threat to the safety of the cargo. So, between the engine room and the tanks there is what is known as a cofferdam. This must extend the whole breadth of the ship and the depth of the tanks to protect the other parts of the vessel from gas. The space between the cofferdam and the tanks must be at least 3 feet. Obviously if the engine room was amidships there would have to be two of these cofferdams. The *Acasta* was one of the exceptions to the rule and had her engine room and funnel amidships.

To go from the middle of the vessel to either the poop or the forecastle would involve going down into the well deck (where all the tank taps and valves were) and climbing up out of the well deck each time. To avoid this it is usual for tankers to have a raised passageway, about a yard wide and with rails on either side, stretching between the centre castle (the usual name for the structure in the middle of the ship) to both poop and forecastle; this is called either the catwalk or flying bridge.

Apparently just before the Norwegians took over the *Acasta* she had been some kind of navy supply ship. She had a large mess deck (presumably where the naval ratings slept in hammocks) and off this deck were our cabins. We did not take long to discover that she had bed bugs.

We crossed the Atlantic with very good weather for the time of the year and dropped anchor in the Hudson River opposite 156th Street in Manhattan. During the last few days of the voyage the bugs had become so aggressive that all hands were settling down on the mess deck to sleep, leaving the bugs to enjoy the luxury of the cabins. It did not take the bugs long to weigh up the situation and follow us.

We asked the captain if the ship could be fumigated, but he claimed that on no account could a tanker be held up for the requisite two days. However, he agreed to have some steps taken to counter the bugs.

Accordingly two gents appeared and sprinkled a yellow powder and a blue powder over various parts of the ship. I asked one of the gents if it would work. He replied that the blue powder was very good but, as it was manufactured in Japan, it was in very short supply. He reckoned it would put the bugs off their stride for a couple of weeks, but that they would return. Apart from the bugs, a heap of cockroaches about 4 inches high was left in the galley!

Our crew was the nearest approach to Babel I had yet encountered. We had 19 Norse, 10 Scots, three Estonians, one Englishman, one Canadian-Scot and a Belgian. Four of the Scots spoke mainly Gaelic, so you can visualise the general smooth-working, well-organised mob we were.

The day before we were granted shore leave, three Scots firemen decided to celebrate with four bottles of the skipper's whisky. The following morning, hoping to throw the Old Man off the scent of the departed spirits, they invited one of the Estonians to partake of a mixture of whisky and a few other ingredients of doubtful origin. The effect was more alarming than expected. The Estonian not only became drunk, but also mad. He finished up by painting the 2nd Engineer a vivid shade of green, using a generous amount of the ship's paint. The skipper decided that he could dispense with the services of the three Estonians and one of the Scots firemen. Four other crew members also chose to dispense with the *Acasta*, and deserted. In their places came eight Norwegians, and this made Babel one language short.

The *Acasta*, without any warning, sailed down to Staten Island, leaving several members and myself to find her as best we could. This was to happen a few times, and each time we made enquiries about our ship we were treated with great suspicion and looked on as possible spies. In the end we located her by some sailors making enquiries in a Norwegian-speaking part of New York.

We made the West Indies in ten days of reasonably calm weather and called in to a village, Point Fortin, in Trinidad, where we loaded a full cargo of crude oil. The only attraction was an English Club where the English-speaking members of the crew were very kindly entertained by members of the British community. Apart from one man, who was a short-wave enthusiast, the members present were all ladies. The cocktail in fashion at that time was known as a Green Goddess, and this was constantly being asked for. The ladies would clap their hands every few minutes, another cocktail would appear, and this all went on to their husbands' monthly accounts.

They were pleasant enough to us, but I had no illusions and knew that in different circumstances they would not mix with lower-deck personnel. I felt a little sorry for them because they had so little in their lives. They made remarks that in two years they would be going home for a spell – home being Britain, not the magnificent houses in which dwelled. Still, as there were probably only about 15 families in the village, we were a welcome change of faces.

After loading, a few hours sailing took us round the coast to the capital, Port of Spain, where we anchored for ten days to await a convoy. This was hell's kitchen. The regular inhabitants consisted of British, Chinese, Spanish, Portuguese, Africans, Indians, West Indians, etc. The three services of Britain and USA, together with merchant seamen of every class, creed, colour, nation and denomination, helped to swell the grand assembly.

Before the USA had come into the war they gave us 50 of their oldest destroyers in exchange for the lease of bases in the West Indies (Port of Spain was one of them) for a period of 99 years. The Yanks got the best of this bargain – their old four-stacker warships were at sea for three weeks and in dock for repairs for up to two months!

I recall an amusing incident at Port of Spain. When in the post office buying stamps I asked the gent beside me where the nearest barber's shop was. He told me that it was in the next street and gave me directions. When I asked whether it was a good barber's, he assured me that it was the very best in town. After writing and posting my cards I arrived at the barber's and sat down. The man that came to cut my hair was none other than the gent in the post office! He was wearing white clothes – but so were most of the population.

Launches took us ashore for $1 and brought us back for as much as the launch men could get out of us. The Americans appeared to be the only ones who cared how their race survived and had first-class clubs for their men and a regular service of launches to bring them back to their vessels. It was true that the British had a club but, since the submarine campaign was at its height, it was always packed with survivors.

One evening I missed the last launch back to the ship and was obliged to spend the night ashore in a hotel. Next day I was back on board at 8.10am and reported for work. The bosun told me not to bother working as I was late (10 minutes) and would be logged. This meant that my name would he entered in the ship's log, and I would have a day's pay deducted.

Now, this was nothing short of iniquitous, for on several occasions there had been sailors lying in their bunks, too drunk to do any work, and they were not reported for this. They were said to be 'under the weather' and it was expected that the rest of the crew would cover for them. I went to the captain to prove that I was cold sober and willing to join the rest of the crew, and he immediately said that I should return to work.

I did not object to anyone drinking, but habitual drunkenness was another matter. It was common practice for drunks to wake their sober shipmates in the middle of the night and ask if they wanted to buy a French battleship. They appeared to think that this was uproariously funny. Nevertheless, there seemed to be a conspiracy among inebriates to look after one another, regardless of how it affected their other colleagues.

While in Port of Spain we were sent on another two-day gunnery course. This time we boarded a corvette and did our firing practice at sea, firing at targets towed by another vessel. I recall that the ammunition for the machine-guns was called TITA, standing for Tracer – Incendiary – Tracer – Armour-piercing. The tracer bullets I understood to be tipped with phosphorus, which made it easy to guide the stream of missiles on to the target, especially at night.

After replacing two of the crew who had jumped ship, we sailed for New York. We departed at 9am and, shortly after darkness fell, a flash of light and a sudden explosion told us that the U-boats had bagged their first ship. As was usually done, we donned life jackets and waited, at the same time cursing the moon for shedding so much light. Soon we found out that she was the next ship astern of us, and a tanker. The vessel did not burn much but nevertheless went down fast. Two explosions in quick succession followed and two more vessels paid the penalty – again, both of them tankers. Three ships gone, and not a day's sail yet from port! There was nothing anyone could do – our escort was hopelessly inadequate.

This was different from the North Atlantic, where a full attack developed and the convoy usually split up. Here they seemed to nibble at you, the convoy sailed on and they came back and nibbled again, tankers being the main objective.

Next morning at about 9.30am, in broad daylight, I was at the wheel and the sea was as smooth as glass. Gazing ahead, I suddenly noticed a white line crossing our bow diagonally from starboard to port. It took a couple of seconds for it to dawn on me that it was the path of a torpedo, and another 2 seconds later it had picked off a tanker close to our port side. Almost at the same time there was another track from port to starboard, and the ship next to us on the starboard side was hit. The tanker was carrying crude oil and did not explode, but burned and rapidly produced huge clouds of smoke.

I remember the Mate panicking and rushing into the wheelhouse to put on the alarm. I also remember the skipper, a short bald-headed man, puffing away at his pipe with apparent lack of concern, and wafting the smoke from the tanker away from his face as if it were from a friendly bonfire. The other casualty was not a tanker but a ship carrying bauxite, from which aluminium is made.

This left the old *Acasta* as the only tanker left in the convoy, and it gave us a feeling of great unease. Admittedly, since we had our funnel amidships and not, like most tankers, at the stern, it would not be so obvious at night to the subs that we were a tanker. Nevertheless, we were still apprehensive after the subs had attacked us in daylight, probably to sink the bauxite ship, and who knew just how much information the Germans had? However, on passing near Curaçao and Aruba, we were joined by another convoy made up of a coaster and 12 tankers. I was never so glad in my life to see a convoy like this one.

Next night the subs struck again, taking a toll of two more tankers. One of them was carrying a load of light spirit as cargo and we were near enough to hear the confused tumult when the 'tin fish' struck. There was nothing we could do but watch her burn, absolutely helpless to offer aid of any kind.

We had no more trouble after that night. The U-boats evidently thought it better to go back to Trinidad and 'escort' the next convoy out. Two days later we received radio calls from the unfortunates behind us.

It was alarming to think that a pack of subs would be waiting outside Port of Spain, and just over the horizon. All they had to do was to follow until darkness set in and content themselves with a couple of ships each night for a night or two, then head back for the next lot.

People at home tend to take their drinking water for granted – they just turn on the tap and out it comes, and always of the same quality. At sea things were a bit different. We would take on about 20 tons of drinking water in addition to water for general purposes, and, if the quality was poor (as so often it was), we were stuck with it until we reached the next port. It certainly made you appreciate Glasgow's Loch Katrine water.

The bugs came back with a vengeance, and again the skipper resisted all requests for fumigation. One day I was chatting to the Glasgow cabin boy.

'Tell me,' I asked him, 'does the captain have bugs? You are in his cabin every day and must know.'

He replied, 'No, I have never seen any.'

At a later time I met him again and gave him a matchbox saying, 'In this box are two bugs. I don't know whether they are male or female and I don't know anything about their mating habits, but if you put them into the captain's bed we'll all find out.'

The weather grew cold very rapidly. The temperature in Port of Spain was around 95°F and we made New York in 10½ days to find it 12°F. The *Acasta* stayed there 15 days and very soon the fumigation team came aboard. It was fine for the skipper to let us suffer in the interests of keeping a tanker moving with its precious cargo, but it was altogether a different matter when he was affected.

The *Acasta* was always expecting to go but never going, and often shifting her anchorage so that, once the crew went ashore, they were never sure where to find her on returning. One night I was obliged to stay ashore and was fortunate in being able to stay the night with my father's cousin. We tied up in Brooklyn for three or four days as a result of a collision with another ship in the Hudson River. One of the crew deserted, one went mad, one refused to go back to sea again, and one committed suicide. Not knowing enough Norwegian, I did not know what was behind all this.

We left on a freezingly cold morning and had not gone very far when we noticed that the ship had sprung a leak, and oil trickled out leaving a trail behind us the whole way across the Atlantic. We narrowly missed collision with a big whale factory ship one dark night when the convoy was struggling along at sixes and sevens.

Then I took some kind of fever and was in my bunk for several days. The Mate, doing his doctor, visited me every day with a different medicine each time. I think that he just started at one side of his medicine chest and worked his way across. However, one day he produced a sulpha drug and this put me back on my feet – minus about 20lb in weight, having lived on orange juice for more than a week.

The trouble was that our deck boy had paid off sick in New York and we had sailed without one. This meant that the 'peggying' had to be done in turns by a lettmatros, and it was just as my turn was due when I took sick. I knew how bad this would look to everyone, and I struggled on for two days trying to do the work until I could no longer cope.

When I was fit enough for some work, fate intervened. The eyes of one of the ABs started troubling him and he could not see to steer. To try to cover up, he had been using binoculars to see the ship in front, and one of the Mates caught him in the act. I was immediately taken off the 'peggying' and he took my place.

Submarines appeared and were beaten off. The weather became stormy and our steering gear broke down. It took us 8½ hours to repair it, during which time the convoy sailed on, leaving us at the mercy of the U-boats and, worst of all, the weather. Fortunately the Norwegians had very good survival gear; we wore these suits and they kept us completely dry. It was nevertheless an ordeal to be battered about by waves dashing on to the poop all the time we were trying to repair the steering.

When under way again, we were so far behind the convoy that the skipper chose to make port alone, as we had a speed of about 12 knots.

Two days later a flying-boat sighted us and gave us instructions to put into the nearest port, Moville in the Irish Republic. Had we been a few minutes later, I do not suppose we would have reached Moville for, just as dusk was falling, we had to alter course for a floating mine.

We anchored off Moville, which is on the western shore of Lough Foyle. With the Republic of Ireland on one side of the lough and Northern Ireland on the other, we would have to undergo the searches of two lots of Customs, another two at the border and yet another on our return to Britain. The *Acasta* paid off in Londonderry on Christmas Day and we set off for Larne to board a steamer for Stranraer.

I went along with our three sailors from Stornoway and, since they were drinking prodigiously, I had a job trying to keep them out of trouble. When I succeeded in this, they expressed their appreciation when we got to Glasgow and were semi-sober. Their regular employment was fishing and weaving the famous Harris tweed. As a token of their gratitude they promised faithfully to send me a bolt of tweed for my sisters. We are now in the 21st century – and I am still waiting!

Boxing Day saw me safely back to Glasgow at 1 o'clock in the morning. It was frustrating to have missed Christmas at home, and by such a narrow margin.

6

Two More Tankers and a Liner

After my leave expired I was offered a job as rigger on the *Empire Mariner*, cargo ship belonging to H. Hogarth, a Glasgow company that was sometimes known as the Baron Line on account of its ships all being named *Baron* this or *Baron* that. Barren Line would have been a more appropriate soubriquet, but they were more commonly called 'Hungry Hogarths' or 'Hungry Hughie's' on account of their frugal fare.

Riggers are usually employed doing sailors' work on ships when one crew has signed off and the next lot have not yet arrived. I went to Barclay Curle's wharf and found that she had been in port for repairs for several months, mainly due to her engines continually breaking down. Her ropes were lying on the deck like spaghetti, and we had the job of unravelling them. It took some time.

Travelling down from home every day for two weeks, the more I saw of her the less I liked her. I remember the cook in the galley picking up a lump of coal, putting it in the fire and, without as much as a pause to shake his hand, lifting a sausage and putting it in a pan.

'Gawd,' said one of our Irish ABs, 'me boots are cleaner than his paws.' It turned out that the cook was the Mate's brother-in-law.

On the last day she was fumigated and we were offered a chance to sail on her. Usually the food in port is a bit better than you expect to get at sea so, when out food was poor in port, it was decidedly a danger signal and we had no desire to pursue the matter. 'Hungry Hogarths' had lived up to their name and not one of us signed on.

I would willingly have stayed on Norwegian ships, with all their advantages, but the UK authorities caught up with me and made me submit to a practical examination of my seamanship. I seemed to have passed the test for they classed me as an EDH (Efficient Deck Hand) and I had now to find a British ship.

On 24 January 1943 I signed on the *F. J. Wolfe*, a tanker of 12,600 gross tonnage. Tankers are usually measured not by their gross tonnage but by the weight of cargo they can carry – in her case it was 19,700 tons. She was a diesel-engined craft built in Germany in 1932. At that time she was reputed to be the biggest tanker in the world, and when I signed on she was reckoned to be about the fifth largest.

At any rate, the ship was now owned by Esso (which some said stood for Eastern State Standard Oil) and run by the Anglo American Oil Company. She had taken two torpedoes on the previous trip and had staggered into Newfoundland – she and three others that were the remnant of a convoy of 33 vessels!

It was a Sunday when I was ordered to join her at Old Kilpatrick on the River Clyde. I went to the bus station in Glasgow but had difficulty getting a bus, so decided instead to take a tram car to Dalmuir terminus, on the outskirts of the city, then try to get the bus from there. As bus after bus sped past the stop, with rows of red noses showing on every one, it dawned on me that it was a hopeless quest. I had to walk to the ship, but fortunately a 'good Samaritan' helped with my kitbag.

The reason for my inability to catch a bus was a stupid bye-law in Scotland prohibiting anyone from buying an alcoholic beverage on a Sunday, unless that person was what the bye-law termed a bona fide traveller. Thus masses of drinkers were heading for Balloch where all they had to do was to sign in a register that they had travelled a certain distance, then they could drink their fill. The bus taking them back at night was known as 'the return of the swallows'.

The *F. J. Wolfe* was a fairly good ship with first-class grub and quarters. Her crew were all decent fellows and included an old windjammer sailor, a soldier from the First World War, a one-time member of the International Brigade fighting in the Spanish Civil War, and a semi-American who had been a skipper, cowboy, lumberjack and student of medicine at different times in his life. Whatever else he was I do not know, but he gained enormous prestige as an accomplished liar and could always amuse us with a yarn on any occasion.

As described previously when giving details about the *Acasta*, the *F. J. Wolfe* had catwalks (or flying bridges) between the fo'c'sle and centre castle, and centre castle and poop. I went to the steward to get my linen and blankets and it took some time before I collected them. Coming out into the darkness I could not see at all well in the complete blackout and wanted to go along this catwalk to our quarters aft in the poop. The entrance to the catwalk and the ladder down into the well deck are very close to one another and, with the blankets piled up over my head, I stepped forward on to what I thought was the beginning of the flying bridge, only to find that it was the top of the

Two more Tankers and a Liner

ladder leading down to the well deck!

I shall never forget that feeling when I stepped firmly into mid-air. It must have been a drop of about 12 feet, and the second I was airborne was terrifying. Fortunately I just missed one of the large metal valves and landed on the metal deck quite shaken. The sailor who was night watchman saw the incident and helped me back to my cabin with the bedclothes.

When I had recovered my composure I was told by one of the older members of the crew to report the matter to the Chief Mate. I was reluctant to do so but he, being wiser and more experienced, said that I might suffer effects later.

I did as he suggested and the first thing the Mate said was, 'Did any one see you fall?'

'Yes,' I replied, 'Andy, the night watchman, witnessed it.'

The Mate would put this down in the ship's log in case there were any future complications.

Losses at sea had continued to rise and by the end of 1942 an appalling total of 1,100 ships had been sunk. More than 30,000 British seamen had had to take to the lifeboats and 10,000 of them had been killed! At the beginning of the war the Germans had 67 submarines – at the start of 1943 they had 393 in operation.

I recall reading in a newspaper, about that time, that a judge had sentenced a felon to six months in jail or join the merchant navy! This was fiercely attacked by the Seamen's Union, who pointed out to the judge that the merchant navy consisted of honourable citizens who were employed in helping the country to survive, and should not be used as a dumping ground for criminals.

We lay off Gourock for two days when RN officers came on board to demonstrate how we should refuel the escort ships at sea. This would mean that the escort could take us right across the Atlantic and not just part of the way.

I believe we were one of the first to employ what came to be known as the 'floating line' scheme. Previously the 'trough and metal hose' plan was used. However, this idea needed the two vessels to sail close alongside each other and required calm conditions. As calm conditions are not the norm in the North Atlantic, any seaman could have told them that the floating line method was by far the superior.

The basic idea was for us to tow the escort vessel while pumping oil into her. The method was to have two balloons covered in thin canvas and separated by 2 fathoms of 'pointline', a Manila rope of 1½-inch circumference. The craft following us would use a grapnel to catch the rope between the balloons and bring this on board, pulling it through the fairleads until a larger rope appeared, then pulling this on board until finally a full-sized mooring rope would be put on her bollards and we would then tow her.

This exercise would then be repeated, but this time the escort would receive a pipeline instead of the mooring rope and, when this was fixed to her fuel inlet valve, we would be all ready to pump. We ran up and down the Clyde with a destroyer behind us while the crew practised running out the mooring rope and pipeline. My post during the exercise was liaising on the poopdeck telephone and, by dint of trying to take orders from it in a half gale, I lost a brand new sou'wester. Said the Royal Navy lieutenant, 'Hard luck old chap.'

Halfway across the Atlantic we were signalled to refuel a destroyer. We dropped the balloons and those on the bow of the destroyer picked up the line between them and hauled it up level with the deck. Now all they had to do was to leave the balloons dangling over the side and pull in the bight of the rope (the middle part, as opposed to the ends) until the mooring rope was on board. We waited for 15 minutes while those at the destroyer's bows seemed to be debating what to do. Finally a leading hand took out a knife, punctured the balloons and drew the ropes through the fairlead.

Our bosun's language was unprintable and we had to improvise by replacing the burst balloons with life jackets wrapped in canvas. We then signalled to the destroyer's crew how to carry out the operation and hoped for the best. We were rewarded with the worst as the destroyer somehow cut through the pointline and sent the life jackets adrift. Finally we had to empty two small water casks from our lifeboats, and use these as floats.

A few days later we were struck by a regular hurricane and had to heave to for some time while the wind ripped the surface off the ocean and turned it into a white expanse. I remember the state of the sea, and the *F. J. Wolfe* scarcely making 1½ knots. One of our lifeboats was almost wrecked, but otherwise no harm was done.

The Commodore ship of the convoy was none other than the *Empire Mariner* and, after breaking down twice, she left the convoy heading for St John in New Brunswick. Why she was chosen to be Commodore I shall never understand. Our crossing took 26 days, which was a bit on the long side as we had encountered the hurricane.

We tied up for some time in Staten Island where we had repairs done to the engine. This lasted 22 days. We had three dock trials but failed in the first two. Many were of the opinion that this was due to Germans doing the repairs. They were, however, naturalised Americans, so no one could say a word. One of these trials took place on St Patrick's Day, and since the Mate, the bosun and two of our crew were Irish, the atmosphere was torrid when shore leave was cancelled for that night. We then went to Bayonne in New Jersey to load about 20,000 tons of oil.

Now, we all craved the bright lights of Manhattan and travelled there each evening. This usually involved a launch to Staten Island, a bus trip to the ferry terminal and thence across to South Street in Manhattan and the subway to Times Square.

The big snag with being berthed at Bayonne was that you had to be escorted back to your ship, as there must be no chance of a drunken seaman throwing away a lit cigarette. So, after having a splendid evening ashore, you had to wait at the dock gates until the authorities accompanied you back to your vessel and saw you safely on board. It was particularly galling when you were cold sober and your ship was just a few yards inside the dock gate. I suppose that this really was the sensible thing to do rather than try to decide which sailors were sober enough to act responsibly.

At West 96th Street there was a Thistle Club and I enjoyed many evenings there; in fact, I learned more Scots songs there than I ever knew at home. Scots who had settled in the USA made us extremely welcome. They all appeared to have good jobs and ran their own newspaper, having the cheek to call themselves 'Scots in exile', when the only time they would ever want to go back to Scotland would be for a holiday!

There were various clubs for servicemen and many were handing out free tickets for shows. I desperately wanted to visit the Metropolitan Opera and kept asking for tickets, but was told that there were none left for that day. I said I would take tickets for the next day but was informed that one had to apply on the day of the performance. I am tempted to think that the distributors were fiddling, but there was nothing I could do for I could not get off work and travel all the way from Bayonne each day.

Martin, the veteran of the Spanish Civil War, and I decided that we would just have to pay for our pleasure and arrived at the opera house for a performance of *Il Trovatore*. The house was sold out but we managed to get two tickets from a bystander who could not attend. They were for what was called the Family Circle, which was midway between the Dress Circle and the Gallery. For this we each paid $2.75. In 1943 the Met was housed in its second building but, as I write, it is now at its third site.

Now, I am well aware that in all countries many folks go to the opera to be seen, as much as to see and hear. Although I despise this attitude, I am conscious of opera being very expensive to produce and needing all the support it can get. If people are willing to pay high prices for an entertainment that possibly they neither understand nor enjoy, it subsidises the seats of the rest and I am not inclined to object. Nowhere in the world is this kind of snobbery more noticeable than in the USA. Above the orchestral stalls was a row of boxes known as the Diamond Horseshoe. In these boxes sat many of the city's wealthy celebrities sporting their jewellery, and, believe it or not, their names and the dates they occupied the boxes were printed in the programme! I have this programme on my lap as I write and can give examples:

> Box 9. Duchess de Talleyrand, Mondays.
> Box 22. Mr Irving Geist, Mondays – Mr Vanderbilt Webb, Thursdays.
> Box 27. Major and Mrs Edgar W. Garbisch,
> Odd Mondays – Lt Colonel Cornelius.
> Box 28. Marquis de Cuevas, Mondays – Mrs Otto H. Kahn, Fridays. V. Whitney USAAF, Odd Thursdays.

So, if you arrived early enough, and the luminaries were on time, there was rare sport to be had by using opera glasses to pinpoint which box was generating the most glittering display. You could then refer to the programme to identify the source of this opulence. Even if the opera failed to satisfy, you had a secondary thrill knowing that you were under the same roof as persons of immense wealth.

We all lived a full life during our stay, and it told on us – we were never on board much before 3.30am.

The USA did not seem to have regular dance halls where you could pay to get in. It was either 'dine and dance' or 'dime a dance'. The first was really a nightclub and, as the money was made on the meals, there were many tables but little floor space for dancing. I believe this extreme lack of room was the reason why so many Americans were unable to do proper ballroom dancing.

The 'dime a dance' was a swindle. In the dance halls there were attractive girls attired in evening dress and known as hostesses. The idea was that one bought a number of tickets at 10 cents (a dime), and each ticket entitled you to a dance with the lady of your choice. The music seemed endless and I assumed that everyone was getting a very long dance for the money; but, being a cautious Scot, I bought only two tickets and handed them to one of the girls. We had barely danced twice round the floor when she asked for another ticket. The music may have been continuous but every 2 minutes or so the drummer gave two taps of his stick on a wooden bar above the drum, and this was the signal for another ticket to be handed over.

You could sit and chat with the girl provided that you bought drinks for both. You would be served with two drinks at quite a high price, but the girl's would be cold tea, or something of that order. The more she encouraged you to drink, the greater her commission.

As well as the usual food, I would buy stockings for my sisters and girl friends. On a previous trip I was advised to buy nylon hose instead of silk. I had great doubts about this but the American shop assistants assured me that they were better than silk and would not ladder so easily. I had given in and had brought home my first nylons, which proved to be all that had been claimed for them.

Leaving New York, our convoy consisted of 21 cargo vessels, 21 tankers and two cargo liners, 30 of which did not see home! Our engine seized up and caught fire, and we put into Halifax for repairs. This was rather fortunate for us for, shortly after leaving the convoy, the attacks began. The engineers in Halifax found traces of sand in the lubricating oil, so it appeared to be more than an accident. Eight days we lay there and were patched up.

Halifax was the capital of the province of Nova Scotia and one of the largest cities of eastern Canada. Its harbour is 6 miles long and a mile wide, and during the Second World War it was the main convoy port for North America.

I had some time ashore and remember going to a cinema there. Now, in the USA one was permitted to smoke only upstairs in picture houses. Fancying that the same rules obtained here, I leisurely took out a cigarette and lit it. At the sound of the match striking the abrasive, two girls just in front of me jumped up in their seats and looked at me. I had barely time to consider what had caused their sudden interest, when an usherette flashed her torch at me with the words, 'Put out that cigarette!'

Off we set homeward-bound. The weather was still very cold and I distinctly remember that all the winches on deck had to be kept running all night to stop them from freezing up. This meant that the watch on deck had to keep lubricating their moving parts.

Cargo ships have four engineers, or exceptionally five, the 3rd Engineer doubling as electrician. The *F. J. Wolfe* had seven, plus an electrician. I made the discovery that we did not have fuses in our electric circuits – they were controlled by circuit breakers. If the load was too much, a button popped out and broke the circuit. So, instead of having to put new fuse wire into the fuse every time one blew, all you had to do was to push the button back into place.

One evening the lights went out for a few minutes then came back on again. This pattern was repeated several times. I went to investigate and found one of the ordinary seamen at the circuit breakers trying to wedge down a button with a piece of wood.

'What are you doing?' I asked him.

'The lights keep going out every time this button comes out, so I'm wedging it in place.'

I had to tell him that the button was supposed to come out when circuits were overloaded, and that by wedging it down he was in danger of setting the ship on fire. A quick visit round the cabins revealed that all deck-head lights and bedlights were on in every cabin and, in addition, four electric irons were being used. One or two items had to be switched off and all was restored to normal.

We had a fairly good passage home and plenty of experience in fuelling warships at sea. There was much speculation where we would dock because our draught was so deep that many ports could not accommodate us. Even though I joined her at Old Kilpatrick near Glasgow, I later learned that she had discharged 2,500 tons at Ardrossan to lighten her load and lessen her draught.

Eventually we turned south and docked at Milford Haven at the western end of the Bristol Channel, one of the largest deep-water harbours in the world. It was very nasty weather on the day we arrived and some poor fellows were doing manoeuvres in small invasion craft. The weather worsened and many barges capsized with great loss of life.

I had half a mind to do another trip on the *F. J. Wolfe* but ultimately made up my mind to leave her.

It comes back to me that it took me 22 hours by five trains to reach Glasgow from Milford Haven. I cannot recall all the stations but remember that it took two trains to reach Cardiff. The third train took me to I know not where, but the fourth one definitely stopped at Crewe for what seemed an interminable time.

When it came to giving a large number of passengers a cup of tea in a hurry, two folk would carry the sort of tray used by bakers for their loaves. These would have scores of cups on them. Another person would be carrying a porcelain pail containing tea that had been 'sugared and milked', and it was a simple and quick matter to dip each cup into this bucket and hand it to the passenger.

We were entitled to two days' leave for every month on ship. As I had signed on the *F. J. Wolfe* on 24 January 1943 and left her on 28 April, I was due only five days ashore. At the end of my leave I reported to the Shipping Federation and was immediately signed on another tanker, the *British Tradition*, owned by the Anglo-Iranian Oil Company, otherwise known as the British Tanker Corporation.

She was only seven months old when I joined her and here was a beauty at last. A British ship fit for humans to live in – was the world coming to an end? Our quarters were superb. We had a tip-top mess-room, a special room for drying clothes and an oilskin locker.

Shortly after boarding I found out that an old school mate, Arthur Fisken, had also signed on as a sailor with his pal Bob Dolan. He had done a year as apprentice then managed to have his indentures cancelled and came back to sea on the lower deck. Arthur had a portable gramophone with about 80 gramophone records of serious music, and had a fair-sized library too.

I do not know how Arthur managed to get his indentures cancelled, but it was a shrewd move. Apprentices were a form of cheap labour for the ship-owners; they were paid very low wages and relied on the generosity of the officers (not always accorded) to give them unpaid tuition on navigation and such like. Dirty jobs, like cleaning out the bilges, were most often given to them and they had no trade union to stand by them in cases of ill-treatment. If, however, they were apprenticed to a better class of line, such as the Clan Line, they stood a fair chance of becoming an officer with that company and their sacrifice would have been worthwhile. Why boys ever apprenticed themselves to tramp companies I shall never understand, for there was no benefit in becoming an officer with them.

Some of the better-class companies signed on lads as cadets. I believe they fared better, had a discharge book and signed on and off every voyage, unlike apprentices, who were imprisoned by their indentures.

One amusing incident took place on our first day on the *British Tradition*. When the ordinary seaman brought in the morning tea one of the ABs gave him a cuff on the ear with the words, 'I've told you before to make sure the water is boiling before you pour it over the tea.'

I tasted it and informed the AB that the water had been boiling but that what we were being offered was China tea and not the usual Indian. Apparently at a previous port China tea had been cheaper than Indian tea, so they bought a large quantity of it. The officers did not care for it and tried to palm it off on us. We protested but had to compromise and accept half China and half Indian in our rations.

This is typical of the policies of most owners. The articles state that sweet potatoes or yams may be used instead of potatoes, and chicory can take the place of coffee. So, if yams are cheaper in some port, you get yams instead of potatoes.

For the first time in my experience the skipper came round our quarters on Sunday morning for an inspection, which was common practice in peacetime. On liners I was told that the Old Man, accompanied by passengers, would go round the ship wearing white gloves. From time to time he would draw his gloved hands under some ledge to see if it was absolutely clean. If it was not, the responsible seaman would be 'logged'. This simply meant that his name would be entered in the ship's log and he would be fined 5 shillings.

We had a very pleasant crossing, with good weather all the way. The only fly in our ointment was the little 5ft 5in bosun, who had previously not sailed on anything but liners and wanted to bundle everything up in red tape.

Sixteen days later we tied up in Philadelphia for 40 hours. Knowing the bosun's ideas, I disappeared for most of the 40 hours, and later found out that he had some of the crew painting the flying bridge. I did all I could in the 40 hours, visiting Anne at Drexel Hill and staying overnight at her house before returning to the ship with food for those at home.

Our cargo was high-octane or aeroplane fuel, a very volatile and highly flammable, if not explosive, liquid, turning the ship into a floating bomb. It was the sort of cargo that caused a great deal of conversation on the road over but, once loaded, we more or less forgot about it. Smoking was prohibited except below decks. The skipper insisted that we wear life jackets on watch, but we felt that it was a useless precaution and wings would have been more appropriate. Unlike other trips, we took off all our clothes when bedding down, as there seemed little hope of having time to put them on in an emergency.

On the subject of ships being sunk, this was one topic that was always taboo. If you talked about previous vessels you had been on, you mentioned the food, the quarters, other members of the crew and so on, but the moment anyone mentioned enemy action there was a wail of disapproval.

I made mention before of the CAM ships that carried an aircraft to be fired off by rocket, and the great disadvantage that the pilot had to bail out and hope to be rescued. The Admiralty now produced a much better alternative in the form of MAC ships (merchant aircraft carriers), which were merchantmen – often tankers – that had part of their superstructure cut away in order to be fitted with a flat deck for aircraft. They were officially known as 'escort carriers' but widely dubbed 'utility carriers' or 'Woolworth carriers' by the seamen.

We encountered a little ice and heard a few depth-charges go off, but the voyage back was uneventful and we docked safely at Bowling in what was then Dunbartonshire. I had been on the *British Tradition* from 4 May until 22 June, so was due only three days' leave.

When my leave was up I reported to the shipping offices and was offered another tanker belonging to the British Tanker Company. Since my last three ships had all been tankers I protested and was fortunate insofar as the master of this vessel had been Chief Mate of the *British Tradition* and said that he would not force me to sign on.

Besides, I was becoming rather tired of people ashore assuming that tanker seamen were given much higher pay. As soon as they knew that I was on a tanker, there came the customary remark, 'Oh, you're after the big money, are you?' Despite my explanation that I did not receive one penny more, I am certain they remained unconvinced or, as the old saying goes, 'convince a man against his will, and he's of the same opinion still'.

The tale was very well broadcast and I do not know how this misconception arose. Perhaps they found it hard to believe that anyone would go on a tanker for ordinary wages. Ships carrying high explosives did not get any extra cash either, although as soon as they reached the safety of port the dockers immediately demanded danger money before they would unload them.

Actually a tanker, when not carrying cargo, is the safest ship on the seas. They have about 30 waterproof (or, even better, spirit-proof) tanks and it would take quite a lot to sink them.

Apart from tankers loaded with light spirit and cargo ships carrying explosives, the most dangerous vessel is the one carrying ore. Manganese ore, iron ore and such like have very high densities. These ships can be loaded down to their marks and yet have very little bulk in their holds. If a ship carrying grain or general cargo is torpedoed it takes some time for the sea to seep through the cargo and fill the hold, but with an ore carrier, where the hold is nearly empty, the sea just flows in and the ship sinks at an alarming speed. I have been told that an ore carrier after being struck by a torpedo can become a submarine within half a minute or less. In addition to this they were often stationed on the outside columns of the convoy, the safer inside columns usually being reserved for cargoes such as oil, munitions, food and so on.

Arthur Fisken, Bob Dolan and I fancied shipping out together again but could not find a cargo ship wanting three sailors. Finally we all signed on a liner, the *California*, belonging to the Anchor Line of Glasgow. Her peacetime
trips had been carrying passengers from Yorkhill Quay in Glasgow to the USA, and her wartime role was ferrying troops. She was a little smaller than the *Reina del Pacifico*, but had roughly the same number of crew. One difference was that the 'peggying' was done and the sailors were looked after by an old AB who was past doing heavy work.

As to the voyage, this was to be something different. Here she was in the beginning of July 1943, heading for an unknown destination with 200 RN personnel and 250 passengers; even stranger, the passengers included civil engineers, missionaries, nuns and priests.

As usual, rumours abounded. The front-runner reckoned that we were headed for India but would put into some port in West Africa to drop off some of our religious passengers.

We left the Clyde in company with the *Duchess of York* (a liner belonging to the Canadian Pacific Railway) and a fast cargo ship, the *Port Fairy*. The *California* was to be Commodore of this small convoy.

Our escort was supposed to consist of the destroyers HMS *Douglas* and HMCS *Iroquois*, and two frigates, HMS *Moyola* and HMS *Swale*, although I cannot recollect seeing all four of them with us at the same time; I think at least one joined us later. Additionally we had a Catalina aircraft, which was seen from time to time. This was reasonable defence against submarines, but was of little use as protection from air attack. It was certainly nothing like the cover we would have been given had we been carrying 1,000 or more troops. Usually convoys bound for southern latitudes make a wide sweep out into the Atlantic, but instead we came close to the coast of Portugal.

The *California* had two crow's-nests. You climbed up the inside of the metal mast to get to the lower one, then had to reach the top one by means of a ladder on the outside of the mast. The upper one was provided with binoculars and had a speaking tube to the lower one, which had a telephone to the bridge.

On 11 July Arthur and I were having a record concert below decks; I had a few records but Arthur had many more. One of our shipmates happened to drop in to listen to the music and remarked that it was quite a risk taking all this lot off to sea. Arthur and I laughed and said that we were as safe as houses here, and informed him that our last ship had been a tanker carrying high octane.

As a sailor, when I was on watch from 4pm to 8pm we had no break for a meal. Traditionally the cook made up a hot dish, stuck it in the oven in the galley when he finished work at 6pm, and we helped ourselves to this at the end of the watch; as previously mentioned during my time on the *Reina del Pacifico*, this was always known as the 'black pan'.

That evening, at the end of the watch, I had just come down from the lower crow's-nest and was tucking into our meal when, at about 8.20pm, we were called to action stations as there was a report of enemy aircraft in the vicinity. My station was Air Raid Precautions on the boat deck.

After half an hour of inactivity three large aeroplanes were spotted very high in the sky – some said about 12,000 feet and others 15,000 feet. Whatever height, they were just tiny specks and hardly any sound could be heard.

Our guns were manned and the gunners stood by in readiness, waiting for our foes to descend. However, they did not come any lower but flew directly above us. As more a gesture of defiance than for any other reason, all our artillery opened up with a thunderous sound, but the enemy were well out of range. Nothing happened for a minute – maybe the Admiralty had something!

Disillusionment came swiftly. Two bombs struck the *Duchess of York* amidships and she was soon a raging inferno. I later learned that communication between the bridge and other parts of the ship was impossible and she immediately lost way.

We all deemed these to be lucky hits, but hardly had we thought so when a bomb crashed into the *California* on the starboard side aft. A minute or two later, when some of our more optimistic members were suggesting that it was a miss, a fireman or greaser burst on to the deck covered in a fine grey dust with blood oozing from his forehead. It was now obvious that somewhere near the engine room had been struck.

I decided that I had better try to rescue some of my belongings and ran down the various companionways to the working alleyway, with the intention of going up forward and grabbing one or two of my possessions. As I ran along this alley a second bomb smashed into the ship. I was lifted off my feet and thrown back in my tracks while a blast of hot air scorched my face. I can remember putting my hand up to my mouth to feel if my teeth were still there. They were. Still thinking of saving my few valuables, I tried to go forward when a third bomb hit us near No 2 hold.

I arrived on the foredeck to find everything near No 2 hatch in ruins. Some 20 or so folk, wounded and too ghastly to describe, were lying there. I think it was the carpenter who had both arms and both legs broken. We dragged the victims under cover of the deck as the planes circled overhead again. The 'abandon ship' had been ordered some time previously and a few of our lifeboats were already in the water. In the hope that one might be left, the injured were hoisted up one deck, but it was of no use. There were still lifeboats there but one of the bombs had made such a mess of their launching gears that we were unable to lower them. *The California*'s lifeboats were double-banked and of the Wellin Quadrant type; the explosions had damaged many of their threaded rods so that they could not be swung outboard.

The planes disappeared and the destroyer HMS *Douglas* swung round and lay about half a mile away on the starboard side. Some time passed and the injured were given life jackets and lowered gently into the sea. A naval sickbay attendant had been standing by them all the while, administering morphine and trying to cheer their spirits – even to the extent of going into the water with them and continuing to help.

Once the wounded were safely away, several of the remaining men decided to swim as there were no boats anywhere capable of being launched. I was as yet uncertain when two or three internal explosions clearly indicated that it was time to leave, and I lost no time in slipping down a heaving-line into the sea, leaving onboard the captain, the Commodore and about four others. I had given away my life jacket to a naval rating whose own (naval ones were inflatable) had been punctured by shrapnel; this was not through either bravery or bravado, but because I was sure I could swim much faster without it.

Just prior to leaving we had heaved a hatch-board over the rail. This we clung to for some time, the destroyer seeming to be a long way off. After the first shock of entering the water had passed, it felt reasonably warm and I made up my mind to strike out for HMS *Douglas*, fervently hoping that there were no sharks around. When I was just about 100 yards from our vessel two more explosions occurred and a piece of some flaming material came hurtling through the air, landing a few yards ahead of me. Halfway to the warship we rested on some floating wreckage for a minute or two.

Pushing off again we were desperately hoping that the destroyer would stay put when a small launch hailed us and asked if we were all right. We assured the occupants that we were and it made off for the liner to take off the half-dozen that were still there.

Without the life jacket I progressed more quickly than the others and soon scrambled on to one of our lifeboats tied up to the destroyer. One of the RN crew gave me a towel and showed me where to go.

The *California*'s surgeon was there busily attending to the wounded and, since many were suffering from burns, gentian violet was being applied all round. It was the first time I had seen it used and the masses of purple faces looked grotesque.

Night was falling. Both liners were blazing from end to end, turning the night sky almost into day and, in the interests of safety, the warship fired torpedoes at both and they eventually sank.

Roughly 600 survivors were aboard HMS *Douglas* and the conditions resembled a railway station platform on a bank holiday. We slept wherever we could and led an existence akin to sardines in a tin. The destroyer was due in port soon and had little surplus grub. Breakfast would be a cup of tea and a small piece of fish on a little bread; lunch was half a cup of soup; supper meant a cup of tea and a small biscuit with a tiny piece of corned beef on it.

Fisken, Dolan and I were exchanging experiences. It is usual

Making Waves   I

**My mother and me on a lock
gate at Fort Augustus, circa 1931
–** *Gondolier* **is behind us.**

Gondolier **leaving Muirton Wharf
at Inverness.** *By permission of
Brian Patton, author and publisher
of* A MacBrayne Memoir

Gondolier **going down the locks
at Fort Augustus into Loch Ness.**
*Courtesy of Stenlake Publishing/
Guthrie Hutton*

Making Waves

Left to right: myself, the pantry man and the 3rd class pantry boy at Banavie.

Posing at the wheel on a Sunday – a bandage on my forearm may be seen.

Left to right: the pantry man, chocolate boy and me on the bridge on a Sunday.

My father's cousin (the purser) and me.

David Watt (the Checker) and me on the paddle-box.

A postcard of the *Reina del Pacifico*. *Author's collection*

HMS *Repulse*. *Maritime Quest*

Making Waves V

The *Highland Chieftain. George W. Howe collection*

The *Newton Pine. Author's collection*

VI　　　　　　　　　　　　　　　　　　　　　　　　Making Waves

A typical corvette.

Balloons at sea – they were much smaller than the shore ones.

The Loch Lomond 'Navy'. *Author's collection*

Making Waves VII

The *Norvarg*. *National Maritime Museum*

An aircraft on the catapult structure of a CAM ship. *Author's collection*

Liberty Ships. *Author's collection*

The *Acasta*.

The *F. J. Wolfe. Author's collection*

The *British Tradition. Author's collection*

to allocate lifeboat space in such a way as to have some deck sailors in each boat, bearing in mind that on a liner of that size there would be a crew of 300, but fewer than 50 of them had any idea of how to manage a boat. In an emergency such as this, folk went to any boat they could get into.

Quite a few of the *California*'s lifeboats had provision for being manned by untrained crews. Instead of the usual oars, they had a propeller powered by a chain to which were attached wooden levers. All that was needed was for people to pull these levers back and forth and this caused the chain to make the propeller turn – no skill was required. Unfortunately Arthur was the only sailor in his lifeboat and the others were predominately nuns, who would not do what he asked but just sat fingering their rosaries.

Two and a half days later we put alongside at Casablanca in French Morocco. HMS *Moyola*, one of the escorting frigates, was already there with 500 survivors, while HMS *Swale* (who had on board seven survivors from the Catalina aircraft, which had been shot down) escorted the *Port Fairy* as she limped in some time later with 55 survivors on board. She had been attacked on two successive nights and, as a result of a hit, her steering gear had jammed.

To swell the numbers of the rescued, HMCS *Iroquois* appeared with 660 on board. The total number of survivors being approximately 1,800, the only place capable of handling them was the US Army camp. They could not have had much notice of our arrival, yet there they were on the quay greeting us with eight large ambulances and 40 heavy wagons. With a delightful lack of formality all the injured (and any that even looked injured) were transferred to the ambulances and driven off to hospital right away. The rest of us jumped into the trucks and were taken to the US Army camp a few miles outside the town, many of the locals throwing sugar-melons and other fruit to us as we sped past.

Arriving at the camp, a US officer met each lorry and handed out a pack of cigarettes and a book of matches to every person. We were given camp-beds, sheets, pillows, mosquito nets, eating utensils, etc, and billeted six to a tent. Soon after this we were mustered and given a meal – all this in a matter of an hour or two. Considering the numbers involved, this was clearly a *tour de force*.

We spent five or six days at the camp and were issued with GI tropical uniforms to replace our tattered garments. The food was understandably not plentiful, but of excellent quality. The Yanks were most particular about hygiene. Three large metal bins – two containing disinfectant and one with plain water – were set on top of fires until they were boiling; all utensils were then dipped in each of the bins before and after eating.

Some two or three hundred yards away was another army camp. We had a sentry on duty and I asked him why this camp was there and so far from the front line. He astonished me by saying that it housed US soldiers that had enlisted but had changed their minds on landing in Africa, and had refused to fight!

We were given some money and leave to go to town, with disastrous results. We had quite a number of Glasgow hard men in the engine room department and they lost no time in getting drunk on cheap wine. I was lying sleeping in my tent with my five mates when a voice woke us up calling for volunteers to fight the Yanks. It was strange behaviour towards the ones that had treated us so well, but intoxication knows no logic. We all pretended to be asleep and the recruiter went away, probably thinking it best not to waste time on the faint-hearted when there would be others willing to swell their ranks.

I do not know what weapons they had, but the Yanks were not for any nonsense and the next thing we heard was gunfire. We all were pretty scared, stuck in our tent at the mercy of any stray bullet, and I confess I was more frightened then than when the ships was being bombed. This naturally resulted on all future leave being cancelled.

On 19 July we all got ready to leave. RAF ratings rescued from the *Duchess of York* were put aboard the *Nea Hellas* to continue their journey first to Freetown in Sierra Leone then on to Takoradi in the Gold Coast (later renamed Ghana). Others who were civilian passengers also started on the same ship but ended up in Nigeria.

The crews of the two liners were to be sent home as DBS (Distressed British Seamen) on the *Dunotter Castle*, but later this was changed to the *Arundel Castle*. Our quarters were cramped. The bunks were three high with little space between. We accepted this philosophically as the rigours of war, but food was a different matter. Despite almost daily complaints it continued to be barely edible and grossly insufficient.

With some amusement I recall Arthur and I taking a particularly revolting bloater to the chief steward and enquiring how he would like this for breakfast. His reply was that it was strange that we were the only ones to find fault with it. Arthur was too sharp for him and asked if he was inferring that all the others were satisfied.

'It would appear to be the case,' said the man.

'Well then,' replied Arthur, 'would you care to come with me and inspect the slop bins?'

The steward had fallen right into the trap.

On the way back our escort sunk two U-boats and possibly a third. It was difficult to be sure about such things as the Germans used to put clothing, equipment and some oil into a torpedo tube and fire it, to give the impression that the sub had been sunk.

During two days in Gibraltar waiting for a convoy we had a first-class air raid and, to liven matters, another at Avonmouth on our return.

On leaving the *Arundel Castle* each of us was given a small paper bag of food to see us home. Unfortunately none of us thought to inspect it before leaving the ship. I opened mine on the train 2 hours out of Bristol and found it to consist of two sandwiches of some foul kind of meat, and an apple. After jettisoning the meat I ate the bread and three-quarters of the apple, the other quarter being a repellent shade of sepia.

There was an amusing incident on the way home. We stopped for 10 minutes at a station somewhere in England and, just after we had arrived, another train full of GIs drew up at the next platform. Quite a few of our party had visited the USA on many occasions and had picked up some of their dialects. We shouted across to them in Brooklynese, southern drawls, clipped Bostonian accents, etc, and, together with our US military garb, they were completely taken in. We had a great deal of fun with this incident and, just as our train was about to depart, we lapsed into broad Glasgow patois – the expressions on the faces of the GIs is something that I shall always remember.

I was told that the total dead from the *California* was a round 100. Ninety-eight were killed directly by the bombs, one died in Casablanca and we buried one at sea on the way home.

No one has ever explained how planes at that height had been able to bomb so accurately. The usual theories and rumours were widespread. One claimed that it was a new kind of glider bomb that was guided on to the target by radio. Whatever the facts, we were not told at the time, but many years after the war I found out the truth and have put it at the end of this chapter.

My gramophone was lost and also the expensive sports jacket I had bought in Philadelphia. For the total loss of my effects I was awarded £13 6s 9d, which scarcely paid for my oilskin and sou'wester. At least I was paid until I returned home. A common practice of many shipping companies was to stop pay (and allotment notes) as soon as the vessel was sunk. As the war progressed, the Ministry of War Transport tried to put a stop to this iniquity, but even as late as 1943 many companies continued with it.

My old shipmate Cromb (from the *Reina del Pacifico*) was even worse off. He had left the catering department and become an ordinary seaman and, after his ship was sunk, he spent four days in an open boat before reaching the USA. Since he had no clothes at all on arrival, he was given a lounge suit of a royal blue colour and a huge ten-gallon hat – neither of which could be worn in the United Kingdom without provoking the greatest degree of merriment. Returning to the UK he was then due £10 compensation for his loss of belongings, but the authorities deducted £8 for the suit and the hat he could never wear outside the USA!

As a result of communicating with others through advertisements on Teletext <internet??>, I have been supplied with much additional information. Most of the details came from the historian Christopher Goss who, together with a German Lufthansa pilot, was researching the activities of a German squadron operating out of Bordeaux in 1943.

First of all, the convoy's code name was 'FAITH', and the sinkings took place at approximately 41°00' North, 15°30' West. We were the victims of so-called 'smart bombs' that were directed by radio. They were not as accurate as we had at first supposed, as will be seen from the following information.

The planes were Focke-Wolfe Kondors and the bombs were all 250kg.

1st aircraft: Commanded by Oberleutnant Ludwig Progner, who was a very successful pilot and later joined Lufthansa as an airline pilot. He dropped four bombs on the *Duchess of York*.
2nd aircraft: Commanded by Oberleutnant Egon Scherret. He dropped four bombs on the *California*. He was later reported missing in action on 13 December 1943.
3rd aircraft: Commanded by Hauptmann Helmut Liman. He dropped four bombs on the *California*. He was older than the others and had been a pilot in Lufthansa before the war. He was shot down by US night-fighters on 27 September 1944.

So, of the four bombs dropped on the *Duchess of York*, two hit the target,
and of the eight dropped on *California*, only three hit.

Hauptmann Liman, together with a Hauptmann Husslein, went to look for the ships on the following day but could not find them.

The matter of merchant ships being non-combatants was quite bizarre. It was most unlikely that anyone could bring down an aircraft by scoring a direct hit. The practice was to send shells up and as near as possible to the aeroplane, hoping that when they exploded the shrapnel would severely damage the plane.

Every few months the Admiralty decreed the fuse settings (that is, the heights at which the missiles would explode) for these shells. It was usually around 4,000 feet, and the theory was that a barrage of shells exploding at this height would deter pilots from coming any lower, the assumption being that above this height they would be unable to bomb accurately. In other words the vessel retained its non-combatant status.

Apparently one convoy on the east coast of Britain was being assaulted by German aircraft that were about 5,000 feet up, when their fuses were set for around 4,000 feet. Being tired of the futility of sending up projectiles that were 1,000 feet short of the mark, the marine DEMS gunner altered the fuse settings to 5,000 feet and succeeded in bringing down two planes. It was said that the skipper and the chief engineer both were awarded the OBE, while the marine was severely reprimanded for interfering with the published settings!

7

On a convoy Rescue Ship

Since I was classed as a survivor I was given extra leave and did not join my next ship until 3 September 1943.

As the Battle of the Atlantic went on, millions of tons of shipping was being sunk; the ships could be replaced but the trained officers and men of the merchant navy could not. The Admiralty, being alive to this, tried out a plan of having the rear vessel in the convoy drop back to pick up the survivors of the ships that had been sunk. This turned out to be no solution. The rescuing ships, when slowed down or stopped to pick up seamen, offered the U-boats a first-class target and were frequently themselves sunk, thus causing more loss of crew and cargo. If they escaped being sunk they were faced with a long, lonely and risky trip back to rejoin the convoy.

Late in 1940 the Admiralty stated that it expected to be able to supply vessels specially equipped for this work. The sort of ships suitable for this work would have to be small, easily manoeuvrable, and fast enough to be able to rejoin the convoy after doing the rescuing. The answer seemed to lie with appropriating some of the peacetime coasters, but would they be strong enough to cross the Western Ocean? In normal times these ships were rarely out of sight of land and were now to face the prospect of crossing the Atlantic in wintry conditions. As the need was now pressing, the Admiralty chose to begin with one or two vessels and see how they fared.

Other than liners, few merchant ships carried a Medical Officer; the medicine chest in the Master's cabin with a few simple remedies and a leaflet describing the most common ailments and injuries was the best one could expect. Having a doctor, operating theatre and pharmacy on the Rescue Ship meant that the naval Surgeon-Lieutenant soon found himself a general practitioner to all sorts of seamen, varying in number from 2,500 up to 6,000 in the case of the big convoys. Removing patients to, or the doctor from, the Rescue Ship while at sea became usual, and many cases of injury or illness were treated.

The job of these vessels was to launch their own rescue boats, pick up the survivors as quickly as possible, and look after their medical needs till port was reached. It was preferable to have two boats with engines, and to have one on each side of the ship so that there would be no need for the parent vessel to turn to afford shelter to the returning boat. When not actively engaged in rescue work she would keep a lookout for stragglers falling out of position.

The task of Rescue Ships grew very quickly as the war went on. As they usually steamed at the rear of the convoy in the central column, Commodores quickly recognised their potential as an ideal help in controlling the tail of the convoy, and keeping the Commodore informed of any difficulties. The Masters found themselves becoming more active in the job of controlling the convoys throughout the war.

In 1941 an effective High Frequency Direction Finding set (HF/DF, but referred to as 'Huff Duff') became available. This allowed rapid bearings to be taken of submarines, and many escort vessels were so equipped. Thus a U-boat signalling near a convoy could now be pinpointed with accuracy.

The size and displacement of the Rescue Ships made it possible for them to be fitted with HF/DF, which meant that cross-bearings could be taken and passed to the convoy escort. With the additional Radio Officers in the Rescue Ships, specially trained for this duty, a very valuable reinforcement of the defence of the convoy was obtained. Many folk reckoned that this HF/DF should have ranked with radar and code-breaking as a top anti-submarine weapon.

But the importance of getting such ships to sea by the end of 1940 meant that few changes could be made to the ships themselves; the provision of additional mattresses and extra wash places and latrines was almost all that could be done in the time available.

They would fly the RFA (Royal Fleet Auxiliary) flag – a blue ensign with a gold anchor on the fly – and when joining the convoy would display the distinctive Rescue Flag, which was green with a white diagonal.

In January 1941 the Clyde Shipping Company's *Toward* and her sister ship the *Copeland* started in the service. This company's ships were all named after lighthouses or lightships and the first two were joined by the *Rathlin*, *Goodwin*, *Fastnet* and *Eddystone*. It did not take long for the first two to show their mettle. Four days out on her first voyage the *Toward* saved a dozen men. Two days later the *Copeland* picked up eight seamen from HMS *Crispin*. In less than a week 40 lives had been saved.

The average size of crew would be about 70 – more than twice the peacetime complement. The deck personnel usually included an extra officer, called the Rescue Officer. There were no deck boys or ordinary seamen, as the Admiralty wanted trained men and not those in the process of being trained. The engine room ratings were pretty much as would be expected, but the catering staff had extra stewards to look after the needs of survivors.

In the radio department there were the customary three 'sparks' and an extra three HF/DF officers. There would be about a dozen gunners – a mixture of Army, RN and possibly Marines. To round off, there was a naval surgeon with his two sickbay attendants, and two Navy signalmen.

Altogether there were 29 vessels employed in rescue work. Six of them – *Toward*, *Zaafaran*, *Walmer Castle*, *Stockport*, *St Sunniva* and *Pinto* – were sunk.

It would be unfair to single out the performance of any particular ship as being 'better' than the rest, as they all did their bit nobly and had no control over what was offered to them in the way of rescue opportunities. But if there was a 'league' it would be topped by the *Rathlin*, which, during the escorting of 60 convoys, picked up 634 survivors. Next would be the *Zamalek*, which rescued 611 and took part in 64 convoys.

A grand total of 4,194 seamen were rescued, including 2,296 who were British or Commonwealth. The remaining 1,898 were from 13 different countries, and actually included four from U-boats!

In the autumn of 1943 I joined the Clyde Shipping Company's *Goodwin* as a sailor. She was a coastal passenger-cargo ship, just over 1,500 gross tons, built in 1917. Just nine months prior to my joining her she had been commissioned as a Rescue Ship. The basic changes had already taken place: her forward hold had been adapted to carry the extra coal needed for crossing the Atlantic, and the two after holds converted to provide living accommodation for survivors. Also, she had six lifeboats (the two near the stern having engines) and was equipped with a small hospital.

There was more work to be done on her to bring her up to standard, but the need for more and more vessels for rescue work was so great that she was put into service early. The final alterations were not made until she put into Halifax in late October 1943.

Her total crew was 73, which included 15 gunners as she was more heavily armed than the average merchantman. All the merchant seamen had to be volunteers and very fit. I recall once, when nosying around in the saloon, coming across a document that was confidential. In it was stated that all sailors had to be both volunteers and healthy. Also, on no account had any men with histories of 'bad backs' or 'stomach complaints' to be signed on, for if they did not fancy the ship they could then use the malady to get paid off. Furthermore, the articles were for six months, and not the usual ones that covered one voyage only.

As mentioned earlier, Rescue Ships had to have a reasonable speed in order to overtake the convoy after doing the rescue work. The cargo convoys were fairly slow – about 7 knots – and before the arrival of these ships one of the rear vessels was expected to do the job. If we imagine her speed to be as much as 8 knots, and if she took an hour to pick up the seamen, the convoy would then be about 7½ miles ahead. Even allowing for zigzagging, this meant that the rescue ship would take nearly 15 hours to regain her station. It was small wonder that many were torpedoed. The *Goodwin* could do 11½ knots and this was a decided advantage; also, her small size might not have appealed to U-boats that were seeking bigger ships and their cargoes.

Since all the deck ratings (bosun, carpenter and ten sailors) were new to this work, we were given some drill in the Clyde estuary before accompanying the convoy. This involved smartly lowering both of our motor launches, making a quick trip round the ship and being taken back on board.

I was in the second boat along with the 2nd Mate, a greaser and an AB. When we came to be winched back on board a mishap occurred. The shaft of the winch, which ran athwartships (from one side of the vessel to the other) with its drums on either side, had its controls in a housing amidships. Our launch was on the port side and this housing obstructed the view of the AB at the starboard drum. This man misheard a command and, not being able to see what was going on, took the fall off the drum, resulting in the stern of the launch suddenly dropping into the water.

By some amazing reflex action, all four of us jumped up off the thwarts (the seats in the boat) and clung to the wire connecting the heads of the davits. Alas, the boat's engine got a real ducking and, despite being thoroughly dried out, was never quite the same again.

We set off for Halifax in our position at the tail of the convoy. Scarcely had we reached Rathlin Island when a ship signalled to say that one of her seamen had been taken ill. The starboard launch was lowered and the man was transferred to the *Goodwin*, where he was soon under our doctor's care.

The trip across to Halifax was typical of the North Atlantic. Rough weather accompanied us most of the way and the *Goodwin* pitched, rolled, corkscrewed and did almost every gyration possible. I used to envy the corvettes. Although they were a bit smaller than the Rescue Ships they were built for ocean work and seemed to ride the swell a lot better.

Three days from Halifax we received a signal from an American ship that one of her crew was ill. I was detailed to go in the port launch together with the 3rd Mate, a greaser and another sailor. The weather was fairly bad at the time, with a strong breeze and heavy swell, and we had some difficulty lowering the boat. We had gone barely 100 yards when the engine gave out – this being the one that had received the ducking in the harbour. The remaining distance of about 250 yards had to be rowed, with the other sailor and myself doing the job.

Owing to the swell, we could pull only a few inches on the oars at each stroke. Eventually we arrived at the ship and the sailor was lowered down to us in a kind of straitjacket. Coming back we had the same bother with the oars and could not take long strokes or we risked falling backwards if the oar suddenly came out of the water.

The man was hoisted on board, then the real ordeal began. A lifeboat is meant for lowering into the sea and possibly being taken back on board again in fine weather; or being lowered into the sea in rough weather when abandoning ship in a storm. What it was never expected to do, or designed for, was to be taken back on board ship in really rough weather. One moment we were in a trough yards below the deck, and the next instant we were level with the deck and could nearly shake hands with our shipmates. Adding to these trials was the *Goodwin* rolling about madly.

The ropes to haul the boat were in threefold purchases; that is to say there were two blocks fore and two blocks aft, each with three sheaves (wheels), and there were six lengths of rope between each set of blocks. These blocks were quite heavy and the lower one had a hook to attach it to a ring in the lifeboat. Trying to fix the hook on the ring while the boat was jumping about wildly was very difficult and dangerous. Getting a knock on the head from one of these blocks would be worth mentioning. However, at last they were secured and we were hoisted back on board.

The man was diagnosed as having appendicitis and it was decided to operate the next morning. The skipper told the man at the wheel to forget about steering the correct course and to try to keep the vessel as steady as possible. There was still quite a swell and not only had the man to be lashed to the operating table, but the surgeon also had to have a leather strap round his waist connected to the table in order to keep him from rolling with the ship's motion. The operation was a success and we kept the man on board till we reached port.

I do not know who leaked the tale to the press, but a Halifax newspaper devoted two columns to this 'epic of the sea'. Reading the vivid account, I wondered at some folk getting all the adventures, and it was only when I reached the end of the article and read about Surgeon-Lieutenant Drake that I realised that we were the ship involved in the exploit.

We were seven days in Halifax. You may remember that on the *Reina del Pacifico* one of the bakers was the brother of our erstwhile neighbours, the MacQuarries. Well, Mrs MacQuarrie had a sister Helen who was married to a Robert Muir. Robert had been more than 30 years at sea as an engineer, and had finished up as Chief Engineer in the Blue Funnel Line. This was a company of large cargo ships trading to the Far East and its ships were all named after Greek characters: *Hector*, *Nestor*, *Achilles*, *Perseus* and so on.

Shortly after the war began Robert was posted to Halifax as a shore engineer to inspect engines of ships in port. He was tipped off that I was on the *Goodwin* and on Sunday he appeared in a huge Pontiac car and took me off for the day. He was the soul of generosity and did this for all sailors with whom he had any connection, and always it was the best hotels he took us to.

In Halifax it was the Lord Nelson Hotel, and I was taken aback to find that he had to pay for the meal and receive a ticket before approaching the table. A waiter appeared and was given this ticket and went off to order the meal. I could understand this procedure in poorer-class eating houses where there was a risk of the diner absconding without paying for the meal, but not in top-class hotels.

Robert and I reminisced about a restaurant, Langs, in Glasgow where the customers made out their own bills from the menu prices, and paid accordingly. Robert said that he told this to Canadian friends but they had not believed him.

On this trip I bought a leather jacket in Halifax. It was made of horse-hide with blanket lining, and cost me $15, which, at the rate of exchange then, was about £3 15s. This proved to be a good investment and certainly helped to keep the Canadian winter temperatures at bay. More than 60 years later my son still wears it.

There was no talk about 'wind chill factors' in those days, but I recall reading the book *Ungava* by R. M. Ballantyne where he claimed that one would be more comfortable at 20 degrees below freezing point with no wind than at 5 degrees below freezing with a wind. He was absolutely correct. Formerly I had worn a coat that kept me warm down to the waist, then flapped uselessly about my legs.

Nothing worthy of note happened on the way home. A few more folk took sick and a little rough weather dogged us most of the time.

One of our sailors had been in Spain during the Spanish Civil War and had smuggled out a book that he told me was banned in Britain. He wanted to translate it into English and, although his Spanish was reasonably good, he wanted help putting it into acceptable English. I offered to give him some assistance and we both laboured at it for nearly two weeks. Unfortunately, he was a most untidy person and left the jotters lying around the fo'c'sle where another sailor took them for scribblings and threw them out. All I can remember is that if the Socialists, Communists and Anarchists had spent less time squabbling and fighting among themselves, the war might have gone on a bit longer.

Another sailor, Willie, was from the Highlands. He had been captured when his ship was sunk in the Mediterranean and taken to an Italian prisoner-of-war camp in North Africa. The treatment he received there was appalling and his diet was a daily dose of couscous. He complained of toothache and their answer was to extract all his teeth without anaesthetic!

As previously mentioned, the Rescue Ships carried an extra officer known as the Rescue Officer. He was responsible to the Master for the readiness and cleanliness of survivors' accommodation, their spare bedding, towels, lifebelts, etc. If a junior 2nd Mate was given the post he had a large list of extra duties including manning one of the rescue launches.

However, one of the office staff at the headquarters of the Clyde Shipping Company, who was apparently frantic to go to sea, was given the job. Naturally he could not be trusted to take charge of a launch and he ended up attending to any clerical duties that arose.

Now, as all seafarers know, shortly before arrival in the United Kingdom a manifest is produced, and all the seamen have to declare any dutiable goods in their possession, and sign this statement. The Waterguard (uniformed officers in Customs & Excise) took away this document and scrutinised it before searching the ship for contraband.

Well, this tyro of a Rescue Officer forgot all about the manifest and there was nothing for us to sign. Consequently, had we had any excess tobacco, spirits, etc, all the Customs could have done was to charge the duty on these items. They could not have fined us or seized the goods, as we had not made a written declaration.

The Rescue Ships usually docked at Springfield Quay in Glasgow where there was no dock gate manned by the police. The Waterguard came out by boat when we passed through the boom at Greenock and inspected our papers, leaving the search until we had berthed. I was at the wheel as we passed through the boom and two of them came on to the bridge and asked me where the skipper was.

'I think he's out on the wing of the bridge,' I replied.

They dashed out of the wheelhouse but returned in seconds saying, 'He's not there. Where is he? Come on, tell us.'

'He was there a minute or two ago,' I asserted, 'and, anyway, I am here to steer the ship and it's not my job to help you look for the captain.'

Apparently on the previous trip he had tried to smuggle a case of whisky, and they were now gunning for him.

I thought it strange that, in all my years at sea, the Customs never seemed to catch stewards trying to evade duty. The reason was simple. The chief steward allowed them to purchase tobacco and spirits duty-free from the ship's bond. This was quite a perk and they would not wish to jeopardise it. I recall that at the end of the *Goodwin*'s last voyage the chief steward was leaving the ship and he made 15 trips with a suitcase and no Customs went near him! When the skipper wanted the Customs to open the bond when in port he had the red ensign hoisted with a knot in the fly.

However, let us go back to the present situation. The Customs, for some reason or other, did not show up until the following day. Now, pause and consider the facts: no manifest, no Customs and no dock gate! I went home, then returned to the ship 2 hours after she docked. The sight that greeted me was an amazing one. People that I had never seen before were walking around the vessel: sailors with their fathers, firemen with their uncles, stewards with their cousins and so on, all minding their own affairs and busily engaged in taking stuff ashore. By the morning I doubt if there was a cigarette anywhere, or enough alcohol to fill an eggcup.

By a strange coincidence Arthur Fisken and Bob Dolan had joined another Rescue Ship, the *Copeland*, and both vessels had two weeks in Glasgow. They arrived a week after us, and we left a week before them, so we were in port together for a week.

They had just finished a trip with the Gibraltar convoy and the ship was crammed with demijohns of wine. The Customs had collected many of them but were unable to link them up with the owners. Apparently the Waterguard received rewards for discovering contraband, but the reward was much bigger if the owner could be found. They were threatening to put a fine on the ship and it was said that the owners would recover this penalty by deducting sums of money from each crew member. Their reasoning for this was that if masses of contraband was discovered, the ship's officers were not doing enough to prevent smuggling. The ship's officers are mainly concerned with looking after the ship's affairs and are not employed to do the work of the Customs, and I, for one, would have refused to pay if it could not be proved that I had been smuggling.

This was one of the troubles with having a small ship with large numbers in the crew. Hiding places were at a premium and it was common for two seamen to choose the same place. Normally the first to return, once the Customs had gone, collected the lot!

Our Captain Campbell, from Skye, was replaced by Captain W. J. Hartley DSC. He also had a Lloyd's medal for bravery at sea and we were more impressed with it than with his others. Lloyd's medals are worn on the right side of the chest.

We were now told that the ship would be in Glasgow for a month so that we could have new quarters built. Most of us were reasonably satisfied with our present accommodation, but accepted the idea in the hope of getting something better. At the end of one week the old quarters were entirely demolished, while we lived in the survivors' berths. Next day the captain received orders to sail for Halifax.

During this second voyage we stayed in the survivors' berths and found this most uncomfortable. Survivors do not have the trunks, kitbags, etc, that a member of a ship's crew is obliged to carry.

Another point I bring to mind was that I had left Glasgow with a severe cold but it had rapidly disappeared when at sea. This set me thinking. Not only did the sea appear to cure a cold, but I can never remember anyone contracting one when actually at sea.

Captain Hartley decided that he would follow naval practice and every Saturday evening all members of the crew were given a tot of rum. This had to be drunk at the time, to prevent anyone trying to save up the ration and have a binge.

Arriving in Halifax, shore workers came on board and fixed up new quarters for us, which, strangely enough, were a good deal worse that the former ones.

Quite an amusing incident took place while I was doing my Christmas shopping. Barrington Street was the main thoroughfare and I had just made a purchase and had a $5 bill as part of my change. I intended putting it into the inside pocket of my jacket but realised, shortly afterwards, that I had actually put it into the space between my jacket and my coat. As soon as I became aware of this I decided to report the matter at a police station. Years earlier I remember my sister discovering a purse with 6 shillings and a few pennies in it. She handed it into a police station and, after six months, when no one had claimed it, the police returned the money to her. With this in mind I approached a policeman who was directing traffic and asked him where the nearest police station was.

'What do you want to know that for, bud?' he asked, still waving at the traffic.

'I've dropped a $5 bill and would like to report it, just in case somebody might hand it in.'

'You've what?'

The traffic was now completely forgotten.

'I know it's not likely but I can tell to the nearest 5 minutes when I lost it, and to the nearest 10 yards where I lost it,' I replied.

'Let me get this straight. You've dropped a 5-spot bill and you expect someone to hand it in?'

'I don't expect it – but just in case an honest citizen does, I thought I might as well report it.'

'Look,' said he, doubling up with laughter and leaving the traffic to look after itself, 'you think someone will hand in a $5 bill. I'm a policeman and I wouldn't hand it in.'

He resumed his directing duties saying, 'Boy, oh boy. Somebody's going to town tonight on your money!'

A point that I have not brought up before was a common practice in port of the Mate saying 'job and finish'. This meant that he required a specified amount of work (usually painting) to be done in one day, and as soon as it was done the crew were free to go ashore. The job was probably a full day's work and the crew piled in like fury and had the task done just before lunch. Obviously this was of mutual benefit as the Mate got a good day's work done and the crew had a half-day's holiday.

As usual, on the Sunday Robert Muir came down to the dock and took me away for the day. This time we went to a valley that was alive with the red autumnal colour of the maple leaves. Every few miles was a kiosk selling freshly picked apples in small casks half sawn through and known as bushels. Robert bought two for himself and insisted in buying one for me. I recall that it held 105 apples.

Another rough crossing and the *Goodwin* arrived back in Glasgow sorely in need of repairs.

As usual the *Copeland* came in about a week after us. They had been to Murmansk and it was not to be recommended. I took my nephews down to see the two ships and they were delighted when one of the *Copeland*'s sailors gave each of them a 1 rouble note.

The normal wartime patching up job was done and we were packed off again to sea. This time we had Christmas and New Year at sea, and this occasioned two meals of much better than normal quality. We reached Halifax one ship short; she had been torpedoed and had to make for Iceland.

The weather was intensely cold and I was given the job of painting the mainmast. Now, since Rescue Ships had radio direction finding equipment this required them to have very tall mainmasts – nearly twice the height of the foremast. Moreover, the top 25 feet or so was very slender and little more than 10 inches wide.

I had just arrived at the top of the mast and had taken off my gloves to fasten the paint pot when the cold got at my hands and I had to scamper down the mast (using the insides of my wrists between the mast and the ladder) before I lost the power in my fingers. It took 15 minutes in the galley, beating the palms together, before they were back to normal. The work was finally accomplished by wearing a pair of woollen gloves below my leather ones and working at top speed. While at the masthead the situation was aggravated by coal being dropped into the for'ard hold and causing the slender part of the mast to shake violently.

The bosun was a heavy drinker and, like so many of his breed, thought that everyone should be similarly inclined. 'Why don't you spend some money and enjoy yourself?' was his constant questioning.

I took this for some time before reminding him of the evening when he had bought a new suit, got drunk, picked a fight with a Swede who broke his nose, then lay in his own vomit until he sobered up in the morning. This, I told him, was not my notion of a good time.

As I said before, the food was extremely poor and I often took lunch ashore at the dock canteen. In the evening, in company with the carpenter and the two RN signallers, I regularly had tea at a restaurant called the Green Lantern where one could get a decent meal for 75 cents. I asked the carpenter if his mate, the bosun, ever thought of joining us, only to be informed that he (the bosun) considered it too dear. It seemed ever thus with boozers. They think nothing of spending pounds on drink but cavil at the thought of paying a shilling or so for a pair of decent socks.

Robert Muir came down to the ship again on Sunday and took me to a place called Windsor. Thanks to him I was seeing quite a bit of Nova Scotia.

Canada had various attitudes to the consumption of alcohol. In the province of Quebec one could drink all day and night without restriction. In British Columbia (which I was later to visit) if you wanted spirits you went to a government office and paid the required amount and got a receipt. This receipt you then took to a liquor store (often in the same part of the building) and were given all the drink you wanted. So, although it was not controlled, the authorities had their finger on the pulse and knew exactly how much was being consumed.

In Nova Scotia they had what amounted to partial prohibition. Each person could get a card entitling him or her to one bottle of spirits or 12 bottles of beer a month! This drink had to be consumed under a roof, but one was not allowed to tipple in a car, as this was considered to have only a 'provisional' roof.

As a result, bootleggers came to each ship and took the few abstainers up to the liquor office where they gave them each the price of a bottle of spirits. Once they got their hands on the spirits, they gave the teetotallers a dollar or two for their trouble, then took the booze to sell to the illicit drinking dens.

Apparently this situation had arisen some years before owing to a strong anti-booze movement with religious connections. They were known by their opponents as the 'Iced-Water Baptists'. Such was their influence that they were able to term all drinking as a sin, and introduced the Liquor Laws that declared that if a person wanted to 'sin' he had to do so in private.

On the way back, one of the MAC ships (merchant aircraft carriers) was carrying New Zealand airmen. In a moment of high spirits one of them dared his pal to push him overboard. Being of an obliging nature, the mate complied with this request and, as the first fellow was going over, he clutched at his pal and both made a rather spectacular double dive into the ocean. Fortunately they were both safely picked up by a destroyer in the escort, much to the annoyance of Captain Hartley DSC, who had immediately pulled the *Goodwin* off her course to rescue the men, and was cheated of adding further laurels to his crown – or medals to his chest!

The decks of these MAC ships were relatively small compared with the regular Navy carriers and it could not have been an easy task to land a plane on them, especially if the vessel was rolling and pitching. A tragedy occurred when one of these planes was trying to return to a carrier. The pilot failed to land squarely on the deck and, to everyone's horror, the plane lurched and fell into the sea. On this occasion neither Captain Hartley nor any of the escort could reach the men in time and the poor fellows were drowned.

It always puzzled me why every tradesman at sea except the carpenter was classed as an officer. On board liners they had electricians signed on as electrical engineers and plumbers designated sanitary engineers. The carpenter was never an officer – always a chief petty officer. His job was naturally anything to do with wood: the lifeboats, hatch boards, wedges for the hatches, etc. In addition he always manned the windlass at the bow when berthing or anchoring. Another duty was to go round all the tanks twice a day to sound them for any water. For this he used a metal rod at the end of a thin rope. The rod was chalked and lowered into the tube leading to the tank. He reported his findings to the engineers for them to pump out the tank if they considered it necessary. It struck me that he had a fairly easy job on board, principally because no one above him in rank knew much about his trade. He laughed in agreement but told me of an exception to the rule.

Anyone that had served on the deck of a merchant ship was eligible to sit for a 2nd Mate's certificate after four years. The time might be served by a sailor, an apprentice, a cadet – or a carpenter. Unknown to our 'chippy', he signed on a ship where the Master was a time-served carpenter before going to sea. Instead of the Mate giving him his daily orders the skipper took on the job.

When they reached the River Plate the carpenter noticed a lot of timber, 2 inches square, being shipped on board. Two days out on the road home he was called to the captain who explained that he wanted him to make wooden gratings for the starboard wing of the bridge, using half-lap joints.

He set about the business and a day or two later the skipper had a word with him, saying that his work was quite satisfactory but he wanted the job done a bit faster. After he had finished the starboard wing the Old Man immediately set him to work on the port wing. He completed the work only to hear the skipper remark that on the way out next trip he wanted him to do 'monkey island' in the same way. That was the end of that ship!

When on the *Reina del Pacifico* I used to ask some of the older sailors to show me some of the fancy knots, but they said that they could not be bothered. At the time I believed them and set about learning from books. In retrospect I think that many of them did not know the knots and were ashamed to admit to it. We had on board the best AB I ever sailed with. He was a lad, Jack Wishart, from the Shetland Isles; he showed me every kind of plait and sennit, and taught me how to make very attractive mats using them.

Arriving in Glasgow we docked at Springfield quay and I was welcomed home by my parents. One thing that used to annoy me was one of the neighbours saying, 'Oh, you're home again – when are you going back?' No doubt the remark was not intended to be irritating, but I could not help resenting it. Others elaborated on some acquaintance that had been away for eight months, never pausing to think that the sailor in question was probably sunning himself off the coast of Australia in relatively safe waters.

My father and mother wanted to wallpaper a room but there was no chance of getting the materials. When in Halifax I saw some stuff that I imagined would suit them and enquired about the number of rolls required. Luckily the saleslady was from Scotland and told me how many Canadian rolls would be the equivalent of the five needed by Mum.

Now, at that time all British wallpaper had plain paper about half an inch wide down the edge of each roll. The idea was that this border would be carefully cut off, leaving the main part of the roll free from any damage that might have occurred through rough handling. This cutting was a laborious and time-consuming task and Dad had just started it when Mum noticed some instructions. Seemingly all you needed to do was to tap the edge of the roll twice against a hard surface, and the border would come away leaving the wallpaper ready for pasting.

The *Goodwin* spent longer than usual in port and our hopes rose as we approached the deadline of the six-month articles. But it was not to be. We shipped out two days before the conclusion of our articles and resigned ourselves to one last voyage.

We had two new cooks this trip. Sea cooks can be strange creatures at the best of times, but these were stranger than usual. They could not cook. This was not in the least strange; in fact, it would have been considered strange had they been able to cook. This odd pair both sported beards and were dressed in brown boiler suits. A cook's normal garb was an apron of sorts varying in colour from a dark white to a pale black – boiler suits were a new fashion for the galley!

The quality of their cooking matched their filthy attire and we soon realised that we had struck culinary rock bottom. At least, that is what we thought until we found their *basse cuisine* deteriorating in a systematic way almost as if it were planned with regard to the Fabian ideal of the 'inevitability of gradualness'.

One day at lunch, after submitting to awful soup and indescribable meat, we tackled the dessert, which was supposed to be apple pie. As was the custom, the apples had been peeled but, upon inspection, the pie was seen to contain something that closely resembled a small branch of the original apple tree. Two of us asked for an audience with Captain Hartley, who took a poor view of this 'orchard pie'. The cooks were summoned, lectured on their shortcomings and given warning that any further experiments would be frowned upon.

Halifax was the same old place, but at least we could get some decent meals ashore.

Canadian girls were like those in the USA insofar as they could not do ballroom dancing with any degree of grace or technique. A few weeks previously two British seamen had given two of the local lassies some tuition in this sphere, and the idea caught on like wildfire. They were begging us to give them some lessons, and by the time we arrived on this last trip they had organised a contest to find out who was the best pair. This was a great success.

In 1942 the British film *In Which We Serve* was released,

concerning a destroyer, HMS *Kelly*. It was closely based on the actual sinking of this ship and was masterminded by Noel Coward, who also played the role of her captain. Most films about wars (especially those made during the conflict) suffer from being too heavily larded with propaganda, but this was an exception. There was no litany of heroic deeds. Even more remarkable was the fact that one of the sailors was portrayed as being cowardly and deserting his post as a gunner during action. It was most lifelike, and about 150 naval ratings on leave from Portsmouth had been employed to give authenticity to some of the scenes.

The film turned out to be an immense success in the USA – both artistically and commercially – and the Yanks decided to make a similar one about an American destroyer. Unfortunately the Americans seem to find it difficult to be objective in such matters, and insist on showing the USA ships and servicemen in the best possible light. Their unlikely tale told of this destroyer being attacked by six planes, bringing down one of them, then, in a crippled condition, going on to sink a submarine.

I went to see the film in a cinema in Halifax. As far as I can remember, the ship sustained some damage from the aircraft, causing her engine room to be flooded. One of her petty officers (Edward G. Robinson) donned a diving suit and, with the aid of welding equipment, went down inside the ship and repaired a leak in her hull. Shortly after this had been effected a conversation between the captain and his chief engineer went, as far as I can remember, something like this:

'How soon can you give me steam, chief?' asks the captain.

'In about 20 minutes,' replies the chief.

'Could you not make it 15 minutes?' is the urgent demand.

'I'll make it 10 minutes, skipper,' then after a pause, 'I tell you what, I'll make it 5 minutes.'

This amazing promise was made despite the water still being about 3 inches below the level of the oil-burners. Halifax being a convoy port, and the picture-house being packed with seamen, many of them firemen and greasers, the audience erupted with laughter. I had never witnessed anything like it before in a cinema.

We sailed from Halifax at 12.25pm on 29 March 1944, passed through the boom at 1pm and dropped our pilot at 1.30pm. By 4pm we were on station in convoy SC 156.

On Sunday 2 April I woke and saw nothing but pancake and slab ice from horizon to horizon. I was told that this was due to the ice patrols being taken off during the war and there being no one left to observe the drift of ice south and take appropriate action. These patrols would land on the biggest bergs and dynamite them, so that what was left would melt more quickly. An American freighter, the *Oldham*, had her propeller shaft damaged by this ice and had to abandon ship. Her crew were taken off by HMS *Porchester Castle*.

The following day at 2.30am a Norwegian tanker, the *South America*, was torpedoed and immediately caught fire. The *Goodwin* at once went to her assistance, but 5 minutes later a second torpedo struck. Curiously this had the effect of putting out the blaze caused by the first one. Captain Hartley performed quite a feat of seamanship, resulting in the entire crew of 42 being rescued unharmed. By 3.07am they were all safely aboard the *Goodwin* and being cared for. Shortly after this a second ship, the *Ruth* (also Norwegian), was torpedoed and her crew were picked up by HMS *Chelmar*, one of the escort vessels.

On 10 April the SOE (senior officer of the escort, usually found on the largest vessel in the escort) asked the *Goodwin* to take off all the survivors from two naval vessels. Since the American ship was abandoned, its crew had time to take off their kitbags, cases and personal effects. Both launches were employed; the one I was in did seven trips and the other eight.

Eventually we arrived at the Tail of the Bank and had to discharge the survivors before proceeding up to Glasgow.

Some of the information concerning this voyage was obtained from other sailors after the war was over. One of them actually managed to get hold of Captain Hartley's official report, and I have included it here. As there are too many terms to be explained I decided not to clarify all of them by adding footnotes; instead I have put the explanation in brackets.

CAPTAIN HARTLEY'S OFFICIAL REPORT
Secret SG156 R/S 'Goodwin'

Wednesday 29th March 1944. Departed from Halifax at 1225. Pilot onboard. Passed through the Boom at 1300 and dropped pilot at 1330. In station as Rescue Ship with SG156 at 1600.

Thursday 30th March. Moderate NNW wind, mod sea. Cloudy and clear.

Friday 31st March. Mod ENE breeze. Mod sea, dense fog.

Saturday 1st April. Similar weather conditions.

Sunday 2nd April. Passed through a field of pancake and slab ice.

Numerous bergs sighted.

Monday 3rd April. Fresh NNE wind, mod sea, fine and clear.

Tuesday 4th April. Fresh to strong southerly wind, rough sea, ss rolling heavily, overcast, cloud

Wednesday 5th April. Moderate easterly breeze, moderate sea, overcast and drizzle.

Thursday 6th April. At 0230 Norwegian tanker No 44 [the *South America*; this was her position in the convoy] was torpedoed, wind ENE force 3, sea calm. *Goodwin* proceeded to assistance at 0232, at that time the vessel was afire amidships with flames mast high. I decided that I would go alongside aft, to windward or starboard – as it looked as if the fire might defeat all attempts by the crew to use the boats. At 0235 *Goodwin* was about 70 yards astern of the stricken tanker and closing her, when a second torpedo struck again on the port side.

This second torpedo had the effect of causing the fire to die out. When this torpedo struck (I noticed two snowflakes well ahead on the port wing of the convoy. I took it that escorts were using illumination) I decided to alter the rescue manoeuvre and turned the ship short round so that the *Goodwin* was hove to [not moving in the water] about 40 feet astern of the tanker, and at right angles to her. This presented the least target to the direction of attack. My ship's bridge was then in line with the tanker's stern.

Two lifeboats and one raft were launched from tanker at 0238 and the crew were immediately helped aboard and taken care of. This operation was completed by 0307. The *Goodwin* remained unscreened [unprotected]. I then proceeded to rejoin convoy and inform the Senior Officer of the Escort by R/T [radio telephone] that I had completed the job and saved the entire crew of 42, including the master.

At about 0320, when within approximately two miles of convoy, R/T messages between escorts were intercepted. There seemed quite a lot of confusion as to whether a second ship had been torpedoed or not. I had enquiries made of Commodore to verify second sinking but he could not vouch for more than one. Only one distress message had been received on 650 yards (from 44). Shortly afterwards I called SOE [senior officer of the escort] and he could not verify then.

At 0333 a R/T message received from an escort – call sign Landmark – telling me that a second torpedoed ship was 000 degrees [due north] – 1 mile – ZZ5. I did not know what ZZ5 signified but decided that I would return to 44 (which I reckoned was still afloat) take a departure from her to try to locate 3 lifeboats which were reported. I turned ship round and headed back, notifying Commodore by R/T that I was about to seek for the second ship's survivors.

At 0337 SOE detailed HMS *Chelmar* to screen [protect] *Goodwin* and asked for a position. This was sent out and at 0420 I arrived at position of 44 and found her still afloat with a broken back. She was then about 12 miles astern of the convoy and *Goodwin* was still unscreened.

I set off on a zigzag with a mean course of 000 [north] and soon found a large quantity of floating lumber – large logs – and also two lifeboats jammed in between. I pushed slowly ahead through the lumber and alongside each boat, but found they were empty. Next I saw a raft which appeared to have men on it, but on closing [coming closer] discovered it was well stacked with seamen's kitbags.

At 0440 HMS *Chelmar* hove in sight and informed me that he had picked up all survivors from No 12 [*Ruth* 1] and was rejoining convoy. I then proceeded in company with him. At about this time the master of 44 came on bridge and I asked him if his CBs and SPs [presumably confidential bag and ship's papers] had been destroyed. On receiving an answer in the negative from him, I immediately got in touch with the SOE by R/T and sent him a coded message informing him of the fact.

The convoy was reached at 0810 and I sent the SOE and the Commodore a report of the morning's work by V/S [visual signal].

SOE informed me at 1115 by V/S that HMS *Kenilworth Castle* had recovered Convoy Instructions, Sailing Orders, and Recognition Signals and asked me to confirm there was nothing else. I then sent for the radio officer who was on watch, and also for chief officer of 44, and questioned him re SPs etc. I was told that SP 28, 29, 30 [confidential documents] and also Incon [I do not know what this was, but it was obviously a secret document] Mersigs vol 1, 2, and 3 [merchant ship signals, which were used by the Allies during the war as the International Code was known to the enemy] were on board and where to find them. I sent this information to SOE and he despatched HMS *Goodall* to get them.

Friday 7th April. Strong SSW wind, rough sea, ss rolling, overcast. At 1215 received signal from SOE saying SPs and CBs were effectively destroyed as when the *Goodall* arrived only the bow of 44 was visible.

Saturday 8th April. Strong to whole westerly gale, high following sea, ss rolling heavily, occasional rain squalls, clear.

Sunday 9th April. Similar weather conditions.

Monday 10th April. Suggested to SOE at 1300 that survivors from No 12 [*Ruth* 1] on board *Chelmar* be transferred to *Goodwin* when weather permitted. At 1504 SOE approved and asked if I could take survivors from No 101 [*Oldham*] on board HMS *Porchester Castle*.

This being the first I knew of sinking of 101, I asked him, 'When, and under what circumstances was 101 abandoned?' He replied that No 101 was abandoned at 1415 GMT on April 3rd due to a broken propeller shaft.

I agreed to take survivors on transfer – numbering 16 officers and 35 ratings.

Tuesday 11th April. Strong southerly wind, heavy following sea, clear and fine.

Wednesday 12th April. Transferred 51 survivors from HMS *Porchester Castle* also survivors from HMS *Chelmar* – using ship's rescue launch.

Thursday 13th April. Passed through boom (inward) at 0810 and anchored at 0830. Transfer of 129 survivors to ABO's charge [meaning not known] begun at 1230 and completed 1530.

Weighed anchor and proceeded to Springfield Quay at 1600, berthing at 1830.

Remarks. In my opinion it cannot be too strongly emphasised on masters their duty in making a distress signal for a ship which has been torpedoed near at hand, and which for some reason has failed to make the necessary distress signal.

In the case of No 12 no W/T distress signal was made, no red lights were shown, and no rockets were fired by her, and no other merchant ship made any of the foregoing signals on her behalf. Consequently the SOE, Commodore and Rescue Ship were unaware for probably the best part of an hour of this vessel's fate.

(Sgd) W. J. Hartley DSC
Master

Hartley's report ended by saying that the 129 survivors had to wait from 12.30pm until 3.30pm – a total of 3 hours – before being taken ashore by tender.

What the skipper's report did not tell us was the reason for this delay. A large blue questionnaire had to be completed by every seaman before he was allowed on to the tender. The Norwegians all spoke fairly good English, but filling in bureaucratic forms was not so easy for them; I recall many of our crew having to help them to do this. Despite some of them having injuries they were kept waiting until all the red tape conditions had been fulfilled.

Contrast this with the treatment the US had given British seamen almost a year earlier when about 1,800 survivors had been landed on them at short notice in Casablanca. The Yanks then had all the wounded transferred to hospital and the rest taken to a US Army camp on the outskirts of the town. Not until the following day were any questions asked.

Many years after the war I was contacted by Captain Hartley's daughter Brenda. She claimed that her father was sure that the second torpedo to hit the *South America* was actually intended for the *Goodwin*. What a fool I was not to have reasoned this out for myself. If a U-boat torpedoes a tanker and sets it ablaze, what would be the point of launching a second torpedo at it? However, the *Goodwin*, being a much smaller target, was spared. Many U-boat commanders had been very decent to merchant seamen, and my first thoughts were that to attempt to sink a ship engaged in purely rescue work was a dastardly action. Then I remembered that in 1944 Admiral Dönitz had issued orders to stop the soft approach, and in future on no account should help in any way be given to folk other than Germans and Italians. That would explain matters.

Throughout the war Captain Hartley had been on other Rescue Ships and had rescued a total of 362 seamen – quite a remarkable feat!

8

My last days on the lower deck

I had a good time on my 15 days leave – sleeping in my own bed, enjoying my favourite food and seeing all my friends.

My next job was completely different. Many convoys left from Loch Ewe in Ross-shire, most of them for Archangel or Murmansk. If a member of any crew took sick they would send to Glasgow for a replacement, but if there was not time enough for this they had a ship there to supply whatever kind of seaman was needed.

This vessel was a steam yacht, the *Iolaire* (Gaelic for 'eagle'), and had once been owned by Sir Donald Currie, a millionaire who had at one time been chairman of the Union Castle Line.

Because the movements of naval vessels from Scapa Flow had to be kept very secret, it was decided that the whole area north of the Caledonian Canal was classed as restricted, and passes would be required to go there.

In company with an Australian AB and a greaser from Bristol, I travelled by train to Inverness. I could have stayed with relatives but wanted to keep in contact with the other two as they had papers concerning all three of us. However, as luck would have it I lost them leaving the railway station at Inverness, and had a good idea that they would immediately go in search of a drink; the day being Sunday, they could have some trouble finding their booze.

After some time, and with no sign of my mates, I tried to find the Seamen's Mission. I was given a wrong direction and finished up at a mission all right – but not the right one. As soon as I entered the hall a massive man seemed to put a wrestling hold on me and pushed me down on a chair with a hymn book in my hand. The congregation were singing 'He's the lily of the valley, ten thousand to my soul' and, as I was unfamiliar with this hymn, I could not add to the volume.

Before I could draw breath they had launched into another effort, chanting 'I'm only a poor sinner saved by grace'. When this was over I approached my wrestling partner and tried to explain to this gent that,

My last days on the lower deck

unlike the rest of his flock, I was not a poor sinner but a poor sailor who was looking for a bed for the night.

'Well,' he retorted, 'you can't book a bed till the service is over so you may as well stay to the end,' and gently, but very firmly, I was plonked back in the chair.

A gentleman rose and for the next half-hour spoke in a dull monotonous voice. Just as I was thinking that the service would end with his peroration, he announced that it gave him much pleasure to call on the main speaker.

This speaker, a young Army officer, was obviously pretty new to the game and found great difficulty in lasting 20 minutes. Another few sailors entered during this period and all were treated just as I had been, so we finished with an extra dozen sinners singing the closing hymn.

My escape was not effected until I had consumed a mug of tea and three buns, after which I found out that it was the wrong place.

By the time I had carted my luggage to the right mission it was 9.35pm and I discovered that lights were out at 10pm, leaving me about 10 minutes to go back to see one of my relatives.

Next day the train took us to Achnasheen, where we were escorted to a bus that was to take us to Altbea in Wester Ross-shire. Here we saw the *Iolaire* at anchor in the bay. She looked every inch a millionaire's steam yacht but for the fact that she had lost the top half of her mainmast when engaged in the Dunkirk evacuation.

This was a naval base and had a mixture of 150 seamen and Wrens at the main part of the base, with another 50 ratings at the boom. I had been to Loch Ewe before (on the *Newton Pine*), but merchant ships went down to the south of the loch to anchor off Poolewe, so I had never seen this base as it lay behind, and was completely obscured by, the Isle of Ewe.

Now, many merchant seamen did not have uniforms, and not all the officers wore the same one, several companies having liveries of their own. On the *Reina del Pacifico* the captain wore three bands like inverted chevrons. The Mate wore two and the 2nd Mate had a thick one and a thin one above it, and so on. In the P&O company they wore their insignia not on their cuffs but on their shoulders.

Using the regular uniform, the captain had four bands, the two at the centre forming a diamond. The Mate wore three with the centre one having a diamond at its middle, the 2nd Mate two, and the 3rd Mate one. Surgeons had red cloth backings to their insignia, engineers purple, and pursers white. Radio officers wore wavy bands.

For the ordinary ratings, or officers out of uniform, there was a special silver-coloured badge worn on the lapel of their jackets. First of all, the top was what was known as the Tudor Crown and was formed with ships' sails; below it the rope formed a reef knot.

Out we went to the ship on 1 May 1944, signed on and settled in our quarters. The ship's four officers occupied the original passenger accommodation, the skeleton crew were billeted in the old officers' cabins, and we were left with the original crew's fo'c'sle.

The *Iolaire* must have had some connection with David MacBrayne (owners of the *Gondolier* and many other Scottish coasting vessels), for much of its silverware had MacBrayne's name stamped on it.

We signed on coasting articles with a special clause in the contract that made us liable to be shipped out at very little notice in any vessel that was short of a man. The person responsible for assigning us to ships was dubbed the 'Shanghai Man' and he was a member of the Ministry of War Transport.

Furthermore, if any seaman lasted three months without being 'shanghaied' he was entitled to three weeks' leave at home. I was told that it was never known for this to happen and I concluded that, rather than give anyone this large amount of leave, they would deliberately send a ship to Loch Ewe one man short. When they said little notice, they meant just that. There were tales of seamen grabbing their wet washing from the clothes-line and bundling it into their kitbags.

Our work was minimal and mainly consisted of an hour each morning scrubbing the decks. Occasionally coal had to be loaded and we were paid extra for this. When cleaning the saloon windows we first of all washed them and dried them, then we polished them with crumpled newspaper soaked in methylated spirits – it certainly gave them quite a shine.

Our wages were the standard coasting ones, with something deducted for our food. The food was good and we were allowed the run of the galley in the evening. Eggs were not rationed in Ross-shire and, since we were permitted to use the ship's boats for fishing, it was common for us to have fish and chips, or egg and chips, for supper.

We were allowed to purchase 40 cigarettes a week at the special low prices from the NAAFI. The steward looked after this and always picked a particular brand called Kensitas. This company had a small extra carton, containing four cigarettes, and this was attached to the main packet and labelled 'K 4s – for your friends'. Stewards being a crafty race, ours shelled all the packets and sold us the cigarettes loose. This meant that the 'K 4s' were for his friends, not ours!

A liberty boat called every evening, weather permitting, and we were taken ashore and brought back gratis. Ashore there was a YMCA that served tea and cakes and also screened a film twice a week (the snag being that it was the same picture each time). It also had ping-pong and an occasional dance. For those with stronger tastes, there was a canteen selling beer and I often went there with the Australian AB with whom I had become very friendly. There was a great shortage of drinking glasses in the country at that time and jam jars were used in their place; a pint would be put in a 2lb jar, and a 1lb jar served for half a pint.

The deck steward on the *Gondolier* came from Altbea so I decided to pay him a visit. Alec Beaton was not there, but a young naval petty officer and his wife were billeted with him and invited me in. Alec, as might be expected, was at a prayer meeting. I amused them with the tale of putting knots in Alec's pyjamas when on the *Gondolier*. Later I touched on Alec's abstemious habits and how they roared with laughter. Apparently Alec did not get his red bulbous nose through drinking lemonade. But they said he was always careful to remove any bottles if there was a knock at the door.

The launch belonging to the Ministry of War Transport was well known, and each time it approached us we speculated on whether they were after a deck, engine room or catering rating – and who would be likely to go. After six weeks it came for me, and I was taken out by boat to join a cargo ship named *Caduceus* belonging to Hall Brothers of Newcastle.

I settled down in the common fo'c'sle that was to be my quarters for the next few months. She was bound for Egypt with a general cargo and I found it rather amusing that a ship capable of doing barely 8 knots would be named *Caduceus*, as that was the name given to the god Mercury's wand. As was typical of vessels from the Tyne, she had Indian firemen.

Now, it is the usual practice at sea to have some fun with those doing their first trips. A common ruse is to send them for the key of the keelson, the key to the fog locker, or perhaps a bar of soft soap. The victim is told to get the key of the fog locker from the Mate.

However, when accosting the Mate he is told that it was recently given to the bosun, and when meeting the bosun the victim is now informed that the carpenter has it, and so on.

On the second day out, the galley boy requested me to cut his hair. I demurred several times and, hoping to put him off, finally said that I had not the necessary implements. But he persisted and said that he could procure them. I kept on refusing but he kept on asking and, as an extra inducement, promised me half of his sweetie ration.

Eventually I swithered. It was not the prospect of extra confectionery but rather the thought that an ability to cut hair might be a useful accomplishment; furthermore, what better way to begin than by using a galley boy to experiment on. I sat him out on top of a hatch and began the learning process. I did my very best for him, but my best was just short of abominable and nothing like as good as mediocre. Two days later I spied him sitting on a hatch with an Indian fireman trying desperately to lessen the damage I had inflicted on him.

It was only then that I learned that he had been pestering everyone to cut his hair and, to get rid of him and have some fun at a first-tripper's expense (as a possible alternative to the key of the fog locker lark) someone had said, 'Do you see that Scotsman that joined us at Loch Ewe? Well, he was a barber before coming to sea.'

The skipper was only 27, the Mate was an old chap and was said to have been on the *Garthpool* (one of the last of the old windjammers), and the 2nd Mate was about 6 feet tall, a non-smoker and strictly teetotal. The bosun had been an apprentice but had failed in his eyesight test for 2nd Mate's ticket.

The officers were very good to me. The 2nd Mate was always giving me lots of useful advice, and the skipper lent me one of his books on navigation.

In writing this book I have relied greatly on perusing many of the letters that I sent home. However, there was a gap in my letters at this point – they just recall travelling to Alexandria. But I certainly remember being out in a lifeboat in the Firth of Clyde with our 2nd Mate, so I think we must have waited at anchor at the Tail of the Bank for a convoy.

The reason this sticks in my mind is that the 2nd Mate said it was his ambition to make the huge liner, *Queen Mary*, alter course for us because we were under sail. I fancied that the liner would certainly alter course to avoid hitting us, but would do it in such a way that we would get a buffeting from her wake.

The voyage was uneventful. This was the first time I had been in the Mediterranean, but the torrid days of the Malta convoys were over and we had no trouble reaching Alexandria safely.

Letters from home informed me that, two days after I had joined the *Caduceus*, the Germans had launched the first of their V-1 flying bombs, also known as 'doodle-bugs' or 'buzz bombs'. More than 8,000 would be launched against London from 13 June 1944 until 29 March 1945, with about 2,400 hitting the target area. However, by the autumn of 1944 the V-1 menace had been overcome by fast fighter aircraft, massed anti-aircraft batteries firing shells armed with proximity fuses, and the capture by the Allies of the V-1 launching sites in northern France.

Our Chief Mate took ill and returned home. We could not get a replacement for him, so the 2nd Mate was promoted to Mate (despite the fact that he did not have a Chief Mate's Certificate) and a new 2nd Mate joined us from the UK. Like the old 2nd Mate he was about 6 feet tall, and also a non-smoker and total abstainer. This was most unusual.

In other countries of the world you can keep any unauthorised persons off your ship, but not in Egypt. There was no way to stop masses of people coming on board, all ostensibly to cut your hair, repair your shoes, etc, but in reality to steal whatever they can lay their hands on. Mooring ropes had to be taken down between decks and anything that was not riveted or bolted to the deck had to be removed for the duration of the stay in port. Also, the practice of leaving portholes open to cause a circulation of air and keep the temperature down could not safely be done; an open porthole was an invitation for anybody passing to reach in and steal whatever was handy.

In Trinidad I always resisted the temptation to go into a taxi where there were two men. I had the opinion that if you were a reasonable height, were sober and walking along minding your own business, nothing could harm you. Egypt proved me wrong. On the first day ashore with two mates I had hardly walked 20 yards when I was waylaid by a young Arab dressed in what looked like a nightshirt and wearing a fez. He had a tray of jewellery and tried to sell me a ring.

I had a suspicion that if he managed to get the ring into my hand, it would be tricky trying to return it to him. This is exactly what happened. How he did it I do not know, but there was the ring in my hand. I said firmly but politely that I did not wish to buy it and tried to walk away. The next instant I saw the point of a knife through his gown or whatever he was wearing. By this time my comrades were slowly walking about 25 yards ahead, leaving me to get rid of the vendor. I looked around for help but there was no sign of anyone in authority – only a few old Arabs who seemed uninterested in my plight.

With all the dignity I could muster I told him that it was a fine ring but that I did not want to purchase it, quickly laid it back on his tray and turned and walked away. The first few steps I shall never forget, expecting at any moment to feel something go into my ribs.

One of the shopkeepers sent his touts down to the ship and they were constantly saying 'Hooch aye' and such like, trying to give the impression that they had some Scottish connection. As I was in need of a pair of shoes I paid him a visit.

'This seems a good shop,' said I to one of my shipmates.

'Excuse me,' interrupted the proprietor, 'Zees is not a shop, it eez a store; and, as you know, a store is always cheaper than a shop.'

He was obviously the type who would venture, 'I sell you cheap because you are my friend.'

Their leather was of excellent quality but the workmanship was poor. I bought a pair of suede shoes from him. A week later, coming back to the ship in a lazy mood, I tried to take a shoe off by pressing on the heel with the toe of the other shoe – and the heel came off. Also, I bought a half bottle of Scotch whisky to take back to the ship and share with my mates. It was labelled 'Distilled on Dumbarton Rock'!

Some of the clubs ran gramophone concerts for the services and I enjoyed a few visits there. One evening I was all prepared to go to one of these clubs when the 3rd Radio Officer appeared and asked if he could go ashore with me. His name was Percy and he was about 17 years old. I explained that I was off to a symphony concert and I doubted if he would enjoy it. He promised that he would keep quiet and told me that all the other officers were broke and could not go ashore. The skipper said that the only way Percy could go ashore would be if he were to be accompanied by me. Somewhat flattered by this, I gave way.

We went to the Montgomery Club where the first half consisted of Beethoven's 4th piano concerto. Although Percy was as good as his word and remained quiet, I could sense that it was not his cup of tea, and this prevented me from enjoying it. Despite his protests I insisted that we left and went for something to eat.

After eating we were strolling along a street when I heard the strains of a piano playing a Beethoven piano sonata. Since in wartime we had no radios, music was the main thing that I missed at sea and, like air to a suffocating man, I desperately needed some. I led Percy into this building.

There was a desk at the door but no one seated there at the time, so we carried on until we reached the sound of Beethoven. Here was an RAF lad at a piano and I began turning the pages for him and encouraging him to play more.

An hour passed pleasantly then he stopped for a rest and enquired who had invited us there. When I replied that we had just walked in after hearing the piano, he nearly swooned.

'This is a YWCA and everyone is here by special invitation,' he told us.

'Percy,' said I, 'it's time to make our departure. Look neither left nor right but follow me.'

When we reached the desk there was a lady there. We bade her good evening and moved swiftly on before she could recover.

Apart from the traders who wanted to sell us their wares, the Egyptian population did not want us there. In a way I could sympathise with them – we had come uninvited into their country. I was not at all sorry when all our cargo was unloaded and we sailed.

Our orders were to proceed to Takoradi in the Gold Coast (now renamed Ghana) where we were to load a cargo of manganese ore. Along the Mediterranean we plodded, then turned on a southerly course for West Africa.

The weather became very hot. The myth that blacks can stand the heat better than whites was exploded when some of the engine room ratings could not cope. For a couple of days I, and other sailors, had to do a 4-hour spell below decks, shovelling coal from the bunkers to where the firemen were working. I cannot recall whether or not we were paid overtime for this, as it could have been considered 'for the safety of the ship'.

Without incident we reached Takoradi and began loading. The larger town of Secondi was quite near and we set off on foot. We passed dozens of women sitting outside their homes all energetically making garments on their Singer sewing machines. One of our sailors had bright red hair – a rarity there – and they delighted in shouting after him, 'Hello Ginger!'

This was my first time loading ore. It is very dense and thus one cannot allow large masses of it to descend at speed into an empty hold as this would damage the wooden flats at the bottom of the hold. Instead, small quantities are gradually dropped until there is a reasonably thick layer of ore. Then one may let the stuff fall freely as it is then falling on to this bed of ore and doing no damage at all.

Leaving Takoradi we headed for Gibraltar to pick up a convoy for home. As I explained earlier, ore is an extremely dangerous cargo; since the holds are nearly empty on account of the high density of the ore, if hit by a torpedo the ship sinks in a matter of seconds.

As well as being dangerous it is also very uncomfortable in a sea with a swell. This is on account of the vessel's centre of gravity now being very low. You may remember toys that were little dolls made of balsa wood with a leaded base. You threw them on the ground and, after shaking very quickly, they assumed an upright position. Our centre of gravity was extremely low and, as soon as we hit a swell, the ship swung from side to side quite violently. To prevent crockery being thrown all over the place we had to put wet cloths on the table when eating. I can assure you that a few days of this can be very wearing.

Bananas were cheap and plentiful in Takoradi and everyone bought a bunch of unripe ones to take home. The other sailors just hung them up anywhere, but I had a better idea of what to do with them. I hung my bunch under the starboard ventilator on the fo'c'sle head and turned the face of the vent on to the wind. I then went to the port ventilator and turned it off the wind. This meant that there was now a steady stream of air passing the bananas. Each watch I checked the position of the vents and adjusted them when necessary.

We stopped at Gibraltar for convoy. Some time previously a certain John Mackintosh, who had a prosperous coal-brokering business in Gibraltar, had visited Scotland in the hope of finding any relatives. He discovered that my relations, who had the small hotel at Fort Augustus, were his second cousins. Being a millionaire he accordingly paid for them to have a Mediterranean cruise at his expense.

This had taken place before the war, but I was told that if ever I was in Gibraltar I should be sure to look him up, and this was my first visit to Gib. Making enquiries I found that John Mackintosh had died some time ago and that his widow had disposed of the concern. I was advised to contact a Major Douglas who had once been the manager of the coal business. Major Douglas asked me many questions about my father's uncle and aunt. I suppose he was checking up to see if my story was genuine, and that I was not some impostor trying to muscle in on the Mackintosh fortune.

After he had established my *bona fides* he informed me that Mrs Mackintosh was in Algeciros and he would arrange for me to get a passport and visit her. This came to nothing, possibly because Mrs Mackintosh had no interest in meeting me – and I certainly had no interest in meeting her, but was merely obeying a request. Nevertheless I made friends with Major Douglas and his family and always went to see them any time I was back in Gibraltar.

When the business folded Major Douglas got the post of Norwegian and Danish Consul, and lived in the Consulate in Gibraltar. This is where I used to visit him. It was a fine building with a flat roof designed for adding to the water supply when it rained.

Gibraltar was always short of water and a small tanker filled with water arrived there once a month.

Major Douglas was a regular Army Major and an Oxford graduate. His blood was so blue you could have used it to write letters. Nevertheless his heart was in the right place. Towards the end of the Spanish Civil War hundreds of people fled to Gibraltar in order to try to cross over to Tangier. He put up overnight in his house a Spanish peasant, his wife and their ten children. While in his home, the woman gave birth to a baby and, to use Douglas's own words, to have let the child go on with the family would have been tantamount to giving it a death sentence.

Although he was old enough to have a son and daughter in the services, he asked the parents if he could adopt the little one and they were very willing to allow him to do this. The child was named Carlos and brought up as his own. English was spoken in the family circle, Spanish was used to communicate with the servants, who came over the border daily from Spain, and Douglas's wife was Swiss from the French-speaking part of Switzerland, so French was her mother tongue. Not only was Carlos (who would be seven or eight at the time) able to converse freely in all three languages, he had books of simple fairy tales in all three tongues in his bedroom.

Spain was supposed to be a neutral country, but it had a fascist dictator, Franco, and many of the population were decidedly hostile. From La Linea, on the Spanish border, they would swim across to the ships anchored in the bay at Gibraltar and fix limpet mines to their hulls. This had been going on all through the war and ships' crews had to keep a sharp lookout for them.

Unfortunately we missed our intended convoy at Gibraltar and this held us back ten days. The bananas began to ripen. There was no point in claiming ownership of a particular bunch; as soon as any lot was ready for eating it was brought into the mess for everyone to share. Some small satisfaction was derived from knowing that mine was the last bunch to ripen. The steward had bought plenty of them in Takoradi (possibly because they were so cheap) and the cook was dishing them up at every meal. It was nothing short of a tragedy that we could not manage to take even half a dozen home, and were almost sick of eating them, when all our families had not seen a single one for nearly five years!

I was still sending in papers to the Nautical College at Southampton University – but certainly not the stipulated one per month. They realised that I would soon have the necessary sea time to sit for my 2nd Mate's certificate and, although I had completed barely 70% of their course, they invited me to finish my studies with them.

The Mate said that he would thoroughly recommend that I go there, but I decided to keep my options open.

We eventually arrived safely in Birkenhead and paid off on 19 October 1944. The ship's officers were a good bunch and the food (despite having an icebox instead of a refrigerator) was not bad. I thought about doing another trip on her, but it was getting near time for me to sit for my 2nd Mate's certificate and I wanted to pick a short voyage if possible. In deciding what sea time is permissible for sitting for a ticket, the Board of Trade was very tough. You could be two days short of the necessary period and have to sail out on a trip that could last a year or more.

However, I was told that you were allowed to sit the examination in India. These tickets were looked down on and scathingly referred to as 'curry and rice' tickets, as it was generally accepted that if the examiner was gifted a bottle of spirits success was assured. Nevertheless they were useful stopgaps and saved a lot of extra time at sea. As long as the final certificate (that of Master) was a proper British one, you were all right.

For my combined time on the *Caduceus* and the *Iolaire* I was due 11 days' leave, so I packed up and made for Glasgow.

On 8 September, when the *Caduceus* had been between Takoradi and Gibraltar, a new type of missile had fallen on Britain – the V-2 rocket. This was a ballistic weapon and the first rocket to exceed the speed of sound. It was also potentially a far more dangerous weapon than the V-1. It could not be shot down, nor did it give any warning of its approach, climbing to about 80 miles before hurtling to earth at four times the speed of sound. It travelled so fast that one could not hear it before it exploded (sometimes in mid-air, with a huge flower of smoke). By that time one was either dead or not, as the case might be.

The day my leave ended I signed on the *Empire Spey*, a tramp steamer belonging to G. Nisbet & Company of Glasgow. She had been built in 1929 and her original name was *Blairspey*, in keeping with the company's practice of giving all their vessels a name beginning with Blair.

This company had a very bad reputation. One of its vessels, *Blairgowrie*, sank in 1935 with a great loss of life. There was an inquest into the tragedy, which revealed that the ship had not sufficient trained deck seamen. I am told that it was largely as a result of this that the Manning Scale was brought in.

At any rate, in the autumn of 1940 the *Blairspey* was taking a cargo of timber from Quebec to Leith when she was hit by a torpedo. The timber kept her afloat for a bit, so the U-boats hit her with another two torpedoes, causing the crew to take to the lifeboats.

Confident that she would sink, the subs then left her alone. However, she did not sink and was eventually towed into the Clyde by a deep-sea tug.

The trip before I joined her she was reputed to have been almost cut in two by a torpedo but, after reaching port in a damaged state, she was successfully repaired and renamed *Empire Spey*. Since all the ships with 'Empire' names were usually managed by the Ministry of War Transport, it was quite puzzling to find that she was still being run by G. Nisbet & Company.

I was beginning to realise just how lucky I had been. Several ships had taken a battering the trip before I joined them – or the voyage after I had left them – but, with one exception, not while I was on them. A friend of mine who had the post of writer on the *California* had gone to sea 18 months after I had, and already had been sunk twice. There was also the case in 1942 where I had been supposed to sail on the *Loch Garry*, but mercifully had not managed to do so. She was shipwrecked on Rathlin Island with a loss of more than 20 of her crew.

It seemed that the *Empire Spey* was not destined to make a long trip, and this suited my purposes. She was lying at Clydebank and had recently had the crew's quarters painted; the smell of paint was very strong and the paint pots and brushes were in the middle of the fo'c'sle deck. Also, there were no seats of any kind in the quarters and she was in a general mess.

The crew kept moaning about the situation but did nothing about it. Having had experience of this type of behaviour, I decided to let them get on with whatever they chose to do, and opted out by travelling down to her daily, so that I could sleep in my own bed at night.

The day of sailing arrived and she was in no better state. There were paint pots and brushes everywhere, a strong smell of paint, and nowhere to sit. My shipmates decided to call on the Seamen's Union representative. This they did, then repaired to the nearest pub so that when the union man appeared I was the only one left on board.

He was the sort of man that wanted the least trouble for himself, and asked me what was wrong. It was quite obvious what was wrong and he could very well see the problems for himself. He asked me my name and this was usually done to intimidate.

The others returned in an inebriated state and I left them to finish off the business, there being no useful purpose served by trying to negotiate on the same side as drunks. At the end the union representative told us that the mess would be cleared up, that the carpenter would be given wood to make benches and that this was the best he could do for us, for it was essential that the vessel sailed. Unlike Norwegian or American ships, where the union representative goes to sea with the crew, this man would be in his dry bed while we were battling down the Irish Sea.

The ship was loaded with coal and it was intended to discharge it in Lisbon. After that, it was anyone's guess where we would be sent, but since there were ports in Spain where iron ore and such like could be loaded, it was quite likely that we would finish up there.

We had barely entered the Irish Sea when it became evident that the coal was of exceedingly poor quality and our firemen, despite their best efforts, could not keep up a decent head of steam. After much deliberation it was decided that the only thing we could do was to was to turn back and head for the Clyde estuary.

The Admiralty arranged for Navy stokers to come on board and try out the coal. This was hardly a fair test as it is one thing stoking a boiler for a few hours, and an entirely different affair keeping a head of steam for days on end. Finally it was resolved to replace the coal in our bunkers, but not that in the holds, so the Portuguese would be importing the inferior stuff. When this was done we set off for Lisbon.

The food was not good and I went to the captain on more than one occasion and made a complaint. He showed some sympathy but said that there was little he could do. I was in the position of being the only one to complain and this put me in an awkward spot. I was the third oldest in the fo'c'sle and the other two older members were being bribed by the steward giving them tots of rum from time to time.

One of the ABs began making a ship to put in a bottle. I watched closely and took a note of what he was doing, but never got around to doing it myself. I thought that he would just fashion a three-masted ship without sails, but was surprised when he took on the difficult task of fitting her out with sails. Many sailors rolled their own cigarettes using special papers for the job, and it was from these papers that he made the sails. However, he told me that the authentic method was to use the thin white skin found in boiled eggs – the part just next to the shell.

The *Empire Spey* carried two apprentices, and one day when I was at the wheel I noticed one of them walking along the deck with a most peculiar gait. On making enquiry I found that he had discovered that he had 'crabs' (pubic lice) and had gone to the steward for help. He was given a strong disinfectant but, not having read the instructions, he had applied it straight from the bottle instead of diluting it!

Arriving in Lisbon we tied up and immediately a member of the Secret Service came on board and gave us a talk. The gist of it was that, now that the continent was being taken over by the Allies, the main German espionage movement had shifted to Lisbon. Their notion was to employ disease-ridden prostitutes to mix with British sailors and try to get as many as possible infected with venereal disease and thus hope to delay the shipping. He went on to say that there were licensed and unlicensed brothels and that on no account should we use the latter.

He then went on to warn us against the two particular bars that the Germans were using, namely the nearby George and the Alecrim. We were assured that free condoms would be issued with our money and we were to be sure to use them. Unfortunately the organisation fell down and the prophylactics were not at hand. The cry went up, 'To hell with the FLs! Give us the cash so that we can go ashore.'

It is always a source of amazement to me that seamen can be relied upon to do the opposite to what they are advised. The overwhelming majority made straight for the *George* and *Alecrim* bars. We were in Lisbon ten days, and just as we cast off the first man reported to the captain with a dose of gonorrhoea. Before reaching home a total of 19 had caught the same disease. By the time the ship paid off the incubation period for syphilis had not ended, so I shall never know the full extent of the Germans' victory – but 19 out of a crew of about 44 was a reasonable success.

We had a pleasant enough time in Lisbon. I remember that some of us astounded the Portuguese by having a dip in the harbour. It was the end of November but we did not feel it cold, while they were all wearing overcoats.

The British Seamen's Institute arranged for us to play a game of football against another British ship. I played at centre-half and we succeeded in beating them 1-0. As I recall it was a remarkably clean game with no fouls of any kind. Afterwards we had an excellent meal at the Institute.

It was quite a few days before I visited the centre of Lisbon. It was magnificent, with lovely broad thoroughfares running parallel to each other – a most impressive sight.

According to crew members who had been in Portugal before I was advised against using a cigarette lighter when ashore. They claimed that the Portuguese Government had heavily invested in matches and, for their own ends, forced people to buy a licence to use a lighter in public. The cost of the licence was outrageous and the local policemen were very keen to catch offenders as they got a high percentage of the resultant fine.

Our next orders were to head for the Spanish port of Almeria to load iron ore. The Spanish habit of planting limpet mines on the ships at Gibraltar was becoming so serious that the authorities chose to have two special men on board to go down every half-hour in diving suits and inspect the bottom of the vessel's hull. The two allocated to us were both university graduates in Spanish and Spanish History.

Almeria was an old Moorish town and its inhabitants were extremely aggressive. They spat upon us, made insulting remarks about our country and did everything to provoke us into fighting. Our two graduates helped to keep a lid on things and I think that perhaps they had graduated in diplomacy too, for they got some of the crew out of a few nasty scrapes.

The skipper was looking through his binoculars one day when he spied the steward climbing over a wall with a sack in his hands. It proved to be full of ship's provisions. Later he asked the skipper if more food could be ordered, to which the Old Man replied, 'Order away all you want, but it will come out of your account of wages!'

We loaded iron ore and set off for Gibraltar to wait to join a convoy. It was here that the graduates earned their corn by inspecting our hull very regularly to see if the Spaniards had stuck any bombs on it. They were exceptionally agreeable chaps and I had many interesting conversations with them – especially about Franco and the Spanish Civil War.

I went to see Major Douglas as soon as we had anchored. Mrs Douglas opened the door and I could hear Carlos in the adjacent room ask, 'Qui c'est?' To which she replied, 'C'est ton grand ami Charles.' Carlos at once appeared and spoke to me in perfect English. I became very fond of him as he was so interested and enthusiastic about so many things. I used to play a bit on their piano and he flooded me with questions about music. He was altogether an extraordinary little lad.

In Gibraltar there was a ceremony of the keys and, as Carlos had never seen it, I was asked to take him there. This was a traditional event: at 6pm a regiment ceremoniously took the keys from the Governor's residence and locked the gate to the town. Carlos was excellent company and I think he appreciated being out with someone a little younger that his adoptive parents.

I learned that on 9 December the blackout was in effect lifted in Britain, as instructions were given that windows no longer needed to be curtained should an air-raid siren be sounded. This did not mean that the attacks on Britain had stopped. Hitler's V weapons continued to fall, 367 people being killed and 847 wounded by explosions in December. Even so, British casualties from V-1 flying bombs and V-2 rockets were light when compared with the deaths caused by these indiscriminate weapons in Antwerp.

In due course we made the port of Workington, just south of the

My last days on the lower deck

Solway Firth, and discharged the iron ore. After it was unloaded we went up to Glasgow to pay off.

The ABs who had been bribed by the steward and also the drunken carpenter all tried to make trouble for the skipper at the shipping office. I stuck up for the Old Man while the steward, the guilty party, slunk in a corner of the office. The shipping master played ducks and drakes with their feeble arguments and they were rightly routed.

I felt that the shipping master was a bit too offhand towards me, and I decided to show him what a sober sailor could do. I pointed out that the articles allowed for each man to be given two enamelled plates. We had been given only one, so he was then obliged to go through every man's account of wages and subtract the price of one enamelled plate!

I had just enough time in to go up for my 2nd Mate's certificate, and was now looking forward to at least three months ashore – and probably in my own home.

9

A SHORT SPELL ASHORE

During my leave I gave some serious thought as to where I should go to complete my studies for the 2nd Mate's certificate. The Nautical College of Southampton University had been warmly recommended, and would have been a new experience for me. Had it been a time of peace I would probably have chosen it, but I finally plumped to stay in Glasgow to enjoy the company of my friends and relations, and so that I could revel in the home comforts of having my own room and favourite food.

As soon as my leave was over I went to the Royal College of Science & Technology (later to be named Strathclyde University) and applied to join the appropriate course. But first I had to have a Board of Trade eyesight test.

After reading letters of various sizes, apparently to the satisfaction of the examiner, he took me to a darkened room and said he would leave me until my eyes were used to the dark. He must have been gone for nearly 15 minutes. On his return he set up three lights – red, white and green – and asked me to identify them, explaining that the white light had a tinge of orange that one could expect with a paraffin lamp. I fancied I was in for an easy time.

Then he set up some gadget that gave lights in pairs and they were very tiny indeed – what you might be faced with at sea when looking at a vessel 2 miles away on a dark night. This must have gone on for fully 5 minutes, with me saying, 'White red ... green red ... green white ... red red' and so on. Just as I thought the ordeal was over I made a mistake by identifying a white light as a red one (due no doubt to this orange tinge) and this meant another gruelling 5 minutes. Still, I suppose they had to be really strict about colours.

The Technical College was not at all like school in as much as you taught yourself and the tutors helped. Another difference was that, as sailors kept coming off ships and joining the class, we were all at different stages of study. It was akin to the cinemas that had continuous showings: you entered when the big picture was halfway through and sat there, through the opening and first part, until it reached the point where you had come in.

A naval architect taught us ship construction, a chief petty officer from the Navy trained us in the various types of signalling, and the rest of the course was left to tutors who had their Master's certificates, or Extra Master's certificates.

The signalling embraced the sending and receiving of Morse code, Semaphore, and International Code. The International Code is quite amazing, and I believe it has versions in many different languages. If you want to communicate with a Japanese ship you merely hoist the appropriate flags; the Japanese look up the meanings of the flags in their version and your message is immediately understood. Should you wish to use some fancy tense, there is even provision for this. There is what is termed the 'modal verb', and the one they picked is one that was most unlikely to be used at sea in its real sense – 'to glean'. So, should you wish to say 'I had had sailed' you picked the flags for 'I had had gleaned' and added 'sail'.

Naturally we could not use this code in wartime, so we additionally had to learn Mersigs (merchant ship signals). I recall with some amusement the Mersigs book where, to prevent the signaller from making mistakes, there were cartoons of an extremely comical nature to illustrate the possible consequences of such errors. This had sound reasoning behind it, for the cartoons stuck vividly in our minds. Mersigs were soon to be replaced by WIMS (Wireless Instructions for Merchant Ships), though I could never understand why the word wireless was used.

When at school I did not apply myself wholeheartedly to my studies. This was different. I listened carefully to everything that was said and worked diligently. I was put beside a young lad who had just recently left the Glasgow High School and was doing a pre-sea training course of two years, which would count as one year's sea time. He was inclined to lark about a bit until I informed him that I was there to study and that, if he wanted to continue sitting beside me, he should take the work more seriously. To his credit he immediately mended his ways.

The signals part of the ticket could be sat separately and I applied to do this in order to get it out of the way and concentrate on the other studies. Unfortunately I caught bronchitis and was off for two weeks. Rather than cancel my application I foolishly chose to go ahead with the exam.

The bugbear was the Morse code – specially the receiving of it. This consisted of individual letters and numbers flashed to you in groups of five, followed by a message. Now, there were two schools of thought about the receiving of the message. The first said that you should on no account try to puzzle over the sense of the text, but should simply decode each letter separately and, in the short time allowed at the end of the sending, try to make sense of it. The second school reckoned you should make some meaning of the passage as it was being sent; otherwise you were throwing away the advantage, and might as well be reading the groups of five letters and numbers. Unfortunately, I subscribed to the second school. It may have had a lot to recommend it, but not on the particular day I sat the test. We were grouped in pairs – one reading the lamp and the other facing the opposite direction and writing down what the receiver was saying.

The message began, 'Chaos in Europe is spreading eastwards…' Now, chaos and chaotic(ally) are the only words beginning with CHAO and it certainly caused chaos. There was an audible gasp when the letter 'o' followed the letter 'a', and to stop to puzzle over any letter as you receive it is fatal. You then have a fraction less time to spend on the following letter, and a chain reaction is set up.

The first school of thought felt it had been vindicated and all belonging to the second school failed miserably as the pass mark was 90%. Nevertheless, I thought that to begin a message with the word 'chaos' was a bit unfair. I made up my mind to leave signals until sitting the main examination.

In the class I paid attention to all that was going on but I did little work at home, preferring to have a good social life. Nonetheless I did have to learn about the International Regulations For Preventing Collisions At Sea – commonly known as the Articles. Formerly all had to be learned off by heart, but at the time I was being examined it was deemed sufficient to know the exact meaning of the first 16 of them, but Article 17 to Article 31 still had to be memorised.

With regard to the question of all the lights that different ships displayed, I drew the lights in colour on one side of pieces of cardboard, and put the names of the vessels on the reverse sides. I would carry these around with me and look at them from time to time, or get my father to question me on them.

In college we had to give practical demonstrations that we knew how to apply the rules. The tutor would have several small bobbins coloured red, white and green, and would place these on the table to represent the lights of ships at night. I recall him putting down a green and a red bobbin and above them two red bobbins, one above the other. He then asked what this signified. The acceptable answer was given (almost parrot fashion) that it was a vessel not under command but making way through the water.

He took away the lower red and green bobbins and asked the same question. The expected response was given that it was a vessel not under command and not making way through the water. I suggested that the vessel might be making way through the water but the observer might not be in a position to see the green and red navigation lights. This, not being the standard answer, was not at all well received and I was bluntly told, 'You'll have an unhappy time at the examination.'

Although it was highly unlikely that you would ever meet a sailing ship, the tutor would put down the bobbins to indicate that one sailing ship was on your port bow (showing a green light), another was on your starboard bow (showing a red light) and a steam vessel was heading straight for you. He would tell you the direction of the wind and leave you to figure out what were the possible courses for the sailing ships (bearing in mind that they were reckoned not to be able to sail closer to the wind than about 65°), what action they were taking to avoid one another (vessels with the wind aft give way to vessels heading into the wind and so on), and what steps you would take to avoid collision with them and the steamship. It was always a prodigious feat of mental arithmetic.

I had an interview with a Captain Latta who had been instrumental in my getting the scholarship for Southampton University. He asked if I had a sextant and, on learning that I had not yet bought one, he showed me one that he had been given to sell on behalf of the widow of a captain that he had known. The price was a lot less than a new one, so I accepted the offer.

It was actually a quintant and had a bigger arc than a sextant – a sextant's arc is 120° and the quintant's is 144°. It had all kinds of extras. In addition to the usual standard telescope and the inverting telescope, etc, it had a pair of binoculars and another eyepiece like the single leg of a binocular set. Moreover, just where the shades were put to dim down bright reflections from the sea, there was an elongator, used when sighting stars or planets. Instead of trying swing the image of the star until it just kisses the horizon, this gadget stretched the star's form into a long line and you just had to pancake this line on to the horizon. The drawback was that it had the old-type tangent screw; also, one had to read the numbers on the arc by peering through a small microscope.

One of our subjects to be studied and be examined on was known as Knowledge of Principles. This was mainly maths and astronomy and was designed to make sure that you really knew what was happening up in the heavens, and not just finding out answers by adding and subtracting figures and looking up tables. It was my favourite subject.

My tutor, Captain Hill, kept asking me to go to the St Andrews

Ambulance Association to get a first-aid certificate as this was a prerequisite to obtaining a 2nd Mate's ticket. I explained that I had already one in my possession, but he advised me to go to their headquarters in North Street, just to make certain.

Together with two other aspiring 2nd Mates I made my way to North Street to be met by a plump man dressed similarly to a 2nd lieutenant in the Army, save for his uniform being navy blue instead of khaki. He asked my mates if they had the requisite certificates and on hearing their negative replies immediately demanded a guinea (£1 1s). When asked, I said that I had a certificate and, if necessary, I could show it to him. He enquired whether it was a Board of Trade one and, on learning that it was not, he insisted on having his guinea.

The class was supposed to be from 4pm till 5pm and we waited until 4.50pm, when a beefy police surgeon appeared and apologised in a *basso profundo* voice for being late. He enquired if there were any new members and, on hearing that my two mates and I were making our first appearance, he said that he had better go over the skeleton again. He put a large diagram up on the wall and proceeded as follows.

'The bones of the cranium are eight in number: one frontal, one occipital, two temporal, two parietal, a sphenoid and an ethmoid. The bones of the face are 14 in number: one mandible or lower jawbone, two maxillae or upper jaw bones…'

This was done at great speed. 'I suppose you did not catch all that, so I'll repeat it,' said the beefy gent. By this time it was almost 5 o'clock, whereupon the doctor made more apologies and said he had to run off to an appointment.

On Tuesday the doctor again did not appear until 4.50pm and asked if there were any new members. This class was the same as the main course for 2nd Mates inasmuch as more sailors kept appearing each day, so it was a repeat performance of Monday. On Wednesday there were no new members and we got as far as the circulation of the blood before the tutor did his customary vanishing act.

My classmates were becoming extremely worried. I had an ambulance book and it was eagerly sought after and went from hand to hand as they began to panic. After five so-called lessons we were to have an examination.

'Come up an hour early on Friday and I'll run through one or two things with you before the exam,' said the gent in the navy blue uniform.

We all came to hear his pearls of medical wisdom.

'How do you set a fractured clavicle?' he asked of the first candidate.

I doubted if the addressee knew what a clavicle was.

'Well,' said the uniformed gent, 'you make a pad and place it under the armpit, then pull the elbow down towards the hip and point the fingers at the other clavicle and secure with roller bandages.'

He demonstrated this, then invited the student to follow suit.

He enquired of the next victim how one should treat a lacerated wound on the sole of the foot using a triangular bandage. Again he was met with a blank stare, so he showed the class how it was done and the pupil did likewise.

At 5pm a different doctor appeared. He asked the first man how to set a fractured clavicle and the second what to do about a wound on the sole of the foot, and so on as each candidate gave the answer he was coached to give.

I was absolutely furious. My certificate had taken 13 weeks to acquire – a total of 26 hours' tuition on a Sunday afternoon in addition to six Wednesday evenings practising bandaging, and it was deemed not to be worth this tawdry pretence. I had sacrificed more than 6 hours of tutoring at the college, and had had less than 10 minutes tuition from the doctor. In addition I had paid a guinea (about £55 at 2000 values) to partake in a complete farce. On top of this, all the other sailors were being sent off to sea in wartime, on ships without a doctor, and without any real knowledge of ambulance work. I stopped contributing to the St Andrews Ambulance Association, and have never since given them as much as a penny.

The examination loomed ahead. It took almost a week. On Monday morning we took our first Navigation paper, followed in the afternoon by English. Tuesday morning was given over to Knowledge of Principles and in the afternoon was the second paper on Navigation. On Wednesday morning we grappled with a combined paper on Ship Construction and Cargo Work, and in the afternoon we did Coastal Navigation and Chart Work. Thursday would probably be signalling and Friday the oral examination.

Signals presented the real snag. If you were to fail in any of the other subjects you would likely be given a chance to resit after two weeks or so. Were you to fail in signals you were shipped out at once to sea. The reasoning behind this was to discourage folk from deliberately failing in signals in order to get an extra week or two ashore.

I recall that the essay we had to write was 'My most thrilling experience'. As I looked around the class I reckoned that, unlike myself, everyone there would have been sunk at least twice and would choose one of these experiences as the subject of the essay.

Remembering the Prince of Aragon in Shakespeare's *The Merchant of Venice* saying, 'I will not choose what many men desire,

Because I will not jump with common spirits, And rank me with the barbarous multitudes,' I decided not to follow what I thought the rest would do. Instead I described how the early morning mist had magically lifted off Manhattan, revealing its wonderful skyline, like a dream city built on air.

I compared this experience with Wordsworth's on seeing London early in the morning, and threw in one or two couplets from his sonnet 'Upon Westminster Bridge' just to give the piece an air of erudition. This was on the principle that, if you cannot be better, then at least be different!

I passed the signals and had a fairly good idea that I had done reasonably well in the other subjects, so it was now all down to the oral exam. I hated this type of exam. With a written paper the die is cast and there is nothing you can do but set about answering the questions as well as possible. With an oral, the examiner can probe, find weaknesses, and concentrate on these.

One examiner – a Welshman named Evans – seemed to strike terror into the candidates (remember that some were sitting for the second or third time). He had disappeared for a time but it was now rumoured that he had returned and was taking the next six examinations.

I managed the intricate mental torture of taking action to avoid the examiner's sailing vessels and set down correctly the buoys to mark out a channel in a river, and several other things. Then came the battle with the sextant.

Now, at that time modern sextants had a wheel just over an inch in diameter and each turn of it represented a degree of arc. On the surface of this wheel were marked the 60 minutes into which a degree was divided, and it was easy enough to read. With the oral exam we were given a very old-fashioned sextant that had no such wheel; one had to look through a small microscope to see the reading and, if the light was not good, this could present difficulties.

Not content with this additional complication, the examiners provided another one. The old sextants had a tangent screw that allowed you to move it very slowly; this screw was described as an endless one, meaning that you could keep turning it as long as you needed to. The ones we were given did not have this endless tangent screw, but could seize up just as you were near your reading. You would then have to disengage the screw, give the instrument a rough setting, then fiddle around again with the screw until you arrived at the right spot.

'Mr Aitchison,' said Evans, 'I want you to set this sextant to 1 degree 35 minutes and 15 seconds off the arc.'

A short spell ashore

Just as I was almost at the correct setting the abominable tangent screw stuck and I had to release the clamp, shift the instrument to an approximate reading, go back to the beginning and twiddle away again. It also did not help that I had a cold at the time and mucus from my nose was threatening to provide unnecessary lubrication to the tangent screw. There was I with the sextant in my right hand and the left hand trying to help, when it was not using a handkerchief to wipe my nose.

Eventually I got it as near as I possibly could and handed him the sextant. I imagined that, regardless of how well one might have done in the other subjects, the dropping of a valuable instrument would be a guarantee of failure by any examiner – particularly this one.

Evans certainly lived up to his petrifying name and I was the only one of six candidates to pass.

I cannot remember how long I was given to get back to sea, but when I reported to the shipping office they wanted me to go as 2nd Mate right away. I protested that I had never been an apprentice or cadet and needed a spell as 3rd Mate in order to feel my way. They protested, but I stuck to my guns and was sent as 3rd Mate to a tanker, the *Athelregent*, which had just discharged a cargo of diesel oil and was lying at Finnart in Loch Long on the River Clyde.

10

A NEW LIFESTYLE

Early on 24 April 1945 I joined the *Athelregent* as her 3rd Mate. She had been built in 1930 and belonged to the United British Molasses Company, although throughout the war she had been carrying oils. When hostilities commenced the line had owned 28 tankers, and *Athelregent* was one of only four that were still afloat!

The officers were a mixed bunch: the skipper was English, the Chief Mate was Irish, the 2nd Mate Welsh and I was a Scot. Captain Cornwell asked me where I had served my time and I told him I was from the fo'c'sle. I did not know what response this would provoke, but he soon left me in no doubt. Some skippers might have resented me, but he seemed to look upon me as a kind of virgin territory – a person that had never been on the bridge before, except to steer the ship, and someone he could therefore mould into a navigator after his heart's desire.

We anchored at the Tail of the Bank for a day or two to await a convoy and this gave me a chance to settle in. I had a very good cabin with wash-hand basin, table, settee, writing-desk, bookcase, bedlight, fan, etc, and the food was excellent. We also had a smoking room for spending periods off duty.

The one minor bugbear was that breakfast when at sea was served at 8.30am rather than 8am and lunch was served at 12.30pm instead of the usual noon. Being the junior bridge officer I was expected to relieve the 2nd Mate for his lunch and the Chief Mate for his tea. It meant that instead of staying on the bridge from 12pm until 12.30pm to let the 2nd Mate get his lunch, I had to come down at noon, hang around for half an hour then relieve the 2nd Mate from 12.30pm until 1pm and have my own lunch from 1pm till 1.30pm.

Our meals were served in the saloon and, in port, there would be seated the Master, Chief Engineer, the three Mates and the three Radio Officers. At sea, of course, some officers had to be on watch. The engineers had a mess of their own and I fancy they preferred this. They wore white boiler suits on duty and could hop into their mess for a cup of tea without having to change into uniforms. The 2nd

A new lifestyle

Engineer (the equivalent of the Chief Mate) was invited to have lunch in the saloon on Sundays.

The 3rd Mate had the two 8-12 watches; the first was 8pm till midnight, and the forenoon watch from 8am till noon. The 2nd Mate had the afternoon watch from noon until 4am, and the middle watch (traditionally called either the 'dead man's watch' or the 'graveyard watch') from midnight to 4pm. The Chief Mate has the morning watch from 4am to 8am and the two dog watches from 4pm to 8pm, enabling him to be on deck looking after other duties, if necessary, during most of the morning and afternoon.

We set off for New York in the first watch and the skipper stayed on the bridge with me all the time, as I had expected he would. I had an idea of how to keep station in a convoy, having heard, when I was a sailor at the wheel, the officer of the watch calling down to the engineer and asking for the speed to be increased or decreased by two revolutions, and the man at the wheel being asked to alter his course as necessary to keep behind the vessel in front.

The Old Man took me in hand right away.

'Never stay in the chart room longer than a quarter of a minute at a time or you will lose your night vision. Also, look upon the ship ahead as liable to break down at any time.'

I said, 'If he breaks down he will raise two black balls by day or two red lights by night.'

'And how long do you think he'll take to get his two red lights up?' he queried. I was to remember this remark a few nights later.

The skipper told me that he wanted me to be able to tell him at any time the true course, the magnetic course, the compass course, the variation (error of the compass due to its pointing to the magnetic north instead of the true north), the deviation (error due to various other causes), the total compass error, the state of the sea and sky and, lastly, what time the moon came up.

'Most of these details are chalked on a board in the wheelhouse,' I mildly protested.

'How can you see them in the dark?' he enquired.

'I have a torch.'

'What if the torch should fail?' he countered. 'At sea you make slips, not mistakes. You only make one mistake and it's your last.'

I had imagined that life would now be a lot easier than a sailor's lot, particularly having a lookout man to report any sightings to me. I was soon to be disillusioned.

'I expect you to see anything of interest before the lookout,' said the captain. 'You are an officer, and he is a sailor and thinking of his probable pay-off and maybe of the girl he left behind him.'

Apart from the duties of keeping the ship in its allotted position in the convoy, there was the compass error to be checked. Before leaving port a compass adjuster came onboard, swung the ship in all directions then messed about with a large iron ball next to the binnacle and a vertical flinders bar. He then produced a deviation chart showing what the deviation was on each course. Apart from the first couple of days, no one consulted this graph. On every watch a bearing was taken of a heavenly body, its true bearing was calculated and compared with this compass bearing, and thus the error of the compass was found.

There was also the question of signalling. We were obliged to know the International Code, which was a system whereby ships of different nations could communicate by hoisting flags without knowing a word of the other's language. Every ship in the world had its four-letter identification, all British vessels beginning with the letter G. I cannot remember the letters of any ship I sailed on, but for some strange reason I recall the *Queen Mary*'s as being GBTT. Additionally, every geographical feature had its four-letter code. Again, the only one I can bring to mind was Beachy Head, which was ALBX.

Naturally this code could not be used in war conditions when every nation on the globe had a copy of it. The Admiralty brought out one named 'Mersigs', or merchant ship signals. It was later superseded by WIMS (Wireless Instructions for Merchant Ships). Both of these books contained the hoists to be used in convoy. I particularly remember the many extremely humorous cartoons illustrating the results of using the wrong signals. As I remarked before, this was an excellent ploy as it firmly fixed the consequences in one's mind.

At the end of each watch the officer would write the compass error in the scrap log (a sort of ship's diary), together with the state of the wind, the sea, the sky and the visibility. Just at the end of the watch, as routine, the standby sailor took the reading on the log (the instrument that recorded the distances) and this was also noted. The scrap log containing all the details was, in those times, written in pencil and every day or two the Chief Mate copied its contents in ink into his 'Mate's Log'.

For two full days I enjoyed my new status and all the advantages that went with it, then the sky fell down on me. We had been given orders that our next cargo was to be *Athelregent*'s peacetime one of molasses. As the previous cargo had been diesel oil, the tanks would have to be thoroughly cleaned. This involved taking into the tanks a cast-iron cylinder called a 'pig' to which was connected a pipe to admit seawater and another one to let in steam. This produced boiling salt water and, with the aid of a drum of caustic soda, the tanks could be given a very good clean.

At least, that was the theory. The Old Man called the 2nd Mate and me and explained to us that the crew were not real tanker seamen, and the Chief Mate would, starting next day, have to go on day work to supervise the cleaning. This meant that the 2nd Mate and I would need to work 'watch and watch', as the saying goes. We would do 4 hours on and 4 hours off, except for the first and second dog watches, which we would treat as 2-hour watches so that this would give us seven watches and we did not have the same watches each day.

This was a nightmare, made worse by their habit of having breakfast at 8.30am and lunch at 12.30pm. Consider the 3rd Mate having just been on the bridge from 4am to 8am; he then comes off watch but, as there is no breakfast till 8.30am, he has to idle away the time for half an hour then relieve the 2nd Mate for his breakfast at 8.30am to 9.00am and have his own meal from 9.00am till 9.30am. In 2½ hours he is back again on a 4-hour watch.

During the first watch that evening the vessel in front of me had broken down owing to her steering gear giving trouble, and turned broadside on to us. In a matter of a minute or so we were up on her and I had to make quite a big alteration of course to avoid ramming her. The skipper was certainly right about not staying any longer than necessary in the chart room. Had I not been keeping a good lookout we would have cut through her. In addition, she did not manage to get up her two red lights (showing that she was not under command) until we were about 100 yards or so past her. I began to have much more respect for the Old Man.

We started 'watch and watch' the next day. The first time I landed the morning watch the skipper came up with me for the first half-hour. He then said that he would lie down on the couch in the chart room, emphasising that I was to call him if there was the slightest doubt about anything. He told me not to think twice about giving him a shake, and assured me that no matter how trivial I might consider the cause, he would not be annoyed.

It was an inky black night and we were the second ship in the column. In front of us was a Dutch vessel with a light on his stern that could best be described as navy blue. So dim was this light that most of the time I had to use night glasses to keep it in sight. These night glasses were binoculars with little magnification but with very large object lenses – thus collecting a lot of light and enabling objects to be seen clearly at night.

I kept altering course so that I would be directly behind her, and also putting the revs up and down to keep the correct distance astern.

This went on for more than an hour when there suddenly appeared on our starboard beam a tanker that was scarcely 15 yards away – an exceedingly short distance in the circumstances.

The ship proved to be a Yank, and immediately began to signal furiously with an Aldis lamp. Ignoring the signals, my first impulse was to yell to the helmsman to go hard a port, but scarcely had this thought struck me when I recognised that if her officer was thinking along the same lines and giving an order to go hard a starboard, our sterns would collide, the turning centres in tankers being further forward than in cargo ships. I shouted to the helmsman to go 10 degrees to port and some of the skipper's caution must have rubbed off on me for I at once climbed up to 'monkey island' to look at the compass and see that he was really following my order. I waited for a minute, still ignoring the Aldis lamp, then ordered another 10 degrees to port. By this time the distance from the other vessel was increasing and the signaller had given up trying to make contact with me. Yanks had special signalling officers on their bridges as well as the navigating officer, and they often delighted in showing off by signalling at top speed. I would have been no match for him anyway.

Towards the end of the watch the dawn broke and revealed that we were not in any column but midway between two columns – and astern of station. I rang down to the engine room for more revs and we gradually moved to our correct station. We were nearly there when the skipper appeared and asked what was happening. I gave him a truthful explanation except that I did not tell him how very close we had been to the other ship. He was annoyed and I got a reprimand of course, because, regardless of circumstances, his direct order had not been obeyed.

I said that I was very sorry not to have carried out his instructions, but had acted in what I thought was the best interests of the ship. I went on to acknowledge that he was an older and much more experienced seaman than me, but stressed that I had my night vision and was aware of the situation, whereas he did not and, on being aroused, might take a second or two to weigh up what to do. He made no reply but I am guessing that he knew that I would have been only too pleased to have given him a shake and handed all the responsibility over to him had my conscience allowed me to do so. At any rate, when danger is imminent the only thought that pervades the mind is how to get away from the threat as quickly as possible – all other considerations appear of little consequence.

Having had years of familiarity with convoys, he knew what had happened, and explained to me that the Dutchman had gone ahead of the convoy, moved over to the right then fallen behind so that he was

A new lifestyle

midway between columns – following him, I had landed in the same plight.

An amusing thought crossed my mind that if ever I sat the Chief Mate's certificate and was asked to write an essay on 'My Most Frightening Experience', this episode would be tailor-made for the job!

I asked the 2nd Mate if he memorised all the courses, compass errors, etc, and he said he used to but his advice was that, if the skipper asked me for them, I was to reply immediately and with an air of confidence; on no account was I to hesitate. The Old Man had not asked for these details for a day or two when, one evening on the first watch, he went into his inquisitorial routine. I rattled off the answers correctly until it came to the time the moon rose. I had not a clue but, heeding the 2nd Mate's advice, I replied without a moment's hesitation that it was due to rise in 10 minutes. The skipper nodded receipt of this information, smiled, and stayed chatting to me for several minutes.

Suddenly the clouds parted, revealing a huge moon (which seemed to be a great deal larger than usual) with an elevation of at least 30 degrees. Captain Cornwell just gave a whimsical smile and left the bridge saying, 'Good night, Mr Aitchison.' The odd thing about this incident was that, while at college, I had read a book *Wrinkles on Navigation* by a famous master named Leckie, and he quoted the same thing happening to him.

The captain continued to give me all kinds of tips about navigation. He was a remarkably good navigator and I was most fortunate to have him as a skipper on my first voyage on the bridge.

At times he was a trifle testy, but it did not trouble me. However, he took me aside and acknowledged that, on occasions, he had been somewhat curt in his dealings with me. He confided in me that he had a stomach ulcer and, at times, it gave him some pain. I sympathised and mentioned that fresh milk might help, at which he at once went into his aggressive mode and scathingly asked, 'Where the hell do you get fresh milk at sea?'

I told him that on Norwegian ships we had fresh milk not only all the time we were in port but also for the first five or six days after leaving port. He grunted but made no further comment.

Jumping ahead to when we were three days out on the road home, he asked if I would help him with the crew's income tax and insurance cards. I gave him an hour or two of my time and he asked if I would like a drink. Thinking it might be beer or wine I said that it would be most welcome, upon which he handed me a glass of fresh milk from the refrigerator. I think that this was a tacit apology.

The *Athelregent* was a curious mixture of the old and the new. We had a gyro compass that had a constant error of 2 degrees and was unaffected by anything else. Nevertheless we kept checking the compasses and their errors as, I suppose, the gyro might possibly break down.

In addition we had an automatic pilot, which meant that in daytime (it was never used at night or in rough weather) the helmsman could be released to do other duties. The course was recorded on a chart and the sailors were, at first, not aware of this and were puzzled at how an officer could admonish them for a piece of bad steering that had taken place some time previously.

One would have expected that a vessel equipped with such gadgetry would have had echo-sounding – but we did not. One day the skipper wanted to know the depth of the ocean where we were, and we had to use the patent sea-sounding machine. This was based on the principle that the pressure on an immersed body increases with the depth to which it is immersed. A glass tube, protected by a brass or copper case, was lowered to the bottom of the sea with the aid of a sinker. This tube contained air and its inside was coated with silver chromate. The tube was open at the bottom, and water was forced into it according to the pressure to which it was subjected. The salt water discoloured the chemical, thus showing how far the water had entered the tube. By comparing this with a scale, the depth of water could be read directly from the scale. It was common to 'arm' the lead; this involved inserting a piece of tallow in a cavity at the bottom, which brought up a sample of the seabed.

On 8 May we heard that the war in Europe had ended. We were not sure what to do about this, but it was decided to keep in convoy until further orders and act as if the conflict was still on.

The steward produced a first-class dinner to celebrate the event. I suppose I should really have called the meal superlative, since all our meals were 'first-class'. We had beer afterwards and the Old Man gave us all a couple of nips of spirits. Two days later we met a U-boat on the surface heading back east. I could not help but admire the spirit of the German submariners, and think many seamen would agree with this. When the U-boat slipped into Scapa Flow and sank the *Royal Oak*, I was told that the general reaction in the merchant navy was that it was a feat of great seamanship, rather than a feeling of hatred towards the Germans.

Incidentally, after the sinking, a gap was revealed at Scapa Flow. Now, the old *Gondolier* was built to fit exactly into the locks of the Caledonian Canal and it was discovered that she was just the size of this opening. Accordingly she was filled with concrete and sunk there.

So, in a way, she was still of some service.

Years after the war the Germans produced a film called *Das Boot*, which detailed the adventures of a particular U-boat and gave an insight into the cramped conditions and hardships its crew endured. The skipper and the chief engineer sat on the starboard side while eating in their mess. During the meal a rating might want to go from for'ard to aft and the officers on the port side had to get up and allow the seaman to go aft.

One particular scene I recall was the vessel ploughing along during a storm and the men remarking that, in such weather, they would have no fears of being attacked by aircraft. I could not help but laugh at this, because in very rough weather we would take off our clothes when going to bed, feeling that we would be safe from submarine attack. There was this kinship between us as we both had a common enemy – the sea.

It was not so with aircraft. There was something grossly unfair about being bombed or fired on by an aeroplane. It was just so one-sided. Here would be a convoy plodding along and doing about 180 miles a day, a distance the plane could easily do in an hour. The pilot could go home to a warm safe bed and come back next day for another assault.

Before I joined the *Athelregent* it had been decided that shipping companies could have the option of putting their officers on either an A scheme or a B scheme with regard to overtime and such like. The latter plan paid officers for all overtime worked and, additionally when in port, the officer who remained on board was to receive £1 for each night. The A scheme meant that officers would not be paid this £1 a night in port, nor would they be paid for any overtime worked, but would get higher wages and 3½ days' leave, instead of the normal 2, for each month served. All the high-class companies opted for the A articles, and the Athel Line, being one of the better-class firms, did likewise. Thus all the extra hours I had worked were for nothing.

To make matters worse, my salary was now marginally above the limit for National Insurance, and if I wanted to stay in benefit I should have to pay the full stamp now as my employers were not obliged to contribute anything. The company's regulations stipulated that an officer was not entitled to leave until it amounted to at least 30 days, and this meant that I would have to wait for nine months before I could go home.

But there is no doubt that the Athel Line was one of the best shipping companies in the UK. A letter sent home from a prisoner-of-war stated that the Athel Line had informed him that they were going to continue paying his wages. This was in stark contrast to other companies. For example, an engineer was torpedoed in October 1941. He got away in a lifeboat and was later picked up by a Canadian corvette. In due course he was landed at a Canadian port from where he obtained a passage back to the UK. When he arrived home three months later he found a letter from the owners saying that they had continued to pay his allotment, but, as the ship had sunk nine days after he had signed on, he owed them for the allotments less his pay for nine days and they asked him to remit the amount owed to them – £37 – which was a lot then. As he would not be paid again until he signed on another ship and made a voyage, it left him with a financial problem. The Government did nothing about this until 1942

Another case was that of a family of a captured seaman where the firm said that his allotment had been stopped the month he had been reported missing, but they were later awarded 50 shillings a week from the Ministry of Pensions. Once they found out that the seaman had survived the sinking and was held captive, they stopped the payments to his wife and she received nothing.

Our convoy split up and we arrived one morning at New York and anchored. Early in the afternoon a USA tanker, fully loaded, dropped her hook quite close to us. I can remember clearly what her name was because the apprentice said to me, 'Sir, what a terrible name for a ship. Imagine anyone asking what ship you were off and you having to tell them her name was the *Bulk Fuel*.'

I remarked to the Chief Mate that it looked too close to us, and that we should perhaps signal and ask them to shift. Apparently it was not so simple as that. The ship's Master must have considered it safe to anchor where he did and, if we thought that it was not safe, it was up to us to move.

At the turn of the tide most of the ships started to swing variously. The *Bulk Fuel*'s stern began to move towards us, and some time later we had to let out more cable on the anchor to keep us clear of her. The Mate got hold of a megaphone and began shouting to the crew on her deck. It seemed that they had no idea what to do as the Mate bellowed instructions to them. It was only then that we learned that her captain and all her deck officers had simply walked off ashore, and the Mate was trying to get some sense out of the 3rd Radio Officer, who appeared to be the senior officer then on the vessel!

We were safe enough for the moment, but at about 4.30am it would be slack water again and the same problem would recur. I was on the 4 to 8 watch and kept a careful lookout from the bridge. As the time drew near, the *Bulk Fuel*'s stern began to swing slowly towards our bow. I watched her movements closely and was pleased to see her stop, then swing back to her original position. This action took place

A new lifestyle

three times. On the fourth time she stopped as usual, but did not move back, then, after a short pause, slowly continued towards us. I immediately rang 'standby' on the telegraph and darted up to the bow as fast as I could.

By the time I reached the windlass and started to let out anchor chain, the skipper was on the bridge and taking command. At the stern of the *Bulk Fuel* were two small platforms jutting out from her hull, and on these were resting smoke floats. We could not distance ourselves enough in time to avoid collision, and these platforms crumpled up as though they were made of cardboard.

On a ship's bridge there was a telegraph for communicating with the engine room. The officer on the bridge rang 'half ahead', 'slow astern' or whatever, and the engineer rang back in acknowledgement. Both bridge and engine room noted the times of these signals. Next day we checked with the engine room and found that their times were all a minute different from ours. As they had used ink and we had used pencil, it was decided to alter ours to match.

Next day the captain went ashore to report the collision. It was certain that he would send for an officer and I was worried lest anyone should detect that our recorded telegraph times had been erased and changed.

The Chief Mate knew a trick or two and said, 'When you go into the launch to go ashore, just drop the book in the water and make sure everybody sees you do this. When it dries, no one will be able to tell what has happened.'

Sure enough, a signal from shore requested the 3rd Mate to meet the captain at the lawyer's office. Once there, the lawyer produced a large-scale chart of New York harbour (a better one than our own) with small models of ships, about 3 or 4 inches long. He then had me place the model ships in positions representing the *Bulk Fuel* and the *Athelregent*.

After that I was subjected to a barrage of questioning about what had happened, and even what compass bearing the ship's head was on at the different times. I thought this a bit much. When another vessel is bearing down on you and threatening to collide, the last thing in your mind is to look to see what the compass bearing is.

Meantime the skipper looked on benignly. He was not drunk, but had 'drink taken', as the saying has it, and was unusually affable. Half an hour of this passed, then the captain said he would leave me with the lawyer and meet me a few hours later to go back on board.

As soon as the skipper left, the lawyer said, 'Just forget everything you told me, Mr Aitchison, and we'll start again afresh.' I feverishly tried to remember all the details I had previously offered and hoped for the best.

'Do you have a bell book?' asked the lawyer. I truthfully said that we had not, but had a good idea that this was what the Americans called our telegraph book.

Luckily he did not pursue the matter. I got to thinking that, if this ordeal were at the hands of our own solicitor, what sort of nightmare would our opponent's lawyer present. I could not but think how utterly stupid and irresponsible the Americans were for leaving a fully loaded tanker at anchor with not one deck officer aboard.

Regarding ships at anchor, it is really the chain that stops them from moving. True, the anchor has to be pointed to dig into the bed of the sea where possible, and also has to be a reasonably heavy, but the weight and length of the chain are of paramount importance. Normally the length of chain let out is three times the depth of water. If the wind blows violently in squalls, the vessel is pushed back and the chain rises off the bottom of the sea. As the wind falls off, the chain drops again, acting as a sort of spring.

If the anchorage is crowded it is customary to put down two anchors – starboard and port – and since the ship rides to only one of these at a time, her swinging is thus limited.

Although there were many things I liked about the Yanks – their lack of formality and red tape for a start – they were immature in many ways. They had a great tendency to show off. I know we had folk that were similarly inclined, but the Americans seemed to have a lot more of them. I recall in New York about ten naval ratings in an underground train; they could not all sit together and were spread out over several seats. They kept shouting to one another about who would do a certain watch and so on. In the UK such behaviour would have been condemned as showing off, but the other passengers appeared to look on approvingly, as much as to say, 'Aren't our boys wonderful?'

When I first came to America, I would offer my seat in a bus to a lady, as was the custom back home. Several times the offer was refused with the impression that I was trying to be familiar, so I dropped the practice. However, in Philadelphia a US Navy rating ostentatiously gave up his seat to a woman who readily accepted it, and he went on to murmur audibly something about 'civilians'. I took this to be directed at me. The creases in his trousers indicated that he had just recently received them from US naval stores and I am confident that I had wrung more salt water out of my seaboot socks than he had sailed on.

While I was on watch one of the US ships in the harbour signalled across to us. As mentioned before, their vessels always had a specially trained signaller on watch at all times. With Morse code, the custom was for the receiver to acknowledge each word in the message by answering with the letter 'T', which is a single dash. If this dash was not given it was assumed that the word was not understood and the sender repeated it. His speed was too much for me and I had to keep waiting for him to repeat a word. After waiting for several repeats he slowed his rate down to an absolute crawl so that I had no difficulty in reading his request for me to 'get a signaller'.

I went at once to our Radio Officer, told him what had taken place and asked him to take the appropriate action. He picked up his Aldis lamp and sent off a message at an incredibly fast speed. This resulted in the Yank having to ask him to slow down his rate of sending – much to my delight.

Possibly the differing attitudes are encapsulated in the following tale. When the Germans retreated in Europe they destroyed many bridges and these had to be replaced by the Allies. One new bridge had a brass plaque on it stating something like: 'This bridge was erected by the 5th US Engineering Corps, comprising of 3 officers, 10 NCOs and 57 men. It took 5 days, 14 hours and 43 minutes to build'. A short distance downstream another bridge had a notice saying, 'This bridge was built by the Royal Engineers. There is nothing remarkable about it.'

In a day or two we departed and made our way, without convoy of course, to Port Everglades in Florida. It was a real pleasure to relax and enjoy the flying-fish weather knowing that there was no one below the sea planning to sink us. In due course we reached our destination and tied up. Port Everglades is very near the bigger town of Fort Lauderdale.

However, another fly was to appear in the ointment. On Anglo-Iranian tankers the engineers do the pumping of oil, and on Anglo-American ones an AB, who is designated the pump-man, is paid extra to take responsibility for this. With the Athel Line the pumping had been left to the engineers until a few years earlier when one of them had turned the wrong valve and poured several hundred tons of molasses into the dock via a pipe that was for discharging cargo into barges. After this disaster the owners decreed that deck officers should do the work. It was left to the 2nd Mate and me to do 16 hours on and 16 hours off until the ship was loaded. Now, I had not many clues about all the different valves and, although I studied the plans of the ship carefully, I was most grateful for the assistance of the apprentice, who had been three years with the company and knew a lot about it.

My main object was to pay a visit to Miami, which was just a bus run away. Unfortunately, although I found myself off watch from 8am till midnight and could get to Miami for the afternoon, I would have to leave there at 11pm in order to be back at the pumping by midnight. This rather spoiled things.

The cabin boy went ashore in a kilt and this caused much interest. He was treated to drinks and had many offers to buy the garment. He waited until we were on the point of sailing, then sold the kilt for a lot more than he had paid for it. Apparently he had done this trick on every voyage to the USA.

We did not have to go to New York but sailed home by the shortest route. Now, the 3rd Mate is responsible for all flags and fire-fighting equipment and has to check all the stores in each lifeboat. Spending 12 hours a day on the bridge outward-bound gave me no opportunity to do any of this, so I had to do it on the way home. Had I been on the B scheme I would have been considerably better off. Without meaning to be cynical, I not could help but wonder whether, if the shipping company had had to pay all the extra overtime the 2nd Mate and I had incurred, they would have been quite so ready to put us on 'watch and watch'.

The worst chore was the checking of all the equipment in the lifeboats. Shortly after the opening of hostilities, there were inquests after a ship was sunk and questions were asked about any difficulties experienced. One ship might state that it had lost its steering oar; the immediate response would be to debate whether or not to put an extra steering oar in each boat. Another vessel would say that its bucket had been washed overboard, and this might occasion a new regulation providing an additional bucket. If the complaint was that there was not enough food, more food had to be provided, and so on.

As I write I have on my knee an old 'sight book' containing the workings-out of ships' positions and also details of stuff in the lifeboats. For food they had in each boat 20lb of biscuits, 27 tins of Horlicks (about 230lb), ten oars and one steering oar, one boathook, ten crutches (rowlocks), three dippers and three drinking vessels, two first-aid outfits, two axes, four smoke floats, one set of charts, 12 flares, six rockets, one tin of massage oil, one rain-catcher, one lamp and two boxes of matches, one grapnel, one compass, one sea-anchor and bag for oil, one aerial, one heaving-line, two painters, two plugs, and a bucket and bailer.

A common criticism was that there was an inadequate quantity of water in the breakers and immediately an order was issued for more water to be supplied. Later on, it seemed that there were still grumbles about there being insufficient water and, believe it or not, many ships had small distilleries put in their boats. I recall that the fuel for them was little cube-shaped briquettes with about a 2-inch side.

All this was very fine in its way, but there was no corresponding

A new lifestyle

increase in the size of the boats. So towards the end of the war we had the best-equipped lifeboats in the history of the sea, but very little room for those who had to use them!

Now that the war was over, we sailed with masthead and navigation lights lit; apart from the short time I was on the *Gaizka*, this was a completely new experience for me. I recall the first time I saw another ship approaching us at night and, for a bit of exercise in Morse and to relieve the boredom, I used the Aldis lamp to ask him, 'What ship and where bound?'

He replied giving details of his destination and what his cargo was, then asked the same questions of me. This was now to be standard practice for, in good weather, there is little to do on the bridge and exchanging words with another vessel relieves the monotony.

Also, when the helmsman strikes the bells every half hour, the lookout man on the fo'c'sle-head turns round and sees if the navigation and masthead lights are on. The custom is for him to shout to the officer on the bridge, 'Lights are bright, Sir.' Of course at that distance every word cannot be heard clearly and many other variations were often given. One can only think of words that rhyme with 'bright' to imagine what other versions were offered!

The skipper chatted me up about my future, saying that, as I was a steady sort of chap, if I stayed with the company I should be able to retire at about 45 or 50. I did not see this as a glowing prospect. The real reason for the possibility of early retirement was the fact that tankers do not spend long in port and the opportunity to spend is thus limited. I could not see myself losing years of enjoyment and trying to buy them back by retiring early. I resolved to leave the company. Besides, I did not want to be carrying molasses for the rest of my time at sea. This was not just the usual signing off and not returning. I was now what was known as a 'company's man' and would have to give them a written resignation, possibly with some sort of explanation.

As the captain appeared to have taken a liking to me and kept referring to what we would do next trip, I became perplexed and sought the Chief Mate's help. I explained my attitude and he understood.

'Leave it to me, Mr Aitchison, and I'll see what I can do for you.'

'How do you like tankers, Mr Aitchison?' said the skipper two days later. 'Do fancy them – or do you prefer cargo ships?'

I knew that the Mate had been at work and replied, 'Well, I prefer cargo ships, Sir, as I like to have longer in port.'

The captained pondered a moment or two, then said, 'Should you decide to leave, I trust you will stay long enough by the ship in port for me to find a replacement for you.'

With considerable relief I assured him that I most certainly would.

The Chief Mate was due for a spell of leave and wanted to hand the ship over to his successor in top condition, otherwise he would get a bad name from the other officers in the company. On the way out all crew members were cleaning tanks, so ten days from home he had the crew painting all the superstructure – he even enlisted the help of the DEMS gunners, who were Army, and unused to this sort of thing.

Seeing them up painting the ventilators I asked him, 'Mister Mate, they're not sailors. Are you not afraid they might fall down?'

'I'll put it to you this way, Mr Acheson,' he replied in his delightful Irish brogue. 'They'll try not to fall down.'

With little in the way of excitement we reached Birkenhead and had to go through a couple of tidal basins before docking. I was on the bridge doing the usual 3rd Mate's duties, that is working the telegraph and conveying the pilot's orders to the engine room, noting the time of the order and relaying the pilot's helm orders to the man at the wheel and observing that he was obeying them correctly. I was also in contact with the shore authorities, who were giving me instructions about where to dock. I was given the title 'grey fox' or something of that order, but what I do distinctly recall was that an ordinary telephone was not used. Instead I had two small pads attached to my throat and they recorded my words as I spoke, so that all the various sounds of the docks were not being transmitted to the authorities, as would have been the case had an ordinary telephone been used.

The first day was an exceptionally long one, and when we docked I had to go round all the tanks finding their ullage. This meant opening their covers and swinging a measuring line so that the end just kissed the top of the molasses. This gave the ullage, or the distance from the tank top to the liquid level, and from this, and provided tables, we found out the amount of cargo in the tank.

I was several days working by the ship and had to take turns at supervising the discharge of the molasses. There was a telephone set up for me to contact our shore staff and to give reports to them on which tanks we were pumping from, and the temperatures of the molasses. Each tank had a main valve that pumped from an aperture about 3 inches above the bottom of the tank. There was also what was termed a stripper valve, the opening of which was in the very bottom of the tank.

Molasses are extremely viscous, which means that you do not just pump until the tank is empty. It is a question of pumping out a certain quantity then turning to another tank while the sticky treacle slowly

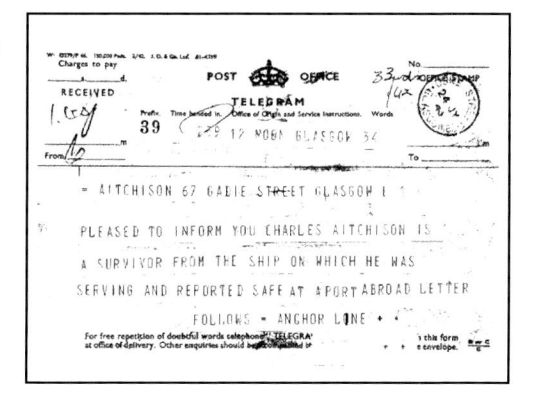

Making Waves IX

The *California*.
Commercial postcard

The telegram my parents received, confirming that I had survived the torpedoing of the California.

HMS *Douglas*.
Author's collection

Myself in USA uniform at Casablanca.

The *Arundel Castle*.
Author's collection

Making Waves · XI

The Rescue Ship *Goodwin* in peacetime guise. *World Ship Society.*

A typical wartime Rescue Ship, showing the very high mainmast.

Willie, crew member on the *Goodwin* and a survivor of an Italian POW camp. *Author's collection*

XII Making Waves

On 3 June 1944 *Illustrated* magazine featured an article on Rescue Ships. In this photograph a Rescue Ship's motor-lifeboat goes to the rescue of the survivors of a torpedoed ship. The lifeboat and survivors come alongside the *Goodwin*. As the injured are hoisted aboard, artificial respiration is given to the needy.

Injured survivors in medical hands.

A typical hospital on a Rescue Ship. *Author's collection*

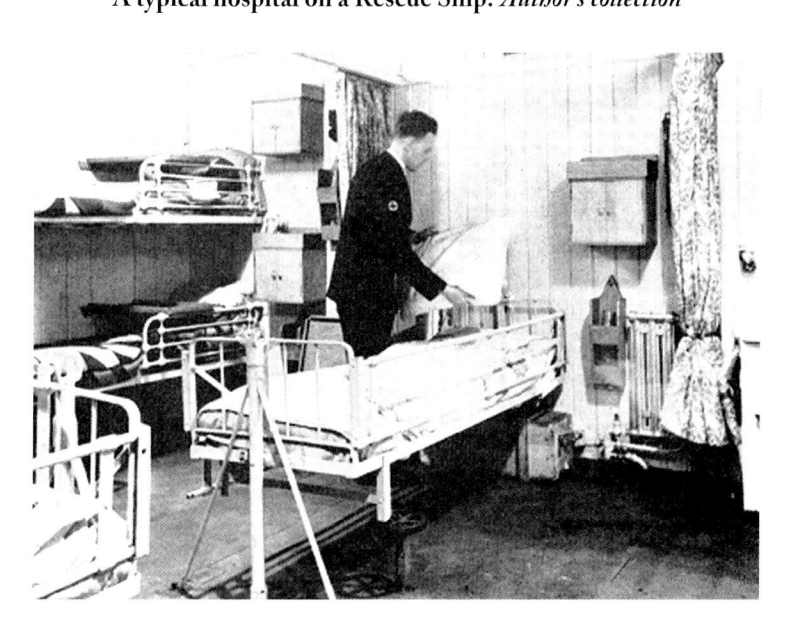

XIV Making Waves

Captain W. J. Hartley DSC, master of the *Goodwin*. He took part in the rescue of 365 seamen and was Chief Officer of the first Rescue Ship put into commission. *Mrs Brenda Shackleton collection*

Captain Hartley was awarded the Distinguished Service Cross at Buckingham Palace on 29 June 1943. Left to right: unknown, Mae Armour, Jim Armour (Chief Officer of the *Copeland*), Capt Hartley, Mrs Hartley, and Captain Hartley's sister Annie. *Mrs Brenda Shackleton collection*

Making Waves   XV

The *South America*. Author's collection

The *Caduceus*. National Maritime Museum

The *Iolaire*.
Peter Newall
collection

XVI   Making Waves

A statue of John Mackintosh in Gibraltar, a distant relation of my family.

The *Empire Spey*. National

A new lifestyle

slides to the bottom of the first tank, and so on.

The Mate rigged up a hose and gave me instructions for the apprentice to hose down the molasses sticking to the sides of one of the tanks. He meanwhile was in his cabin with the company's cargo superintendent.

This helped in two ways. It quickly washed down quite a bit of the molasses sticking to the sides of the tank, and it added to the total tonnage. I was on edge hoping that the cargo superintendent would not suddenly appear and find a first-trip 3rd Mate and an apprentice engaged in what I could only think was an extremely dubious practice. Later, when the relief bosun appeared, I mentioned it to him and he said it was a common practice.

I had sent my resignation to the captain and was anxiously awaiting my relief, but had to wait several days for it to arrive.

What irritated me was the habit of members of head office appearing at the ship about 11am – usually on some flimsy pretext – and waiting to be invited to have lunch with us. The food on the *Athelregent* was outstandingly good and, as food rationing was still severe, here was a chance to have an excellent meal and at no cost. As the junior deck officer, I was always asked to give up my place in the saloon to these scroungers. After three days of this I rebelled. I maintained that I was crew and if anyone should wait on a place at the table it should be those that were not crew. I do not think my attitude pleased everyone but, as I was leaving the ship and they were under some obligation to me, I could not have cared less.

On 14 June 1945 I reached home. It was wonderful to know that the European war was over and to find the nation was still in a state of jubilation. I had been away for just over seven weeks and was due only three days' leave. However, for some reason or other there were not many jobs at the time and I finished up having 30 days at home before signing on the next vessel.

It was a sobering thought that at the beginning of the war Britain had more than 4,000 merchant ships, but at the end of hostilities 2,246 had been sunk and 29,180 merchant seamen had perished – or, to put it another way, one in three had lost their lives!

11

ON A GLASGOW TRAMP

My next posting was a complete change. She was a cargo ship belonging to the Kingsborough Line (P. D. Hendry of Glasgow), who had only three vessels: the *Kingsborough*, the *Kingsland* and the *Radcombe*. This last was a captured Yugoslavian ship and it was to this one that I was sent.

She was a typical tramp ship, berthed in a quiet spot in the little town of Burntisland in Fife, and was discharging iron ore when I arrived on 21 July 1945. Her Chief Mate had had his ship sunk by the *Admiral Scheer* early in the war and had spent more than five years in a German prison-of-war camp. This was his first ship since his release and he was a bit rusty in many matters. Our 2nd Mate was a few years older than I and hailed from St Johns in Newfoundland. We were signed on the B articles and, after my last experience of working many hours for nothing on A articles, I welcomed this.

We stayed in Burntisland for nearly two weeks and the 2nd Mate and I had night about as officers of the watch. There was a small pub whose upper room overlooked our gangway and the 2nd Mate used to go up to the window of this room where he could have a drink, keep an eye on the ship and be paid £1 for doing so. When we did set off we were bound for Huelva, a port on the Atlantic coast of Spain.

I was on the first watch (8pm to midnight) and the skipper appeared on the bridge with a bundle of small charts, each about 8 inches by 6 inches. Without any explanation he laid these down on the desk in the chart room and began messing about with them. It dawned on me that these were charts of the North Sea and he had been given them, before we left port, because the ordinary charts did not show where our minefields were. His breath smelled of drink and, used to the tight discipline of the *Athelregent*, I found this disconcerting. Eventually he got the charts arranged on the table so that we went from one to the other as we navigated through the dangerous waters.

After a couple of days we found ourselves clear of the British coast and heading south. With reasonably good weather we arrived at

Huelva, which is a few miles north of Cadiz, and began to load iron ore.

This was a different Spain from the one I had experienced at Almeria. Germany had lost the war and Fascism was now a dirty word. I think that Franco, Spain's dictator, was at that time a bit unsure of how he would be treated now that Hitler had departed from the scene. There was no more spitting on us in the streets and we were made welcome. If you pulled out a packet of cigarettes, you would be quickly surrounded by people offering to buy some from you. Many commodities were in very short supply, especially soap.

About 6 miles up the Rio Tinto from Huelva is the little village where, in 1492, Columbus set sail on his historic voyage. There are many streets and monuments named after him.

Now, in these dictatorships the rate of exchange is rigged at a rate favourable to themselves, and grossly unfair to outsiders. Naturally there were market forces afoot and you were constantly being besieged by seedy characters offering four times the official rate. This could be very tempting, but woe betide you if you got caught: Fascist jails were best avoided. As was usual in these circumstances, cigarettes were the best commodities with which to barter.

The Spanish customs officials came on board to enforce their rules and regulations, whatever they were – I am sure they were not above inventing a few of their own, and who could gainsay them? Their duty ostensibly was to stop us from taking cigarettes ashore to trade with, but in reality they were there to corner the market and offer us poor-quality rayon stockings in exchange for tobacco.

We were glad to see the back of this country. On the way down the river, the pilot hinted that he wanted some coal, as there was a shortage ashore. In order to empty ashes from the furnaces there was a hole cut in one of the ventilators, and a large metal cylinder, about 18 inches in diameter, was hoisted up and down to do this work, only this time it came on deck filled with coal, which was transferred to a basket for lowering into the pilot launch.

On the dog watches (4pm to 8pm), the senior officers were on watch and the juniors below. This was the time when you could make as much noise as you liked, for no one was expected to be sleeping. The 2nd Radio Officer, 3rd Engineer and I used to go to the 2nd Mate's cabin for a drink.

At the start of each voyage you could buy, duty-free, one bottle of whisky, one of gin and one of either port or sherry. One whisky was the limit, but you could get more wine if you wanted. The 2nd Mate would pour out drinks and curl up on his settee while we made conversation.

He thought that the Glasgow accent was the funniest in the world and delighted in hearing samples of it from me. Something like 'Hey Jimmie, get oan yer hookerdoon an' we'll awa' to the gemme' ['Jimmie, put on your cap and we'll go to the game'] put him in ecstasies. But his favourite was the two Glasgow women and a baby down at Rothesay for the Glasgow Fair.

One says, 'Haw, Sarah – the wean's bum's a' saun'.' ['The baby's buttocks are covered in sand.']

To which the other replies, 'Dip it in the watter, well.' ['Well, dip it in the water.']

On hearing this he was convulsed with mirth. I can still hear his high-pitched laugh as he rolled about helplessly on his settee. I had to say this one every day. After being in his cabin for barely half an hour he would say, 'Go on, Jock. Say it now,' and he would be keyed up with expectation.

As well as drink, cigarettes were also very cheap and were issued in cylindrical tins containing 50. Since we did not pay for tobacco until the end of the voyage it was almost as if cigarettes were free. If you went into a shipmate's cabin you just helped yourself to his fags without asking, and he did likewise when visiting your cabin.

In due course we got orders for Antwerp and discharged the cargo there. I took the train to Brussels and had a very enjoyable day there with the 3rd Engineer. If I recall correctly we had a couple of games of football against other ships. I did my best for the team but was never very good at the game.

My father, having been a professional footballer, taught me how to shoot and I was really good at that. I could also cross a ball reasonably well, tackle competently and run fast with the ball at my feet. My two failings were that I did not have a football brain and could not read the play and take action tactically, and that I had no idea how to head a ball.

Leaving Antwerp in a moderate gale, shortly after casting off we struck a Dutch barge that was tied up near us. It could hardly be helped as the wind forced us down on it. These barges are usually run by families and, in this particular case, the menfolk were ashore. The two women panicked at first but soon regained presence of mind and, with the aid of a wire hawser, kept the barge from being cast adrift.

We narrowly missed a floating mine in the English Channel, and were troubled by fog, but eventually docked safely at Newport, Monmouthshire, in the Bristol Channel, and paid off. Two weeks before docking we got the news that Japan had surrendered and the world was now at peace.

Now the skipper was a great snob. The Labour Party was

anathema to him and its victory occasioned an almost daily diatribe of disapproval. I had leanings to the left in those days and resented the fact that he was denigrating a party before it had any chance to show what it could do. He was wildly class-conscious and this sparked off an interesting conversation.

'You consider yourself middle class surely?' he enquired.

'I've always worked for a living, and always looked upon myself as working class,' was my reply.

'Oh, I can understand that, when you were a sailor, but now that you're an officer surely that must make you middle class,' he reasoned.

'Just where would you say the middle class ends and the upper begins?'

'About £120,000 a year,' he put forward.

'And where do you reckon it begins?' I ventured.

This took him somewhat aback. He had not foreseen this line of questioning and he now had to think furiously to arrive at a figure that put me in his cherished class, but excluded the bosun, who was the highest-paid rating on the ship. Eventually he blurted out a figure that was somewhere above the bosun's wage, but a little below mine. He tried to announce this figure in a casual manner but he had obviously done a quick calculation. The *coup de grâce* was not original, as Robert Muir had outlined it to me more than a year before, but it was nevertheless devastating.

'Do you not think that I would have an almighty cheek to put myself in the same class as a person earning £120,000 a year, but yet in a different class from someone getting about £60 a year less that I am paid?'

I had won the argument and left the skipper with not a leg to stand on, but the reasoning was fraudulent. The question of class does not relate entirely to wealth or earnings. There were dockers during the war earning almost as much as brain surgeons, but they would never be in the same class because of their spending habits. They had enough money to send their children to a private school, buy their own house and take a holiday abroad. But the vast majority chose to live in a council house, next door to a man earning not a quarter of their pay, and to spend their extra money on cigarettes, alcohol and gambling.

These dockers were a constant source of trouble to us. Apart from the usual stealing of anything they could lay their hands on, they raided our lifeboats, particularly for anything that had a saleable value. This went on all through the war and judges were very soft in sentencing them because they were said to be 'so important to the war effort'. As a result, a man earning £40 a week would be ordered to pay a fine of £5 – hardly a discouragement! In addition to this, they were frequently on strike.

I had not much leave due to me and decided to have another trip on the *Radcombe*. With the war over, secrecy had become a thing of the past and we had orders to proceed, after some repairs were carried out, to Wabana in Newfoundland (then a separate country from Canada) to load iron ore, thence to St Johns for bunkers and finally to report to Hampstead Roads for further orders. This openness was overwhelming.

On board we had a good-looking ginger-haired AB just over 20 years old. I remember seeing his signature on the manifest as Robert Gordon. I later discovered that he was completely illiterate and that the only thing he could write was his name, because someone had taught him to do so.

As he was a very intelligent lad I was appalled to discover this and asked him how it had come about. He told me that he was a bargee's son and had never stayed long enough in any spot to have proper schooling. I had seen film documentaries about special schools for the children of bargees, but he assured me that that was the theory, but the practice was very different. I offered to teach him but he declined.

Our crossing had no fog or rough weather, which was exceptionally good for that time of the year. By arrangement with the Old Man, as soon as we docked at Wabana the 2nd Mate went off to his home in the capital, St Johns. This was his first time home since a few weeks before September 1939 and you can imagine how excited he was about it.

Wabana was a very small mining town with nothing much doing. There was to be a dance, and I walked 3 miles to the venue only to discover that it did not begin till 11pm. For a change I did the sensible thing and went back to the ship – add to the 6 miles 339 steps from the pier to the main road!

I took over the 2nd Mate's duties as well as my own and after the cargo was loaded we set off for St Johns, which was only about 4½ hours' sailing. As we rounded the north part of Newfoundland it was the 8am to noon watch, and I was on the bridge with the skipper. Now the Old Man was no great shakes as a navigator. To be charitable, he might have been a lot better in his younger days, but he was now approaching 60 and maybe had lost the plot a bit. He was looking for a way of identifying the entrance to the passage leading to St Johns and got into a panic when he could not think of any way to find it.

I looked at the chart and saw a promontory a little north of the passage, drew a line from the passage entrance to this promontory and found the direction of this transit bearing. It was a simple matter to convert this to a compass bearing by applying the compass error. All we had to do now was to wait till the promontory was on this bearing and the land immediately behind it was sure to be where the passage began. The skipper was not entirely convinced, but, as he had nothing better to offer, acted on this suggestion and we arrived safely at the passage.

At the time I thought little of the episode, but 60 years later, one evening when lying relaxing in a hot bath, it suddenly dawned on me why the skipper had panicked. The Chief Mate was only a few weeks out of a prisoner-of-war camp, where he had spent almost the entire war and was very much out of touch with navigational matters. The 2nd Mate was an excellent navigator but he was ashore at the very place we were trying to reach. That left the captain having to rely on his 3rd Mate, who he knew had just over two months' bridge experience.

Now that I come to think of it, the Mate should have done a trip or two as 2nd or 3rd Mate, then eased himself into his former rank.

Talking to the Mate about his experiences in the German POW camp, he admitted that he had been fairly well treated, and that when the time came for his release all the possessions that had been taken from him when he entered the camp were, with typical German efficiency, returned to him. Despite this, when I asked him what should now be done to Germany his answer was, 'Erase the race!' I found his reply quite chilling.

One thing that intrigued me was how the Newfoundlanders would pronounce the name of their country. Most people at home said New*found*land, but on radio the BBC announcers always insisted on calling it *New*foundland. Neither appeared to be correct, for the inhabitants did not accent any of the syllables.

Once docked, I went ashore to see about buying food to take back home. I had it on my conscience how bad the rations still were, and there was nothing I could lay hands on during the last trip in either Spain or Belgium. Here I managed to buy some raisins, tinned salmon, tea and other stuff.

The 2nd Mate was desperate to show his gratitude for my doing his job for what amounted to 12 days, and took the 3rd Engineer and myself to the famous Colony Club together with his sister, Hope, and two of her chums. We had a most enjoyable time.

After bunkering we loaded ten bags of mail to take home, and we were also to carry two supernumeraries who were coming to Britain to study medicine.

Despite previous orders, we sailed straight back to the United Kingdom. As we neared home, it was mentioned on the radio that a storm was sweeping over Ireland, and it was lifting roofs off many houses. About 350 miles off the Irish coast we ran into it and passed close to the centre of the depression – the wind changing from south to north-west in less than 15 minutes. It certainly blew.

Unscathed, we docked at Port Talbot in Wales on 28 September and began discharging the iron ore to go to the famous iron works of Guest, Keen & Nettlefold. I had a pleasant enough time there and sent home the food I had bought in Newfoundland together with a bottle of sherry I had got from our steward.

My mother and sisters had been pestering me to have a photograph taken in uniform. I was still quite shy about this sort of thing and it took a considerable effort to go to a photographer. Two girls set me up and wanted to try out various poses, but my one idea was to get in, get the job done and get out as quickly as possible. The result may be seen on page XVIII.

We left Port Talbot with orders to go to Sfax, a town in Tunisia. It was still a novelty to know exactly where the ship was going and not have to make a guess. There were no convoys to bother about – just sail to your destination by the shortest possible route.

We arrived in Bizerta nine days after leaving Port Talbot. This was a record time for an old tramp considering that we were held up in the Straits of Gibraltar by the Levante (a strong easterly wind) and lost 12 hours steaming time. We had to call at Bizerta for route instructions and, though we had radioed them 6 hours in advance of our coming, we had to drop anchor and wait for the night – losing another 10 or 12 hours.

We made Sfax about 11am and were working from a sun position we had got at 1pm the previous day. No one had been there before and we were all on the bridge looking for buoys and markings.

Sfax was not much of a place. It was typical of North Africa, having its French and Arab sections. No one spoke English, so I had to take out my French again (last used in Antwerp) and give it a bit of a dusting. The only decent evening we had here was at a dance at a French club. The rate of exchange was rigged but we could easily get four times the official one.

A cargo of phosphate (fertiliser) awaited us and we learned that we had to take it to somewhere in Europe. Phosphate was something like sand, only much finer. It was a real messy cargo, and seemed to find its way into every corner of the ship.

The dynamo, which had been giving trouble ever since I joined the *Radcombe*, broke down here. We did not manage to have it repaired, so we left for Gibraltar for orders – without degaussing gear, using paraffin navigation lights, and with no radio.

The steward was a lazy fellow who did not bother to clean the paraffin lamp in the saloon. I used to sit in there and do some study for my Chief Mate's ticket and, a few days off Gibraltar, a pile of soot dropped on to my text book. I made up my mind to leave off studying for the time being.

Years later I happened to look at Nicholls's *Concise Guide II* (the navigation manual for Chief Mates and Masters), saw the mark of the soot and turned over the page where there was a problem in navigation and its solution. Now, someone had given me a puzzle about a box 4 feet square being put at the bottom of a wall, and a ladder 20 feet long being placed against the wall so that it touched the edge of the box. The problem was to find out how high up the wall the ladder reached. After many weary hours I had solved this by algebra, but now here was basically the same problem, and it was solved more elegantly using trigonometry.

Nearing Gib we struck a strong westerly wind and this added about 12 hours to the trip. This was a bit unfair when we had already had to battle with an easterly wind on entering the Mediterranean. We anchored at Gib for five days while the dynamo was being attended to, but I managed only one day ashore. This time I determined to load up with food and took an empty suitcase with me.

Our chief steward asked if I would change some Tunisian money at the Army Paymaster's Office. I did not fancy this but I did not want to refuse him, so put the money down my socks.

However, the case aroused the curiosity of the Customs, who took me to their headquarters. I was asked why I was taking the case ashore. I truthfully told them that I intended to buy a lot of tinned food and they were aghast at this admission. Seemingly there was a ban on any food being taken out of Gibraltar. It ended with them taking the case from me, and asking me to show them how much money I had. They then relieved me of most of the cash, saying that I would get the case and cash back when I returned. The most annoying thing was that other members of the crew were taking food back (as I had done many times before) through the usual gate. It had certainly been a wise move to put the steward's cash down my socks!

I paid the usual visit to Major Douglas's establishment and saw little Carlos again.

The voyage home was uneventful except for a severe storm in the Bay of Biscay. Although we were not aware of it at the time, we had sprung a leak in one of the holds and water got to the cargo.

We sailed up the River Scheldt to the Ghent Canal and tied up for the night at the Dutch town of Terneusen. Next day we had a sail lasting 3 hours along this canal to Ghent. I was sent ahead in a launch with the ship's papers. At the border I gained clearance and rejoined the *Radcombe* without her having to stop. Like our trip on the Cape Cod Canal, it was a pleasant change to be sailing along a waterway, high above the surrounding country.

Ghent proved to be a fine town full of ancient buildings, and there was very little war damage due to the Canadians advancing too quickly for the Germans to do much sabotage as they retreated. The skipper and I went to the British Consulate on business and the Consul very kindly took us on a car journey round the town, showing us all the places of interest.

The skipper, Chief Mate and I had to go to court to 'swear protest', as the legal saying goes. This was because some of the cargo was damaged in the storm when crossing the Bay of Biscay. The business was conducted in Flemish, but we were provided with an interpreter. Passages from the Mate's log (relating to the stormy weather) were read out to me and I had to attest to the truth of his statements. This was to make sure that it really had been the bad weather that had caused the leak, and not any other reason.

After unloading was completed we left Ghent and sailed back along the canal and into the North Sea. Our orders were to go to North Shields to pay off.

Heading north we had to navigate by picking up buoys to guide us through the minefields, and they all had different characteristics, as was shown on the chart. It was the first watch and I checked the error of the compass and set a course allowing for leeway (caused by the wind) and the effect of the tide. I managed this quite well and was picking up the buoys near enough almost to be able to spit on them.

After an hour of this the captain came on to the bridge and asked how we were doing. I informed him that we were sailing past all the buoys without experiencing any difficulties. He asked how much I was allowing for leeway and I told him 5 degrees. He sniffed at the air and said, 'The wind seems quite fresh – give her another 2 degrees for the leeway.'

Against my better judgement I complied and he went below. Twenty minutes later he came back and claimed that the wind was stronger and asked for me to allow another 3 degrees for the wind. There was nothing I could do but obey. We now had 10 degrees instead of 5. Less than a quarter of an hour later he returned and demanded another 3 degrees to be added, then amended this to 5. I could not understand why he had to interfere, since we had been finding all the buoys quite easily.

By this time we should have been sighting a buoy, but none was to be seen. The skipper became a bit alarmed and asked me to check the compass error. Then I had to check it a second time. He was now seriously worried.

'What's gone wrong?' he asked. 'We've confirmed all the details twice and we still can't see a buoy. The only changes we've made is a degree or two on the leeway, and that's neither here nor there.'

A change from 5 to 15 degrees was being dismissed as 'neither here nor there'! As a Glasgow comedian once said, 'If a thing is neither here nor there – where the hell is it?'

One of the shore lighthouses came into our view and I took a bearing of it. This did not give a position but told us that we were somewhere along a line from the light, and the line showed that we had missed three buoys! I persuaded the captain to take off some of the leeway, and 10 minutes later the lookout reported a red light 5 points on the port bow. We turned and headed for the buoy and arrived safely, much to my relief.

In a way I was glad when the watch ended – but in another way I was anxious about what the Old Man was getting up to. Next day I conferred with the 2nd Mate, who laughed and said that the skipper kept going down below for a tot of rum then, returning to the bridge, imagined that the wind was stronger and added more leeway.

Said he, 'It's a good job he had only half a bottle broken out. Had he had a full one, we might have had so much leeway that we would have been heading back to Belgium!'

The skipper had told me once that he had put one of his ships on the rocks, and this did not surprise me in the least. I was happy that he had not been my first captain, and that I had been given a firm grounding in navigation by Captain Cornwell.

North Shields was not much of a town and a deal smaller than South Shields. All round that region from the Tyne to the Tees was an area of deprivation, and the shortage of goods was much more severe than in other parts of Britain. Pubs usually ran out of beer about 7 o'clock in the evening. Cigarettes were in very short supply and you were lucky to get any at all. When they were sold it was mostly in packets of five, seldom in 10s and never in 20s.

Most folk preferred Virginian tobacco to Turkish, and there was a Turkish variety of cigarette called Pasha that no one really wanted, but you often had to accept or go without. The worst of the lot was one that went by the name of Spanish Shawl.

Any complaints about shortages during hostilities were met with the customary, 'Don't you know there's a war on?' But peace, at the moment, did not make much of a difference. The only consolation was that the people in the area were very friendly.

After three voyages I decided that I was not learning much from the captain, who was a definite liability. I resolved to make this my last voyage on the *Radcombe* and, after paying off on 21 November, returned to Glasgow.

For the four months that I had spent on the ship I was given eight days' leave. It was another ten days before I was found a ship, so I had nearly three weeks ashore.

12

The *Masunda*

After leaving the *Radcombe* I would have enjoyed spending Christmas at home, but my leave rapidly passed and I had to report for another vessel almost as soon as my leave was up. This time I was sent back to South Shields to join the *Masunda*, owned by MacLay & MacIntyre – commonly referred to by the sailors as 'Muck and Misery'.

Seamen had a habit of making up phrases based on the initials of the company. As I said before, they referred to the PSNC as either 'passengers should never complain' or 'poxy sailors never cured'. H. Hogarth were said to be 'Hungry Hogarth's', while Shaw Saville & Albion was always named 'Slow starvation and agony'.

The *Masunda* had been built in 1929 by Stevens of Linthouse in Glasgow. The owners were holy people who, at one time, were supposed to have provided a bible at each seaman's bunk, much in the manner that the Gideons did in hotels.

On her previous trip she had picked up iron ore in North Africa and was now discharging it here. She was slightly bigger than the *Radcombe* and had a speed of 10 knots, which was faster than most tramps. The captain hailed from Wick, the Chief Mate from Greenock and the 2nd Mate from Burnside on the outskirts of Glasgow. The 2nd Mate's name was Tommy Aitchison, and having two officers with the same surname seemed to present difficulties.

'I can't call an officer by his first name,' said the skipper. 'Have you any middle names?'

I replied, 'I have two middle names – Alexander and Mackintosh.'

'Very well then, I shall call you Mr Mackintosh.'

The *Masunda* had just had a Board of Trade Survey (a routine check on the safety of the ship) and was in quite a mess, with all the lifeboat gear lying around on the deck. I could not imagine her sailing but sail she did, with orders to proceed to the River Plate for more orders. I had quite a lot of work to do, stowing all the stores and equipment back in the lifeboats.

Up on 'monkey island' I was taking bearings when I heard this frantic voice calling, 'Mr Mackintosh, Mr Mackintosh!' Eventually I got the message and settled down to my new name.

'Mr Mackintosh, here are the ship's articles. Make up the lifeboat stations and return them to me,' adding that I was to be very careful to keep them in pristine condition.

On each voyage every member of the crew was allotted a place in one of the lifeboats. Small cargo ships usually had four boats, Nos 1 and 3 being on the starboard side and Nos 2 and 4 on the port side. It was usual to put the skipper and Chief Engineer in No 1, the Mate and 2nd Engineer in No 2 and so on, spreading the deck officers and ratings evenly over the four boats.

My cabin opened out on to an internal alley on the starboard side, the fore door and aft door of this alley usually being kept open. Going down the English Channel on Christmas Day, heading into a force six breeze, I stepped into this alley and the articles were neatly plucked from my hand by the wind and carried swiftly to the side of No 3 hatch.

In a matter of seconds I reached the spot but, just as I was about to put my hands on them, they took flight and flattened themselves against the outside of the galley. Again, at maximum speed, I reached the galley just as they decided to take off in an afterly direction. Cursing the innate perversity of inanimate matter, I sped towards the end of the bridge deck, where they were presently coiled around a bollard but, no doubt, cunningly waiting for my approach before they deliberately took off again, probably heading for the well deck and thence possibly for the English Channel. There was now no time for the niceties of using hands. I halted their progress by stamping on them with a dirty big sea boot.

I think I must have stood on them for several seconds with pounding heart, partly from exertion but mostly from the horrifying possibility of arriving in Argentina *sans* the articles. At that time I was told that a manifest had to be submitted in octuplicate, giving details of all stores from the number of shovels in the stoke-hole to the number of bottles of aspirin in the chief steward's medicine chest. Unlike British Customs, where one may err on the safe side, the Argies would fine you if you under-declared or over-declared. To arrive without the articles would be the end. A duplicate set would have to be flown out and the owners would be mightily displeased, any expense, however small, being frowned upon.

Taking the wet and dirty articles into the galley I dried them off and applied soft bread and other remedies, but their condition continued to be very much 'unpristine'. The captain received the articles with little enthusiasm. As P. G. Wodehouse would have it, he may not have been disgruntled, but he was very far from gruntled.

On 24 December, in preparation for Christmas, we went to work in the saloon. The engineers fitted up fairy lights, the 2nd Mate and I draped it with the red ensign and the house flags, while the stewards decked the mirror with cotton wool (to represent snowflakes) and the various compliments of the season.

By New Year's Day we were off Madeira in beautiful warm weather and had another very fine dinner with nuts, dates, figs and mince-pies. We went on to sail through the Cape Verde Islands, where we reported to Lloyd's so that we would be mentioned in the shipping news.

The captain's name was Sinclair, but he chose to pronounce it as 'Saint Clare'. He had some quaint idea that only senior officers should smoke on the bridge. Not that he was a non-smoker – he sported a dirty big briar which, if you were unlucky enough to be on his lee on a windy day, could give you an eyeful of top-quality ash. Nevertheless, he stood by this decision and came up halfway through every watch to let the junior go below for a smoke.

One day at lunchtime he was still in the saloon having a cup of coffee when I sat down to eat.

'Pass me the sugar, Mr Mackintosh,' he requested. As I did so, I was conscious that the hollow of my right hand was showing a dark mahogany shade. I think he must have noticed, but chose not to remark on it.

At the table one day he proclaimed, 'Last trip down to the Plate, if we had caught another 8 pounds of fish we should have landed a ton.'

This was greeted with modified amazement by his fellow officers, so he went on to elaborate. It appeared that the fish were benitos, and all one had to do was to bait a hook with a piece of white cloth and the ignorant mutts mistook the cloth for a flying fish.

'Just wait until we get into flying-fish weather,' stated he, 'and I'll show you how it's done.'

At length the great day arrived. He announced that the time had come to reduce the population of benitos in the South Atlantic.

'Get me some white bunting Mr Mackintosh, and we'll make a start after lunch.'

At 1pm Captain Sinclair, arrayed in a white boiler suit, stood at the bow with an 8-foot pole to which was attached some line and the prepared hook. The benitos sported about close to the bow, reminding me of a line from a Thomas Gray poem: 'Alas, regardless of their doom, the little victims play.'

About a dozen or so members of the crew had assembled to witness the one-sided battle between man and fish. Smoking his foul briar and looking quite relaxed, the skipper pulled the rod slowly back and forth to give the fish the impression that a tasty morsel was there for the taking.

After 10 minutes some of the onlookers mentioned that many of the benitos had moved from the port to the starboard bow. The skipper murmured a grateful acknowledgement and moved accordingly. However, after another 10 minutes they were seen to be back on the port bow, and once more this was made known to Captain Sinclair, who changed his locus again.

After half an hour – and a distinct lack of cooperation on the part of the benitos – he was told that the fish had once more moved, but testily replied, 'I can see that for myself!'

By 2 o'clock many of the spectators had lost a little of their confidence in the Old Man's prowess, and had drifted away. Came 3 o'clock the skipper was alone at the bow – no fish ... and no fans.

In some ships the engineers have a mess-room where they can pop in attired in boiler suits, but the *Masunda* did not have one and the engineers had to dine in the saloon. This being the case, boiler suits were strictly *verboten*.

At 5 o'clock I was on the bridge relieving the Chief Mate for his tea. From there I could see the skipper, still at the bow, but could not judge of the success or otherwise of his enterprise. Coming down for my own meal at 5.30pm, I was joined by the 4th Engineer while the 3rd Engineer was still eating in the saloon. At 5.55pm we were joined by the captain, still in white boiler suit, as he sat down in his accustomed place.

'I hope you don't mind my sitting down in the saloon in a boiler suit,' said he, addressing the 3rd Engineer. The man had scarcely time to express his lack of concern for this breach of etiquette when the skipper muttered softly, but with great intensity, 'It wouldn't matter a damn if you did!' He had not caught one single benito!

Fish were never mentioned for the remainder of the voyage, and many benitos lived happily ever after.

By this time there was no longer a requirement to have three Radio Officers and we set off with only one. I felt sorry for him as his was now a lonely job. He did not go on watches but had spells of duty based solely on Greenwich Mean Time. As the ship went east or west the clocks were altered so that they showed 12 o'clock approximately at noon. Naturally all our activities were governed by the ship's time, but the 'sparks' had to stick with GMT.

We entered the River Plate and were more than halfway to

Buenos Aires when new orders came telling us to turn back and head for Montevideo. Apparently the orders contained instructions to proceed to Bahia Blanca to load grain for South Africa. Coal being cheaper in Uruguay than in Argentina, we took on 1,800 tons. At £4.20 a ton, this would come to £7,560, and it filled the bunkering space, while the excess was heaped in the open on top of No 3 hatch.

I had a gut feeling that only 1,700 tons was actually loaded, and this meant a saving of £420, which would be split between the Old Man, the Chief Engineer and the shore agent. Where there was no one to keep a watch on such activities, a deal of dishonesty went on at sea.

We were looking for the wreck of the scuttled *Graf Spee*, but only the control tower and part of a mast were visible. I remembered that the Government of Uruguay were protesting about its hampering shipping, but this was not true and I fancy they were just out for more compensation.

I went ashore for a whole day with the 2nd and 4th Engineers. We walked all over the town and saw the sights. After having tea at Liberty Inn (a restaurant run by the British community) we went to a big fair and had half an hour in one of the cabarets before catching the last launch back to the ship.

Most of the ratings had bought leather suitcases at £5 a time. I suppose this was a bargain if you wanted a suitcase made of leather; but they seemed heavy enough to tote around even when empty.

Two and a half days after leaving Montevideo we came into the small port of Ingeniero White. The bigger town of Bahia Blanca (Spanish for White Bay) was quite a few miles away from Ingeniero White – I recall that it took about 20 minutes to reach it. Smoking was prohibited on the bus and I recollect the captain saying that to do without his pipe for 20 minutes was sheer purgatory – this from a man that forbade his junior officers to smoke on the bridge!

As expected shifting boards were erected for the cargo. We would load a considerable quantity of maize then cover it with layers of bagged grain. Usually South Africa has enough maize, not only to feed its population but also for export. This particular year there had been a severe drought, hence the need to import.

South American countries presented a problem for tramp skippers. The authorities had to be bribed and regular lines – such as Donaldson South Atlantic or the Grange Line – knew precisely how much to offer. Possibly our contribution fell short of expectations as the following episode might suggest.

I was officer on watch on the first night and was standing talking to the bosun when there was an almighty noise and we both rushed up to the windlass, thinking that the anchor had not been securely fixed and had dropped into the dock. It had not; but we soon noticed that one of our rafts was floating next to the ship. We had four of them altogether and they were lashed to the shrouds on either side of each mast. I examined the lines that were holding it and they had obviously been tampered with. I took hold of the painter and made it fast to a cleat on board, as nothing could be done until we had the help of the crew in the morning. I reported the incident to the Mate, and that was that.

However, when next morning dawned there was no raft to be seen anywhere. Captain Sinclair came on the scene and said, 'Mr Mackintosh, before you have your breakfast you'll take a launch down river and look for the raft. Take my telescope with you.'

The agent quickly arranged for a launch and two Argentinians to take me downstream. After sailing for 2 miles I could see our raft lying on a sandbank. I started giving orders to the two locals when I discovered that they had not a word of English. When I was trying to suggest what I wanted by gesture, our launch ended up on this sandbank.

I got every piece of rope in the boat and tied them together so that the raft could be jerked off the bank. But first we had to get ourselves off. One of the Argies took off most of his clothes and went down under the boat, and together we managed to free it. We successfully got the raft in tow and brought it back in time for me to have a late breakfast. I am certain someone deliberately tampered with the ropes holding the raft.

The Argentinian Customs were as corrupt as those in Spain, and put various petty restrictions on us. Coming back to the ship at lunchtime (the only time we could shop) we were told by them that there was a port order forbidding any goods from being taken on board between noon and 2pm. There was no way of knowing if this was true or not, and the practice was to hand them 10 cigarettes and suddenly the port order became irrelevant.

In a foreign port it is the custom to fly the flag of that country at the starboard yard-arm of the foremast; this is known as a courtesy flag. Not, however, in Argentina, where it was deemed essential. Tramp vessels could not be expected to carry the national flag of every country that had a coastline. Fortunately, the letter 'J' in International Code is in every ship's flag locker, and it is the same as the Argentinian flag.

The weather was not too hot – 85°F – and the mosquitoes let us off lightly. Some of the fair-skinned lads had blistered badly, but I had been doing a little sunbathing every day on the way south and had safely acquired a deep tan.

On the third evening it was my watch on board. The rest of the officers and some men, 15 in all, went to the church service at the Seamen's Mission. The 2nd Engineer was an excellent organist and played for a service lasting 35 minutes, with free supper afterwards. The joke was that the ABs had just come out of the pub to go to the service and later went back to the pub!

The mission had a boxing ring and gloves, etc, and was always looking for victims. I was inveigled into going three 2-minute rounds with the 2nd Engineer. Early in the second round the 2nd's nose began to bleed freely and some of the blood got on to my glove. After that my glove touched his chest and left a red mark. His glove then got gore on it and similarly my body had red marks all over it until it looked as though we had done serious damage to each other. Everyone was worried except ourselves, so the bout was called off for appearance's sake.

At the mission I met a girl, Señorita Fuentes. We agreed to go to the cinema and I, in a fit of chivalry, said I did not mind sitting through a Spanish film. She replied that she preferred one in English. Apparently when the Americans wanted to dub one of their films in Spanish, the cheapest way was to get the job done in Mexico, and she and the other Argentinians did not like Mexican Spanish.

We were challenged to play another British ship, the *Stankeld*, at football. Despite being the superior side, we were beaten 2-1. No one had wanted to go in goal and, eventually, one of our black firemen was pitchforked into the job at the eleventh hour. He had not much idea of the game and let through two very soft ones. I began at centre-half but switched to centre-forward and surprised everyone (including myself) by scoring our only goal. Admittedly I was given a perfect pass just 10 yards in front of an open goal and could hardly have missed.

There were usually about 14 or 15 pairs of football boots on a ship, and getting a decent pair was a lottery. I had an ill-fitting pair and contracted blisters on the soles of my feet, resulting in being confined to the ship for three days.

We took 15 days to load the grain. The reason for this was their lack of coal, which meant that the grain arrived in small lots; the normal time would have been about three days. A shortage usually means higher prices, and this would explain why we loaded so much coal in Montevideo.

There was no need to have a feeder above the shifting boards as the bags of grain kept the maize from shifting too much. These bags came down to the dock to be taken on board in cargo slings, but, before this, they had to be tested by the exporter for some reason or other. The man doing this had an implement like a hollow stiletto. He jabbed this into each bag, then turned the blade point upwards and the grain came tumbling into his hand out of a hole in its handle. He put this into a tin container, announcing its number as he did so. As this was done in batches of 50, I distinctly remember him crying almost triumphantly, 'Cinquento' as the last bag in the batch was sampled.

On 10 February we set off for the port of East London in South Africa, and it was just as well, as the Argentinian elections were about to take place and trouble was predicted. It was a real Fascist country, yet I was informed that only a small minority actually supported the dictator, Peron. No doubt he would fiddle the election and get himself re-elected. From talking to some Britishers they averred that most civilians were against Peron. Argentina's Navy, which was run on British lines, was 100% pro-British and the Army, which was organised on Fascist lines, was one-third for Peron and one-third against him, with the remaining one-third sitting on the fence. I had no way of verifying this.

The captain, knowing that I was from the fo'c'sle, remarked that I would probably be good with a palm and needle. I merely said that I was average, having an idea what was in the offing. The next thing I knew I was being given a lifebuoy and requested to repair it while on watch. My first captain had impressed on me that my job on the bridge was to keep a good lookout and do only duties related to keeping a watch. I felt I could not refuse, but I took such a long time over the work that the skipper got the message that I neither wanted to do the work of an AB, nor considered it part of my duties. This would be the equivalent of the Chief Engineer asking his 4th Engineer to shovel coal into a furnace.

During the depression in the 1930s I was told that often the Mate, during his bridge watch, would be on deck working with the men, having given his whistle to the man at the wheel with instructions to blow it if anything unforeseen happened. From sailors who had been lucky enough to have a job at sea during the depression, I learned a great deal. Apparently they worked many hours of overtime but were never paid for it, the reason being that if they asked to be paid they were not offered any more work on that ship.

Also, when they wanted a crew, the Mate would go down to the shipping office to sign them on. Dozens of sailors would be waving their discharge books aloft crying 'Wife and three' and suchlike. Now these discharge books had reports on the behaviour and proficiency of the bearers, so the Mate would ask to see them, ostensibly to check on the seaman's character, etc, but in reality because he knew that most of the books would have a 10-shilling note inside them as a kind of bribe. He collected all the cash before choosing the sailors.

Although I have previously been scathing about the dockers and their behaviour during and after the Second World War, I believe they too fared very poorly during the 1930s depression. It was expected that on their way home they would visit a pub and pay a sum of money to the owner of the pub so that their foreman could have free drinks with his buddies. If there was not enough cash in this kitty the foreman would enquire into the payments and anyone that had not contributed, or had paid too little, was not selected for work the following day. Many public houses in the Yorkhill area of Glasgow had little alcoves specially made for these foremen and their friends.

Back to the *Masunda* I had the feeling that Captain Sinclair was the kind of skipper who belonged to the breed of masters who wanted something for nothing, for I recall that when the ship was leaving South Shields he asked me to take the wheel and steer her out. The 3rd Mate's job on these occasions is to give the pilot's orders to the helmsman and to use the telegraph to convey his wishes to the engineers.

Another annoyance was the painting of the board carrying the ship's name. During hostilities all ships had their names painted out and, when in port, they displayed at the gangway a blackboard (just over a yard long and about 10 inches deep) with the name of the ship painted on it in white. It was not a matter of painting the board black, then, after it had dried, adding the name in white. The two colours had to be applied at the same time, which was known as 'cutting in'. In some companies this practice continued long after the war and, when in Ingeniero White, the skipper told me to paint this board. I did so, but put in a claim for 2 hours overtime – which was not at all well received.

We reached East London on 2 March, which was not bad going. One thing of note on the passage was that the captain asked the carpenter to make a small wooden collar, about 2 inches wide. To this he attached a long line, after baiting the collar with fish. We floated this on the sea and had not long to wait when an albatross swooped down for the fish and caught its head in the collar. We had to let out the line very quickly to stop the bird breaking its neck. It soared aloft at quite a speed and we gradually checked its flight by letting out the line more slowly. Ultimately it stopped rising and, with great care, we slowly pulled on the line until we had the albatross on the deck. The skipper measured its wing-span and it was found to be about 13 feet!

East London was known as Buffalo City as it lay on the Buffalo River. It had not rained there for ten months (hence the drought), but, as luck would have it, our arrival was heralded by a thunderstorm and there was a fair bit of rain during our visit.

I should have bought food in Bahia Blanca, but the shopping area was so far away, and the language so difficult, that I chose to wait until we got to South Africa. This was a mistake, as they had rather a lot of grub on ration. I turned the charm on a little blonde salesgirl who took pity on me and gave me seven tins of corned beef, 4lb of sugar and four tins of pears, which was a lot more than I was entitled to.

South Africa was a fine country to visit – if you were white. We reckoned that the grain would be sucked out in two or three days but this was not the case. The bags were unloaded in slings, and when the loose grain was exposed they sent men with pails and sacks down into the hold. They bagged the maize and sewed up the bags, which were then lifted out in cargo slings on to the dock. This delighted us as we could look forward to two weeks or more in port.

Usually the 2nd Mate was in charge of the Nos 4 and 5 holds when loading or discharging cargo, and the 3rd Mate had Nos 1, 2 and 3. With the 2nd Mate was an Afrikaner to supervise their dockers, while I had a British ex-Navy rating doing a similar job.

The rates of pay were quite interesting. The men down the hold were paid £1 10s a week. Their foreman (rumoured to be a Zulu chief) was very efficient, and was paid £3, while both the white supervisors got £14 a week. The Zulu really ran the business for them. He would come to them with a suggestion and they would appear to consider it, then give consent, but it was very much a formality.

We were called for one day and taken away to the beach for a day by some British residents, after which they gave us tea and entertained us. At the beach they did surf-riding; no boards were involved and it was very tricky. What you had to do was to go out past the breaking waves, swim along with the swell then, at a precise moment, swim as quickly as possible and throw yourself flat and rigid just as the wave broke. This required some practice but, if achieved, gave a lovely feeling as the wave broke just under your abdomen. I had mixed success at the sport and usually ended up doing a cartwheel and ploughing up the sand with my nose.

To guard against our catching malaria we were given a daily dose of quinine and mepacrine. I had never had quinine before and simply put it into my mouth; I had partially chewed it when I discovered that it had the most abominable taste. It comes to mind that I tried jam, liver salts, plain sugar and various other substances, but the horrible aftertaste remained in my mouth for two or three days.

After this experience I took a mouthful of lime-juice, popped the quinine tablet into my mouth and endeavoured to swallow it whole. Even at that, there was a slightly disagreeable flavour. I learned afterwards that one ship had administered its quinine in liquid form, and this must have been a terrible ordeal.

We bought South African cigarettes to be put in the ship's bond for issue to the crew. One variety was named Commando and, since they were quite strong, people joked that only a commando could smoke them.

One of the other varieties was 'C to C', and various explanations were put forward for the name. Some said it stood for 'Coast to Coast' and others claimed it meant 'Cape to Cairo'. The British soon had their own interpretation, and reckoned it was 'Cough to Coffin' – other variations offered were 'Cough to Consumption' or 'Consumption to Coffin'. The explanation that really appealed to me was that offered by the Yanks, as it showed a typical transatlantic sense of humour. It was simply 'Camel to Consumer'.

With regret we departed for Lourenço Marques (now renamed Maputo) in Mozambique, Portuguese East Africa. Here we had to anchor outside the harbour for nine days, as there happened to be eight ships before us, all waiting to load coal, and there were only two coaling berths. Just as we hoped to go alongside, another two ships arrived and, for some reason, were given priority. This caused a delay of another three days.

The coal came in huge trucks almost the size of a railway carriage, and was dumped on to a chute that fed the coal into the hold. As the trucks carried 33½ tons and dropped it 15 yards, it was a very messy business with coal dust everywhere.

The town was not of much account save for a casino that was said at one time to have rivalled the one in Monte Carlo. We paid a visit there and saw some fools being quickly parted from their money.

I was very glad when we finished loading the coal and the ship was washed down. We had an uneventful passage to the Cape Verde Islands and landed up off Mindelo, a town on the island of Saint Vincent. Seemingly this island got 2 hours of rainfall a year, so its golf course was mainly baked earth. Other islands had mountains and enjoyed more rain.

This Cape Verde Islands provided a coaling station for ships going to South America. We did not go alongside but remained at anchor and discharged the coal into barges. This was another messy business as the trade wind blew at force six, more or less constantly, and scattered dust everywhere. If the wind rose above force six, the barges became difficult to control, so much so that discharging was impossible and was cancelled. This resulted in our taking 16 days to unload the cargo.

At East London I thought that the men had a raw deal having to work for £1 10s a week. Here it was much worse. Noticing their dismayed faces when the weather got too rough, I made enquiries and found that they were paid £1 10s, not per day but per ship! So, bad weather meant idleness – and idleness meant no pay!

Some members of the crew bought several guinea fowls here. I suppose it was to give them a supply of fresh eggs. Whether or not they achieved their end I cannot say, but the fowls kicked up an almighty din all the way home and proved very annoying. This sort of thing was very common on Greek ships where live poultry and goats were regularly carried.

There was nothing ashore and I was pleased when we departed for Freetown. Arriving there, we sailed about 15 miles up the river to the small village of Pepel, where we took on a cargo of iron ore.

Leaving Pepel I was giving a hand with the moorings when I suffered a cut from handling a hawser. It was near the knuckle of the index finger of my right hand, and I thought little of it at first but, after a week, it began to swell and turn septic. The skipper told me to see the steward about it and I did so.

He was a huge portly man who had some throat affliction and could speak only very huskily. His intention was to lance the swelling and he reached for a scalpel contained in a filthy leather wallet. I did not fancy this and suggested that he either dip the blade in a flame or, at least, boiling water. He took umbrage at this criticism and refused to treat me.

I carried on for a few days and remember seeing the lights of Las Palmas in the Canary Islands as I asked the 2nd Mate if he had ever heard of a ship leaving her route to take a member of the crew to another port for treatment. His disturbing reply was that, if any member of a crew was in such a condition as to require this, he would probably not survive anyway. Another worry was that two red lines appeared on my forearm. Lay opinion on the lower deck judged this to be a very bad sign, possibly with terminal consequences.

At this point I must confess that during the war U-boats and aircraft did not scare me as much as they did some of my mates. This was not because I was braver in any way or even more foolhardy than my fellows. It was because I had a far greater fear – and a greater fear drives out a lesser one.

My continual dread was to be taken ill at sea 1,000 miles from the nearest doctor. I often imagined the captain telling me that the Mate and he were of the opinion that I had an appendicitis. They then speculated that I would die if they did not do anything, but could give no guarantee for my recovery if they did. I thought of possible anaesthetics and came to the conclusion that it was either a half bottle of rum, or more likely the carpenter's mallet.

In addition to the 2nd Mate's books of study, those going up for Chief Mate's certificates get *Meteorology for Masters and Mates* and such like. Those after a Master's certificate have extra books on maritime law, and one more that used to send shivers down my spine merely to read it in print – it was called *Simple Surgery at Sea for Masters*!

The following evening the swelling was such that I could not get my arm into my patrol jacket and I contacted the skipper. He advised that I should see the steward in the morning and have him put kaolin poultices on it. This was tried without success as the kaolin formed a hard surface through which no matter could penetrate.

The captain decided that it had to be soft bread steeped in boiling water. He would take my place on the bridge during the forenoon watch so that I could be treated by the steward, and intimated that, if he could not hear me yelling, the water was not hot enough.

The steward's idea was to place the bread in a sieve and put this in a pot of water. When the water reached boiling point he quickly lifted the sieve and clapped its entire contents on to my hand. The pain was intense and I pointed out to the steward that there was no need to scald the whole of the hand, only the small part at the seat of the trouble. He husked away that he knew what he was doing and that I was not to complain.

This was done every 2 hours, and as I yelled he husked, 'Bear the pain … bear the pain.' I think he must have had a streak of sadism in him. After six doses the hand began to leak horrible yellow pus, followed by clearer stuff with some black matter in it.

The last poultice was administered just as we were entering the Bay of Biscay. Being a sailor, I knew that we were about to alter course to starboard and the ship would most likely roll a bit. Just after he had applied the hot bread I felt the ship turning but, out of spite, I made no remark.

He had the pot of hot water precariously balanced on a table and, as the vessel listed a little to starboard, the pot slipped off and landed on his foot. Since he was wearing socks it was for all the world like a poultice. He rose in agony, tearing the socks off and grasping the side of his bunk with such passion that I thought he would tear the bunk off the bulkhead. Being unable to yell, he emitted what can be best described as a very loud husk. If I had had a bit more courage, and/or he had been a bit smaller, I should have counselled him to 'bear the pain'.

Just outside the River Tees we picked up the pilot. He had a fresh complexion and rosy cheeks, causing the skipper to look at me and remark how yellow I seemed. I replied that he also had the same look, and we realised that the constant dosing with quinine had given us this appearance. We arrived at Middlesbrough where I agreed to stay by the ship while the 2nd Mate went home on leave. I now had 13 days leave due me.

Since the war was over, officers could bring their wives on board for short spells. On this occasion two of the engineers had their wives down to live on the ship for a few days. I dare say it would be a welcome change for these women not to have to think about food rationing.

As part of our tea one evening we had tinned red salmon and, while ashore, we were all looking forward to having the remains of this for our supper sandwiches. Coming back in eager expectation we were horrified to learn that there was no salmon left – the women had given it all to the ship's cat!

13

The 'run job'

My next trip was to be what was known as a 'run job'. During the war, sailors might be sent to the USA to join a new ship and always there would be a week or two before the ship was ready for the crew. Given that there was a great shortage of labour ashore, they could take up employment while they lived in a hotel and were on ship's wages. It was something devoutly to be wished. But after hostilities ceased, and there was plenty of labour ashore, the prospect was not so enticing.

Ninety ships had been built by the Canadians that all had 'Fort' in their names. They were purchased by the USA Government and transferred to Britain under the Lease-Lend terms. I joined the oil-burning *Fort Aspin* at Middlesbrough on 16 July 1946, and she was supposed to sail to Montreal where we were to pick up the coal-burning *Dentonia Park* and bring her back to Britain in exchange. The oil-burner was presently owned by Thomas Dunlop & Sons and the other was to be taken over by Watts Watts of London.

When on the *Masunda* in Middlesbrough three weeks earlier I had dated a girl called Audrey, but she had not turned up one evening. I met her again by chance and she apologised and explained that she had had to work late. Unbeknown to me, the 2nd Mate of the *Fort Aspin* had met her before my arrival, and we had shared her night about for four days, as one of us had to stay on board each evening on watch. It was quite a joke with the others.

The Chief Mate had recently left the Burmah Oil Company. They had offered me a job when I left the *Radcombe*, but as they signed off and on in Asia and the period was for two years, I had declined. Our Mate looked as if he had spent too long in the company for his skin was a little yellow and he had a distinctly oriental look about him.

The 2nd Mate, David Robb, was a very decent lad whose parents ran an hotel past Clachnaharry on the way to Dingwall in Scotland. He had served his apprenticeship with Andrew Weir (known as the Bank Line, because all its ships had a name ending in 'Bank') and had spent nearly all of his time on the Australian run.

As I write this I have the old sight book on my lap and can see that the *Fort Aspin* was having days when her average speed was 10.45 knots and her general average speed from Middlesbrough to Montreal was 9.6 knots.

Our Atlantic crossing was without any incident until we reached the Straits of Belle Isle, which is the strip of water between Newfoundland and Canada, and is famed for fog. Now, rain does not bother a sailor nor, up to a point, does wind. His two chief enemies are fog and ice, and the Straits of Belle Isle are where you can meet them both at the same time!

I thought of the time on the *Newton Pine* when I had to carry sacks of wheat from one side of the ship to the other, and thought how wonderful it would be to be an officer. I, of course, then knew very little of an officer's life.

For 4 hours on the bridge I spent the time peering through night glasses at the fog and watching for ice. Other ships were in the vicinity and sounding their whistles. But fog can be most deceiving: you hear a ship's whistle and estimate that she must be about four points on the starboard bow. But the fog plays tricks with sounds and when the mist clears a little you find she is dead ahead and steaming straight towards you. After 4 very weary hours doing nothing but watch out for ice and other ships through the fog, I felt like a worn-out rag – yet I had lifted nothing heavier that a pair of binoculars.

Captain Douglas was on the bridge without a break for 27 hours and finally collapsed and had to be carried off the bridge. Those who think physical work is more stressful than mental have a great deal to learn.

The master is always in charge of the ship and this is a fact of life that all masters must face. They are always responsible for the safety of the vessel, regardless of circumstances. If Captain Douglas had come down off the bridge badly in need of sleep, and left the Mate in charge, he would still be liable for anything untoward happening to the vessel. Many folk think that once a pilot is on board he can be blamed if any accident happens when he is manoeuvring the ship. This is not so. The pilot is there to 'assist' the master. The captain is always in command for, if he does not think the pilot is up to the job, it is his duty to ask for a different pilot.

We cleared Belle Isle and started the two-to-three days sail up the Saint Lawrence River to Montreal. At one point the Jacques Cartier Bridge spans the river and it seems to be some kind of optical illusion, for you will swear that your main mast will never go safely under it.

We safely berthed in Montreal and the rumours began. One

said that a Greek concern was buying our ship, but that a Canadian company was going to run her for two years. Another favourite claimed that we were to load pit props in Quebec. One thing was sure, and that was that the *Dentonia Park* was not to be seen anywhere.

An official representing the British Ministry of War Transport boarded us. I imagined that he would do a very thorough check on our stores, since the ship was to be disposed of, but he did not seem to have any interest in this, and spent a very short time on board.

Montreal is the largest city in Canada and is nearly 1,000 miles from the Atlantic Ocean. It is situated on Montreal Island and its great harbour stretches 16 miles along the river. It takes its name from Mont Réal (Royal Mountain), which rises 750 feet behind the city; on its summit is a huge cross that is lit up at night and may be seen for miles.

As it looked as if we might be a considerable time on the *Fort Aspin* doing nothing (because there was nothing to do), we asked the Mate if we could seek employment ashore as riggers. The engineers had already found jobs at $1.20 an hour and we wanted to do likewise. The Mate said he could not release us as something might turn up.

This ship had an office equipped with a typewriter and I began typing all my letters home. It was a great saving in weight for airmails. One day the Mate asked me if I would type out an inventory of the ship's stores. This I did, and two days later he claimed to have made a mistake, and asked if I would type the list again. Having nothing to do, and looking for practice in typing, I readily agreed. The only change I could see was that he had scored out six mooring ropes and replaced the number by five. I was just at this point when I fancied a break for a smoke. I went out on the deck, where the deck crew were engaged in lowering a mooring rope over the side on to a small lorry marked 'Happy Harry – Ship Chandler'. Now, mooring ropes were many fathoms long and their price new was £1 per fathom, so I was watching some serious money snaking (or sneaking) its way over the ship's side. I do not know what price Harry was paying the Mate, but both certainly looked happy.

Two days later the Mate alleged to have made another error and wanted his inventory of stores retyped. I scanned the list and found that this time he had substituted three wire hawsers for the original four. So it was no surprise to see the same chandler's vehicle on the dock and a wire making its way on to the back of it.

The radio was on when we were lunching and we had our first taste of commercial radio. Every day at 12 noon we had to listen to some odious woman named Aunt Lucy who told a short story about how white she got her husband's shirts by using Rinso. This was an entirely new experience for us, and how we loathed it!

Talking of radio, there was a never-ending stream, from the USA, of anti-Soviet propaganda, which I found most depressing. The magazines and papers joined in this and gave me the impression that another war was likely.

There was a radio programme on this subject called *Town Meeting of the Air* and it broadcast a debate between Max Eastman (then editor of *Reader's Digest*) and a Mr Laski, who was chairman of the British Labour Party. Laski won so overwhelmingly that it lifted my gloom somewhat. Laski was an outstanding orator. When the debate was thrown open to the audience he was asked some awkward questions. Hardy had the questioner stopped speaking when Laski began his response. There were no pauses at all in his reply. It was almost as if he had had a week's notice of the question, had done a considerable amount of research, put it into first-class English, typed it out and was reading it. Never again have I heard anything like him.

The crew were fairly keen to play football and I was elected to be sports officer. I therefore arranged for the deck department to play the engine room and we were defeated 6-3. From the 22 players on show, a first 11 was picked and it was fixed up that we played the Canadian firm Vicker's. The evening before the match, money was dished out to the crew with the result that only six of the chosen team were sober. The sailors were a respectable bunch but the firemen could not resist a drink.

We fielded a team of sorts and relied on Vicker's to supply the boots. This was disastrous. Some had no laces, some had soles hanging off, and most had a fair quota of nails in them. Vicker's had four substitutes, as was allowed by Canadian regulations, and they were allowed to come on to the field at any time if the referee was given notice.

Despite all the odds, we were beaten by only 4-0, and luck was against us at that. I thought it very unsporting of Vicker's not to have seen that we had decent gear. I was also extremely annoyed that certain of the crew were too drunk to play, so I washed my hands of the whole business. I was reserve for the first 11, and had to take the place of one of the drunkards. But what angered me most was that, if our picked team had been there and had half-decent boots, Vicker's would have had no chance. The ship's team was really good. Given some training and practice they could have beaten any team in Montreal.

The Mate asked David Robb and me if we would like to earn some money and we eagerly assented. He wanted the stores in all four lifeboats to be removed, the boats cleaned and painted and the stores returned to them. The crew were to do the work and David and I were to supervise. We both thought that, as we were not acting as officers, we should get into boiler suits and muck in with the crew. The Mate did not care one way or the other, and we were all paid the same rate of 70 cents an hour. After this was over he wanted the masts, the funnel and the ventilators painted.

Slowly it dawned on me what he was up to. It now seemed that the *Fort Aspin* was to be taken over by a Greek concern who wanted her painted, and we were a lot cheaper than hiring Canadians to do the work. I think that he must have contracted a price with them and was, in addition, using ship's paint.

The bonus for the Mate was that Dunlop's peacetime garb was a stone-coloured funnel with black top and a small white ring, about 4 feet deep. The Greek colours were identical except that their small ring was royal blue. The Mate would have needed to buy about a quarter of a gallon of blue paint out of his own pocket. That must have hurt.

As a change from rumour, we had definite news now that the *Dentonia Park* was at present in Cyprus and not expected in Montreal for at least another five weeks. The *Fort Aspin*, under her new owners, was supposed to load general cargo in New York on 5 September.

After five and a half weeks in Montreal, the crew were taken to the Seamen's Mission to board there. Three days later we were taken by bus to the Hotel Papineau, named thus because it was at the corner of Papineau Street and Ontario Street. No one was expecting us, so we had to wait an hour for them to get the rooms ready. They had no porters or lifts, so we had to take all the luggage up to the rooms ourselves. Fortunately David and I had packed a long piece of log-line and, with the aid of this, we hauled the cases and sea-bags up the fire escape.

When the 11 rooms were prepared, the 2nd Mate and I could not get adjacent rooms and were offered a double room. At first I was against it but, on seeing that it was more than twice the size of any of the others, I accepted. It also had its own bath and toilet and, above all, a piano.

We were not aware of it at the time, but it was the Bridal Suite, and this later caused much merriment. As was typical of many Canadian hotels, all the rooms had beds that folded up and disappeared into the wall during the day. Likewise the tables and benches we used when eating, so that when we were neither sleeping nor eating there was considerable space.

The captain had gone to the Hotel Windsor and, it was said, had it not been for a sudden demand by tourists we would have been there ourselves. Although the Windsor was a superior hotel, we fared much better. The Hotel Papineau had a cafeteria and we could come down at any time for meals. If we had had a late night and wanted to sleep in, we could have breakfast at 11am and lunch at 3pm. I doubt if the Hotel Windsor would have offered that.

The Hotel Papineau was staffed entirely by French-speakers. Here was a chance to try out our French, but the French spoken in the province of Quebec was not much like that spoken in France, and finally we all gave up.

At first we were not sure just how much food we were allowed. Rumours mentioned $2.50 a day, but as time went on and no queries were made we ate more and more. Our breakfast usually meant a glass of fruit juice followed by a cereal and two boiled eggs. Later we found that we could have half cream and half milk with our cereal instead of milk, so we opted for that. A great favourite was steak, egg and chips. There were two meatless days every week. I suspect this was a token and nothing more for, on these days, one could eat a whole salmon or half a chicken.

The only snag was the jukebox. At that time the current popular song was *Doing What Comes Naturally* and the jukebox 'naturally' had this on its menu. We would be having a meal when someone would put on this tune. A few minutes passed and somebody would enter from outside (a non-resident) and, sure enough, the jukebox would begin to play the song again.

At first we locked the door of our room every night but, as some nights we did not get to bed until very early next morning, there was a tendency to oversleep. The maid had orders to wake us no later than 10am, but she could not get us to stir, so we decided to leave the door open so that she could give us a shake. This would ensure that we now did not sleep too long.

However, one particular day we came back very late and just flopped into bed. About 8am the old Chief Engineer came into our room and gave me a shake. He told me that he had gone to the bathroom but, when returning to his own room, had found a man coming out of it. Investigation led to his discovery that £20 of his money was missing. I was half asleep and resentful of being woken so early and lay there drowsy for a few minutes. I saw my trousers where I had left them with the braces hanging over the wardrobe door and silhouetted by the morning light coming in through the window. Surely we were safe from this intruder – I had certainly heard nothing. Still half asleep I casually put my hand into the pockets of the trousers and woke up very abruptly – both pockets were empty!

Immediately I woke David and asked if his cash was all right, and he felt for his wallet, which he had wisely put under his pillow. It

The 'run job'

was still there. I cursed my stupidity at leaving the trousers so exposed in an unlocked room.

We all had an early breakfast that day and the 2nd Engineer asked the Chief if he could recognise the man. The old Chief was fairly certain that the man was sitting two tables away from us. The 2nd Engineer suggested we jump on him and search his pockets. I agreed, but the Chief backed down and began to express doubts. The 2nd then asked me if I still agreed, but I had nothing to offer as evidence. I had had $15 stolen, but finding 15 Canadian dollars in this man's pockets would prove nothing, whereas the Chief had lost four £5 Bank of England notes and, if these were in the man's possession, he would need to have a good reason for having them. So the affair fizzled out and I had to borrow some money from David until our next sub was due.

We had a wonderful six weeks in this hotel. What a change from the fare onboard ship, and how we appreciated it. But all good things come to and end and we had to join the *Dentonia Park*. It seemed that we were to load grain. This would usually take two days but, since there had been a railway strike that had tied up masses of rolling stock and it had only just ended, we had to join a queue of vessels waiting to load.

I used to date a Canadian girl, Pauline, who was a widow; her husband having been shot down and killed as a pilot in the RCAF. She was good company, though she had not yet got over the loss of her husband. I felt sorry for her and preferred her company rather than risk a serious attachment with a single girl. I was introduced to her husband's sister and later David partnered her and we made up a foursome.

She worked in Morgan's, one of the big stores, and she did not stop work until 6pm. As she lived a fair bit out of town at St Zotique, by the time she got home and had a meal we were not ready for an evening out until about 9pm. Not that this mattered, for the night life continued in Montreal into the small hours of the morning.

Often we finished up at a restaurant called the Old Mill. Instead of the usual jukebox, they had a trio of piano, violin and violoncello playing good music, and all round the walls were pictures of the great composers.

On a Sunday morning I used to take her and her girlfriend to Mont Réal, which was a big park where many folk were riding beautiful brown horses with platinum manes and tails. These were known as palominos.

There were two large cathedrals being built and these were almost finished. To get to them one had to climb about 100 steps, and there were many folk kneeling and saying a prayer on each step. On reaching the top we went into the first building, which was completely empty apart from a table holding little jars with lighted candles in them and a notice saying 'Brûlez pour vos intentions'. The place was deemed to be so holy that I had to give each girl a handkerchief to cover her head. Despite this, the first thing that one saw when entering was a 5 feet by 4 feet metal plate on the wall advertising Sweet Caporal cigarettes!

Our evening jaunts continued, but one night we overdid it. By the time I had seen Pauline back to her home in St Zotique, trolley cars were becoming scarcer. I arrived at 4am at a depot about 2 miles from the ship. Now, at 4am, even the night life of Montreal was winding down, and there was no immediate prospect of getting a trolley back to the ship. I was told that I would have to wait for 25 minutes.

Reasoning that, by the time the trolley reached the depot, I could have almost walked back to the ship, I decided not to wait and set off at a brisk pace. Now, I have always loved walking and, from an early age, developed a habit of walking very quickly – even if not in a hurry -- so much so that if I am accompanying someone who walks slowly I tire readily as, to me, it is unaccustomed exercise and more akin to balancing on one foot then the other rather than walking.

It was a warm autumn night and I was striding along at more than 4 miles an hour when I was abruptly stopped by a policeman's truncheon sticking out in front of me. He had been standing in the doorway of a shop.

'Where are you going, bud?' he asked.

'Back home,' I replied.

'Where's that?'

'To my ship,' said I, mentioning the name of the dock.

'Why are you not taking a trolley car?' was the next question.

'I can be back just as quickly by walking,' I ventured.

'But do you not know that there's a trolley leaving the depot in a few minutes?'

'Yes, I know, but I prefer to walk.'

'You prefer to walk?' he exploded.

In a country where few people would walk 200 yards if there was a taxi available, this must have sounded to him as if I was trying to be insolent. After a few seconds to recover from this seemingly irrational reply, he resumed by asking if I had my papers with me to prove that I was a sailor. I searched my pockets in vain. This was the one night I had left them on the ship.

'I'm sorry, I don't appear to have them with me.'

'Did you come round past that bank?'
'What bank?' I answered, not knowing the district.
'The one over there,' he indicated, pointing his truncheon.
'I don't know the area and I don't know of any bank here.'
'All right,' he ended. 'You look like a sailor. On your way.'

I suppose my dialect might have helped him make up his mind but, on thinking back on the incident, it was more than likely that he was not used to seeing anybody race along at my speed, and decided the best course of action was to stop me. If I had been up to mischief, or if someone was pursuing me, a delay of 10 minutes might have caused me to panic and run off.

Talking of trolley cars, Montreal had huge ones nearly twice the length of a British bus. Inside, the breadth would be well over 2 yards. In busy tines they would hook up a second trolley to the main one and I never saw anyone not being able to board one because it was overcrowded.

We had been altogether 20 weeks in Montreal and I was beginning to tire of it. The French were not very cordial and if asked a question in English would pretend that they did not understand.

The town's authority ended at Rue St Laurent. If a Jehovah's Witness was selling *The Watchtower* on one side of the street this was accepted. But if he was to cross to the other side he was liable to imprisonment. Quebec was more Roman than Rome; there had been a time when things looked bleak in Italy and they were all prepared to receive the Pope if the need had arisen.

Time was moving on, winter was about to strike and if we waited much longer we would be frozen in until April, as had almost happened to the *Newton Pine* in 1941. As it was, we were the last vessel to go down the river – another day later and we should have had no pilot, or no insurance, I forget which.

The *Dentonia Park* was not quite as comfortable as the *Fort Aspin*, but nevertheless better than most British ships. The crossing was no worse than could be expected for the end of November and beginning of December, and we finally berthed at Meadowside Granary on the River Clyde. Again, I have the old sight book to hand and see that her speed was somewhat similar to the *Fort Aspin*'s.

I remember, as we came within range of British radio, hearing a voice say, 'Good evening, this is the BBC and here is the 6 o'clock news.' A spontaneous yell of delight went up from all the listeners, thrilled to be back hearing non-commercial radio with none of the infantile advertising interruptions. Aunt Lucy making shirts white using Rinso was now a thing of the past!

14

My last ship: part 1

Some time during my leave I met Arthur Fisken and we had a long chat. He had failed in his signals examination and was forced to go back to sea for several months before coming home to pass his 2nd Mate's ticket at the second attempt. We thought that we would like to ship out together after our leave was up.

The first ship to come up with vacancies for 2nd and 3rd Mates was owned by Nourse, a subsidiary of the P&O Line, I was told. She was brand new and we went down to see her. It was most disappointing to find that a new ship did not have hot and cold running water in her cabins and we declined the offer, after telling them what we thought of the accommodation. This was a mistake. We were not to know that the first time the ship reached the Orient, her quarters would be completely overhauled and brought up to a very high standard.

Next there were two jobs going on the *Celtic Monarch*, belonging to Raeburn & Verel Ltd of Glasgow. We knew that we could not both be 2nd Mates, and that one would have to go as 3rd. I had a feeling that Arthur, having sailed as 2nd Mate, did not want to drop a rank and, more than willingly, I offered to be 3rd Mate.

The position was this. My basic salary would be £5 a month lower than Arthur's, but I would receive a bonus of £3 because I had a certificate superior to my station. Arthur would get his basic pay and no bonus, as he did not have a Chief Mate's certificate. In other words, he would receive £2 a month more than me and, when income tax was deducted, he would be only about 5 shillings a week better off.

The 2nd Mate had the middle watch, of midnight to 4am, and went on watch again at noon. However, he could not sleep all through his period off watch as, apart from it causing him to miss his breakfast, he required to be up on the bridge to take his morning sight. Down in the tropics this is a simple matter of a few minutes, but in the North Atlantic it is vastly different. The sun does not beam down invitingly on you for minutes at a time, but shyly peeps out from behind clouds maybe for a few seconds only. You could wait a very long time for a mere glimpse.

Arthur would come off watch at 4pm and, even if he wanted to, there would be not much chance of having sleep during the dog watches (4pm to 8pm) as this was traditionally when all the noise occurred; the senior officers were on watch then, and anyone was at liberty to make a din. At any other time of day, if there was any noise there was a reminding cry of admonition, 'Watch below', meaning that some members of the crew are trying to sleep.

So the poor 2nd Mate could never get an unbroken sleep. The 3rd had to check the lifeboats, fire-fighting equipment and flags, but the 2nd has to keep all the charts up to date by amending them. Hardly a day passed without the Radio Officer handing him a note of various amendments to the ship's charts.

I had successfully refused 2nd Mate's positions on more than one occasion, and had made up my mind not to accept one until I had my Chief Mate's ticket. Then I would receive a bonus on top of 2nd Mate's pay, whereas I doubt if the shipping companies would pay a double bonus were I to continue as 3rd Mate after acquiring a Chief Mate's Certificate.

We ambled down to the head office on 13 January 1947 and enquired after the jobs. The clerk asked who was to go 2nd and I indicated that it was to be Arthur. He asked to see our certificates and immediately protested that mine was a superior ticket, meaning that I had had mine longer than Arthur. I replied that we had made our decision and it was not up to a clerk to dispute with us; all he was required to do was to sign us on. I had no great love of head office staff and it maddened me the way some skippers would treat them like Royalty when they were only glorified office boys.

Thus on that day we signed on the *Celtic Monarch*. For the privilege of sailing together again we were to pay a heavy price. Her engines were in a poor state and were to be like a leaking sore. The cabins had been removed from the wings of her bridge, leaving it very draughty. The wheelhouse was unbelievably small; in fact, there was room only for the man at the wheel.

One of the first things I noticed when inspecting the bridge and chart room was that she had various instruments like an anemometer (for measuring the speed of the wind), a rain gauge and, in addition to the usual aneroid barometer, a Torricellian one; this is a type of mercury barometer and is much more accurate than the ordinary aneroid, whose main virtue is that it is very sensitive and will detect changes in barometric pressure very quickly. The Torricellian has a gadget called a 'Gold Scale' (named after the naval officer who invented it) and this allows adjustments to be made easily so that weather reports from various ships and areas can be compared. There has to be a standard latitude, temperature and height above sea level, and the Gold Scale does the job admirably. All this pointed to one thing – the *Celtic Monarch* was a weather ship.

Obviously there were other vessels, such as liners, that would send in weather reports, so why was an old tramp steamer chosen? It could possibly be because we would visit remote corners of the earth where regular lines never ventured.

I began to feel elated at the prospect of sending information about ocean currents in distant parts of the world when I recalled a conversation I had previously had with the 2nd Mate of the *Athelregent*. He had told me that if ever I found out anything worthwhile I should not send the information to Greenwich, but should prefer the US Hydrographer. He went on to recount how some old skipper had furnished Greenwich with findings over a period of 30 years and received a small diary for his pains. Others who had sent their stuff to the US Hydrographer were given masses of useful charts and advice.

On the first evening I was given a sandwich for my supper. On opening it I discovered it to be full of red ants. I had never come across this before and no one had warned me about them. I had to throw the stuff out. Afterwards I learned to wrap the sandwiches in greaseproof paper and hang the parcel from a string on the deckhead – this gave me a 2-hour start on the ants.

The captain, John Keir, aged 44 from Glasgow, was an old sailing-ship man. Her Chief Mate was a very pleasant young lad from Fochabers in the Moray Firth, and very young for a Chief Mate. Her Radio Officer let me know that we gave him weather reports every 6 hours and he transmitted them to Greenwich.

We had hardly left the dock when the engines gave trouble. I envisaged another few days in Glasgow but we managed down to Gourock where our compasses were adjusted, and we left at 6am. Nothing seemed to work properly. The telephone to below was a creature of moods, working when it took the notion, the whistle on the funnel was as hoarse as a crow, and the chronometer had an unpredictable error. Chronometers were very accurate clocks placed in gimbals like the compass, so that they were not affected by the ship's movements. They were set to Greenwich Mean Time and their errors checked whenever possible so that their rate of gain or loss could be predicted.

Every spot on the earth's surface has its own time. Indeed, before the railways appeared each town in Britain had its own time. Even after the railways had altered this anomaly, I recollect that

Ireland's time was 20 or 25 minutes later than the UK's. So basically the morning sight determined the ship's apparent time and, after this was converted to the ship's mean time, it was compared with the chronometer and the difference was the longitude in terms of time.

At noon each day the skipper, 2nd Mate and 3rd Mate took the altitude of the sun as it rose higher and higher in the sky. When it reached its maximum it was relatively easy to calculate the ship's latitude. Earlier on, a position line giving the ship's longitude was worked out by noting the chronometer at the time of taking the sun's altitude. This line was run up to the noon latitude and the ship's position was then determined. From it the distance travelled that day and also the average speed and the general average speed from the start of the voyage could be assessed.

The first time we took our noon sight and agreed it, the Old Man almost immediately proclaimed the ship's position and shortly afterwards the distance sailed and the average speed. Arthur, who was not much good at mathematics, was completely baffled, but I had a good idea how it was done by using pre-calculated data, and explained this to Arthur so that we could now compete with him. The Old Man had the advantage as it was he who decided which of our three noon altitudes we would use – usually his own.

Just after we entered the Bay of Biscay the weather turned very bad and our boiler gave trouble, slowing us down to 5 knots. Two days later our speed had dropped to between 2 and 3 knots and we had done only 85 miles in 24 hours. It was nigh impossible to steer at this speed, so the ship seemed to be on every point of the compass except the correct course. This caused her to roll heavily. The worse she rolled, the longer it would take to fix the boiler, and the longer this took, the more she rolled.

After we left the Bay, the boiler was repaired and the weather improved, although there was still a swell. We had a few concerts on Arthur's gramophone and, as he had brought a violin, I practised a bit on it and played duets with one of the apprentices who had a mandolin.

Every 6 hours (based on Greenwich Mean Time) we had to assess the state of the sea, the direction and force of the wind, the height of any clouds, the visibility, the temperature, and the barometric pressure – suitably corrected. We then consulted a chart to give all of the data appropriate letters. For instance, 'u' stood for an ugly, threatening sky and possibly the precursor of a hurricane. I often thought what would happen if I popped this into the reckoning, and how much alarm it would cause. After this was done, the whole report was transferred into blocks of five letters and given to the Radio

Officer to transmit to Greenwich.

For the first few days out this did not pose a problem. Once we got further from home our 'sparks' had no means of transmitting the message direct to Greenwich and had to contact other ships to see if they would relay it for us. Now, many Radio Officers know one another and, when there are no official duties to be done, they merrily chat away among themselves. Their speed of sending is so fast that no other person can find out what they are talking about.

As soon as our Radio Officer cut in with a request for somebody to transmit a weather report to Greenwich, these conversations abruptly ceased and the air went quiet. Sometimes we had to wait for 5 hours before anyone was willing to oblige us, and by this time we were nearly ready for another report.

I recall the 'sparks' gloomily remarking to me, 'There would appear to be a sad lack of cooperation among my colleagues.'

On 7 February we passed the Canary Islands and the temperature was just over 68°F, but four days later it rose to more than 72°F when we were abreast of the Cape Verde Islands.

We reached Freetown on 13 February. I went ashore with the Old Man, who had been a pilot there for 20 months during the war and knew many folks in the town. One of them kindly offered to get me syrup, raisins and peaches (but no sugar) to take home. The temperature was 95°F but the mosquitoes did not give us much trouble.

The west coast of Africa has a rainy season. Before the rains come the heat is stifling, but the real discomfort is caused by the humidity. Everyone looks forward to the rain as it takes away much of this clamminess. Tropical rain comes down in torrents and to cope with this Freetown had gutters at the side of the streets; these were about 12 inches wide and nearly 16 inches deep, and in the rainy season they were usually overflowing!

On board the *Celtic Monarch* was a junior apprentice making his first trip. He had never been outside Scotland before and Freetown was another world to him. As we were walking along the street together a young African woman was gliding along, stripped to the waist and carrying a bundle on her head. Years of doing this had given her a magnificent carriage – and pair! The apprentice was more interested in the pair and had never seen anything like them before, so he kept giving her furtive glances. His object was to see as much as possible, without being seen to be seeing. Paying more attention to the damsel than to where he was going, he suddenly stumbled into one of these big gutters and fell down, much to the amusement of his shipmates.

Without much ado, we loaded the iron ore up river at Pepel. We did not load the ship down to its marks on the Plimsoll Line because the water where we were loading was almost fresh. With the use of a hydrometer we measured the density of the dock water and from this calculated how much more cargo we could load, so that we would be on the proper Plimsoll marking when we were in salt water. For the average tramp steamer the TPI (tons per inch immersion) at the Plimsoll Line would be about 40, and this would mean that, if we had 2½ inches to play with, we could load another 100 tons.

We headed back home for Middlesbrough. The temperature plummeted and I remember coming up the North Sea with 6 inches of snow on our hatches. We tied up at the LNER berth and I found, to my disgust, that all trains to Scotland had been cancelled. As we had been away for just about six weeks my leave entitlement was only three days.

Now, I required 18 months as a watch-keeping officer to entitle me to sit for my Chief Mate's Certificate. This certificate covered much the same ground as the 2nd Mate's but had more difficult applications and the candidate had to work at a greater speed; in addition, it had the extra subject of meteorology. A simple calculation revealed that I had served the necessary 18 months plus 26 days!

The winter of 1946-47 turned out to be the coldest since 1880-81. This had exacerbated fuel shortages that had already brought short-time working to many factories and steel mills. Lack of coal had also curbed supplies of electricity and gas, making more than 4,000,000 workers idle through power cuts. Now coal was piling up at the pits, unable to be moved along roads, and rail lines were blocked by snow. Many shivering domestic consumers of coal had been without heat or light during the daytime for much of February. To rub salt in the already festering wounds, the meat ration was reduced again.

I did not have much use for spending my three days leave in Middlesbrough, so I asked the captain where our next trip was likely to take us. He reckoned that it would possibly be another trip to Pepel for iron ore, lasting probably about six weeks. So Arthur and I signed on again; there was little else we could do.

This decision was to alter the course of my life, although I did not know it at the time. When the war finished, the Government had taken the decision to give university grants to all members of the services, and to order the universities to take 90% of their entrants from these former servicemen – which was a bit rough on those leaving school then. I had put in my name some time earlier for one of these grants, and had been hoping to be awarded one so that I could get a BSc degree in civil engineering. Had I been able to get to Glasgow I might have managed to clinch the deal or, if not, to sit the Chief Mate's examination.

Very soon it became obvious that a six-week voyage back to Pepel was out of the question and we would be six weeks in Middlesbrough getting repairs!

Round about this time our Federation and the National Union of Seamen hammered out a new deal about conditions at sea. When I got round to reading it I could not believe how crass our representatives had been. The contract was full of loose phraseology like 'when suitable' or 'at the master's discretion' or 'when convenient', etc. We were to be allowed an extra day's leave for every Sunday at sea but – at the master's discretion – this could mean getting leave for a day up in the jungle at Pepel!

Our Chief Mate had several days leave due to him and chose to pay off and go home. We were without a Mate for six days and the usual rumours proliferated, one stating that we were to get a former officer from P&O. This I found hard to believe, as P&O was a very classy company and I could not envisage any of their officers joining what, I had discovered, was a very poor tramp. P&O used to ape the Royal Navy and I believe that they had dress uniforms that included a sword. We joked about this and often commented that it would be useful for cleaning out the scuppers. But for once a rumour turned out to be true.

Our new Mate was about 48 years of age and came from Kirkcaldy. He had a double-barrelled surname and would dearly have loved to have been addressed by his full title but never got it. As one half of the name was much shorter than the other, that was what he was always called.

He had served his time as apprentice on some sailing schooner and had joined P&O, rising to the rank of Chief Mate. According to his tale, he contracted some ailment that was aggravated by heat. He was thus advised by his doctor to leave P&O as its runs were invariably to the tropics. He became skipper of the *Empire Blackwater*, a ship run by the Ministry of War Transport.

Now, the question everybody was asking was, why had he landed on us as Mate? He turned out to be an arrogant man and very stubborn, and I had my own theory about the circumstances that brought him to us. You see, when a seaman of any capacity went to the shipping office for a post, he was offered a total of three vessels. This in effect meant that he had two choices, for if he refused the first two on offer, the third was sure to be the most undesirable one on their books and one that they desperately wanted to be rid of. I could just imagine our Chief Mate refusing all three and being demoted to Mate.

Having served his time in sail and having had a reasonable education, I think he thought that he might lord it over his fellow officers. The first shock he received was to discover that both the 2nd and 3rd Mates had their Scottish Higher Leaving Certificates. However, the real jolt was when he learned that, not only had our skipper served his time in sail, but had also been bosun of the *Archibald Russell*, a four-masted barque running down to South America.

He wanted to impose liner standards on us and we would not have it. On tramps, dress was informal and the officers normally wore battledress with a navy blue jersey; wearing collar and tie on a Sunday if they felt like doing so.

'In the P&O, every man's feet are on the deck at 7am,' was his proposition.

Our argument was that we were not getting passenger ship accommodation or food, and were not going to countenance passenger ship dress or discipline. He had to settle for this, getting no support from the Old Man.

One day he was regaling Arthur and me with stories of life in the P&O. According to our new Mate the living quarters were palatial and the food was plentiful and outstandingly good. As to booze, you did not ask a man how much he wanted to drink – you handed him the bottle and let him help himself.

They carried lascar crews and, in port, there was always a quartermaster (in Hindustani called the 'secuni') at the gangway. The real stunner was that all their officers had to have a working knowledge of Hindustani. I was tempted to enquire if their lascars could not speak English and was told that they all could but it was a matter of principle. The officer had to be considered the bilingual one, and any attempt by a member of the crew to speak to an officer in English would be dealt with very harshly.

Two days later a P&O cargo liner, of about 12,500 gross tons (nearly three times our size), berthed about 200 yards away from us.

'I'll take you on board and let you see what a real ship looks like,' said our Mate.

He and I walked across to see this nautical paragon but, arriving at her gangway, there was no sign of anyone on duty there.

'Secuni! Secuni!' yelled the Mate several times without any response at all from above.

After bawling another ten times, a rather shabby quartermaster appeared and demanded to know why he was being summoned. The

Mate spat out a stream of what I imagined to be Hindustani but the quartermaster did not appear to understand what was being said.

'The stupid bugger doesn't know Hindustani,' claimed the Mate.

I had serious doubts about this but said nothing. Eventually the Mate managed to convey to the quartermaster that he was a former employee of the line and wished to be taken to meet the officer of the watch. That evening it happened to be her Chief Mate.

We trooped up to the cabin. Neither the P&O Mate nor our Mate knew each other but, after some name-dropping of past ships and acquaintances, it seemed that our *bona fides* had been established and we were ushered into the cabin. Although hardly lavish there was a dayroom and a small sleeping cabin attached.

After some conversation that was over my head, my companion remarked that it was a long ship. This apparently meant that it was a long time between drinks. Our host hastily produced a bottle of Scotch, with scarcely an inch left at its bottom and, while apologising for this being all he had, poured out two ungenerous nips.

The conversation was not going too well. I could see that our Mate was aware that his rosy picture of life on such a liner was slowly fading from view. The final blow was dealt when the ship's 3rd Mate and the Radio Officer appeared with three fish suppers, and they all fell upon them ravenously as though they had not seen grub for a week. Nothing was said on the way back to the *Celtic Monarch*, and no further references were ever made about life on P&O liners.

It seemed to be one repair after another, particularly to the boiler, and there was no sign of our leaving port. The company had a superintendent who had developed frugality to an art form. One idea was to cut expense by shutting off lights during the day and blaming it on the Coal Board. I later found out that Raeburn & Verel paid their Chief Engineers a bonus of £40 (about £2,300 at 2000 values) a year if they could reduce expenses. Any outburst on the part of the superintendent was always greeted by the Mate with a show of excessive politeness; but I doubt if the superintendent understood that this was intended as a rebuff.

Boilers are of two types: the Scotch, or fire-tube boiler, in which the fire passes through tubes surrounded by water; and the water-tube boiler, in which the water circulates inside tubes surrounded by the fire and hot gases. Ours was the fire-tube type and it was its constantly leaking tubes that were giving the trouble. Several times we were all ready to sail when another tube needed repairing.

Our 2nd Engineer had left and we had some difficulty finding a replacement. The shore company that was servicing our ship had an engineer that seemed to know what he was doing and impressed everyone. In the end we signed him on as 2nd Engineer although he did not have a 2nd Engineer's certificate and had never been to sea in his life. I do not know how these things were done. It was like the time our Chief Mate took ill in Alexandria when I was on the *Caduceus* and our 2nd Mate was made Chief Mate although he did not hold a Chief Mate's ticket. This might have been understandably allowed when the ship was abroad and in wartime, but surely in a home port a certificated 2nd Engineer with sea time should have been insisted upon.

Finally we did manage to leave the River Tees and headed for Jamaica. The *Celtic Monarch* was an odd vessel. Most ships have plain portholes at the fore end of the saloon, but she had four large windows: one had Lord Raeburn's coat of arms, one had the escutcheon of Verel, another had the Glasgow coat of arms and the fourth had some other design, but what it was I knew not.

We had two new officers. An Irishman from Dublin signed on as Radio Officer. He was quite a wag and could play jigs and such like on the fiddle. The other was a new 3rd Engineer who could talk the handle off a door – mostly about gruesome operations that he had suffered.

Arthur and I had a gramophone recital nearly every day. Once we arrived at the really hot weather it was found that our records had warped a little with the heat, and instead of the needle having a flat surface to play over, it moved up and down as the record revolved. Arthur was nothing if not resourceful and got some porthole glass from the carpenter. We sat the records one by one on this glass (which was absolutely flat and an inch thick) and they were gradually restored to their former condition.

We broke down seven times on our way to the West Indies, and each time it was due to a leaking tube. This of course caused a waste of water. At each port we took on drinking water as well as water for general purposes, and the engine room shared the latter. There was always a need of water for the engines, but when the tubes leaked it caused the engineers to make hefty demands on our general-purpose water, and made them very unpopular.

If we were some distance off land there was an attempt made to repair the tube. But if we were just a day or so off port, the engineers' practice was to run the boiler on sea water, which was just heaping up problems for the future.

We tried to find an accurate position each day by calculations based on the sun's altitude. Unfortunately the sun was not always obliging and we had to recourse to what is termed 'dead reckoning'. This meant that we used the compass course (corrected to give the true course), using allowances for currents and leeway, and the distance as given by the log. This was not very accurate and, if the sun did not put in an appearance for a day or two, any errors were compounded.

This might happen when the ship was nearing the coast, and we were then forced to request radio bearings. Our 'sparks' called up an appropriate radio station and asked for a bearing. The station immediately asked for the ship's identification. Every ship is allotted four letters and, as stated before, all British ships' letters begin with a 'G'. Once this was settled, the bearing was given and the owners were sent a bill for the service.

Now, this single bearing did not fix the position of the vessel but merely showed that it was somewhere along a certain line. Of course a second bearing from a different station (provided it cut the first one at approximately right angles) would clinch matters, but this was seldom done.

If we were sailing on an easterly or westerly course, the master would ask for a bearing running roughly north and south, so that he would know how far we were from land; he would then hope that the following day we would see the sun. If this did not happen, he would ask for a bearing running east and west. I cannot remember exactly what the cost of these bearings was – I am sure that it was either 15 shillings each or for the pair – and the frugality of shipping companies never failed to amaze and shock me.

At Jamaica we stopped for coal. A football match was arranged between the local team and ourselves. Only their captain had boots, the rest had bare feet. Nevertheless, the feet seemed to be phenomenally hard and the lack of boots appeared to be no obstacle to their performance. As usual, we had about 16 pairs of boots on board and if you were lucky you might get a pair that was passable. The result was a draw.

It did not take long to coal us and we soon set off for Chile, but first we had to go through the Panama Canal, one of the finest organised businesses in the world. The ship was towed into the first lock where six electric cars – three on each side of the vessel – manoeuvred the vessel into position. They were known as 'mules' (probably a throwback to horse-drawn days) and each had a capstan on its top; this contained a wire hawser that was connected to the ship. The mules ran on a track and, by going backwards and forwards and tightening or slackening the wire, the ship was wonderfully controlled. There was no fuss of any kind, just an occasional whistle from the pilot and a tinkling of a bell on the mule. All the locks were in pairs and could be used by ships going in either direction.

Once out of the lock and into the lake we were guided by leading marks, which were vertical lines painted on nearby hills. We sailed straight for one set, which formed a single vertical line. Meanwhile another set appeared, but, although at different heights, they were a distance apart. As we progressed this second set gradually came together, and when they presented a single vertical line we turned and sailed directly towards them – and so on. The pilots certainly had an easy job here.

The canal does not run from east to west as one might suppose, but from NNE to SSW. It is a great distance-saver; before it was built a voyage from Liverpool to San Francisco would have been an extra 5,666 miles.

In the chart room of every merchant ship is a bookcase containing 'pilots'. These are books giving detailed information when sailing along the coast of any part of the world. For instance, if you were sailing along the coast of Brazil you would use the appropriate South American East Coast pilot, which would provide many facts and illustrations that could be most helpful. When passing Sugar Loaf Mountain, for example, it might not be readily identifiable due to the angle of view. But by consulting the pilot you could find a photograph of it taken from a different angle and making it instantly recognisable. I found these books a great help during this voyage.

15

My last ship: part 2

After sailing some distance down the west coast of South America we arrived at Tocopilla, a small town midway between the two larger towns of Iquique and Antofagasto. Seemingly Tocopilla means 'el rincón del diablo', which translates as 'the devil's corner'!

Here we started to load sodium nitrate. The nitrate wagons had to go up more than 9,000 feet to the mines for this chemical, which is used as a fertiliser, and commonly known as Chile saltpetre.

One good thing was that we took on board fresh crockery as the stuff we had been using since leaving Middlesbrough was most horribly chipped – on occasions one man had to wait for another to finish to get his soup plate! The food was deteriorating and I began to write *The Rime of the Modern Mariner*, a satire on the ship's shortcomings; the bosun, being a good freehand drawer, supplied sketches to match the poem. As well as *The Rime of the Modern Mariner* I wrote other parodies, such as this:

Sea Fever (apologies to John Masefield)

I must go down to the sea again
To the lonely sea and tide,
Where the good ship *Celtic Monarch* lies,
Old Raeburn's joy and pride;
For all I ask is some rotten food
And a dirty pokey room,
And a draughty bridge and a stinking fridge
And a stained-glass port saloon.

Oh, yes go down to the sea again
To see that my shares are paying.
For the call of cash is a clear call
And a call that there's no gainsaying.
For all I ask is a luxury yacht
With the Monarch house flag waving

> And a five-course tea is enough for me
> So long as you do the slaving.

It had not rained in Tocopilla for several years and there was no vegetation of any kind. The only industries seemed to be the mining of nitrates and fishing. Everything was imported (mostly from the USA) and prices were very high. The USA price plus Chilean taxes and the cost of shipping made many items very dear.

One of my teeth gave trouble and I told the captain I wanted to see a dentist. The ship owners would meet the cost of up to three extractions (they reckoned that any more meant that you were not looking after your teeth), but considered fillings a luxury and would not pay.

I did not mind this quite so much as my having to pay every week into my insurance society (Prudential) and get nothing in return – were I at home they would be forced to contribute. The dentist asked if I would pay or whether the agent would foot the bill. Having a notion that the agent would take his cut out of it, I elected to offer cash.

As he approached with his drill revving furiously I became apprehensive. I knew that the pain associated with a tooth being filled is caused by the heat generated by the friction of the drill on the tooth and, from the speed of this drill, I feared the worst. However, it proved to be a new high-speed drill from the USA – where else? – and, as it was exceptionally sharp, I did not feel any discomfort. I mention this because it must have been at least 20 years before this drill put in an appearance in Britain.

A football match was arranged between us and the local bank. Both Arthur and I played, together with the 4th Engineer, who was a very good player and had much experience. There was, of course, not a blade of grass on the pitch. Our football boots, with their studs projecting half an inch, were designed to be used on soft grass, and we found them most awkward to play in. Our opponents had very fine footwear with thin pliable leather uppers and, on the soles, little bars of leather hardly a quarter of an inch in depth. This meant that they could make sharp turns on the baked surface.

A short distance off the coast was a little island and close to it was an area of water in a kind of basin. Fish came in and out of this and, when the tide was low, many of them were swimming about in very shallow water, possibly content to stay there until the next tide.

The local birds seemed aware of this. About 20 minutes before low water they congregated there and one could scarcely see the surface of the island for birds, many of them pelicans. At the appropriate moment – it almost seemed as though the boss bird had given them a signal – they all rose off the island and descended upon this basin. The fish had no chance whatsoever and the birds gorged themselves before returning to the island for a rest. This happened every day and was quite fascinating.

Although I did not actually see it happen, I am fairly sure that the locals called at the island from time to time and picked up the excrement. This went by the name of guano and was used as fertiliser. I had heard of ships transporting the stuff from port to port and was assured that it was the smelliest of all cargoes.

Life ashore had pitfalls. Our 4th Engineer was walking along a street when police suddenly surrounded him, and without any explanation he was bundled off to jail, where he spent the night. Next day he was taken to court where their equivalent of a magistrate pronounced sentence to be '300 pesetas or ten days'. The engineer asked, in English, what he was being charged with, only to be told again, in a louder voice, '300 pesetas or ten days'. It was obvious that this was about the limits of the man's knowledge of English so he had to pay up.

This type of revenue-raising was quite common in the southern states of the USA. A certain tanker loading fuel in Galveston, Texas, had most of the crew in jail on very flimsy pretexts and the skipper had to pay all the fines to get them out.

Although we had been some time in Tocopilla our departure was quite sudden and I dashed ashore eager to spend my remaining pesetas before sailing. In a record shop I saw two records (the old 78rpm discs on the USA's RCA Victor label) with the name of Gigli on them. My funds were almost exactly what was required and I made the purchase without further thought.

Coming back on the ship I scrutinised the record catalogue and found that they were the first two records in an Italian recording of *La Bohème*. Thinking that there was not much point in having only these two records, I wrote home and told my father to buy the remaining two records to complete Act 1 of the opera.

The British ones were on the famous HMV (His Master's Voice) label, as they were financially tied up with RCA Victor. When I finally arrived home and played them there was a dramatic improvement when we started playing the HMV ones. Although all four were pressed from the same master discs, the British surfaces were vastly superior. I mention this because so many British people make the assumption that American techniques are always superior to ours.

Our orders were to take the nitrate to Alexandria. Since coal weighs the ship down, we did not take on enough to see us there, but intended to stop at Jamaica and Gibraltar to top up the bunkers, thus

My last ship: Part 2

allowing us to load more cargo. Our Government was not keen on our bunkering at Gibraltar, I was told, because they would rather sell the stuff to US ships and receive payment in dollars, which was considered a 'hard' currency. This will let you know how bad our country's finances were then.

We made Jamaica and had another football match with the barefooted brigade that we had drawn with on the way down to Chile. This time we were beaten by two goals, due to some extent to our lack of fitness. We were glad to leave Jamaica as all doors and portholes had to be kept tightly shut to keep out the dust, and the resulting high temperature made sleep hardly possible.

Apart from our lack of fitness, the *Celtic Monarch*'s food was hardly nourishing. It was becoming steadily worse and we kept protesting but nothing was done about it. Eventually we decided to contact our union and lodge an official complaint.

Here was the rub. Our captain (not that he was going to help us) was in the Master's Guild or something of that sort, as was the Mate and Chief Engineer. Arthur and I were in the Navigating & Engineering Officers' Federation, as was our 3rd Engineer. The 4th Engineer was in the Marine Engineers' Association, while the 2nd was in the Amalgamated Engineers' Union, which was really for those working ashore. The Radio Officer was in a special union run by Marconi, and the ratings were in the National Seamen's Union. Six different unions were representing only 44 men!

Notwithstanding this, I resolved to try to use the apparent weakness to our advantage, by having all five unions knocking on Raeburn & Verel's door at the one time. I contacted the bosun who agreed to draw up a letter of complaint and have all the sailors sign it. The 4th Engineer had a cousin ashore in Jamaica and he agreed to post the letters without the skipper having to know anything about our plan.

Although the Mate had been badgering us for some time to use the unions, he now would not register a complaint, saying that, as he had been a master, it would be against his principles – whatever they were! The 2nd Engineer, the 4th Engineer and the Radio Officer reckoned that it was useless for any of them to register their objections, as each was the sole member of his own particular union. To compound my disappointment the 3rd Engineer pulled out of the plan, saying that he did not want to be the only one of the engineers to carp about the grub.

So, we ended up with a letter of protest written by me and countersigned by Arthur, together with the one given to me by the bosun.

This was not the bottom of the pit. The letter given to me by the bosun was a fake, and was concerned only with claiming short-hand money because a sailor had paid off and had not been replaced. It contained not a word about food or conditions.

Later I learned from one of the sailors that the bosun – a professed communist – had said, 'These officers want us to pull their chestnuts out of the fire. Why should we send a letter when they won't have sent one themselves?' Shades of Stalin?

In the end, there was only one letter signed by two men out of a whole ship. Our Federation did nothing apart from forwarding our letter, without comment, to Raeburn & Verel, so that by the time we reached Gibraltar my letter was in the captain's hands. I did not know of this, or of the bosun's treachery, for some time to come, and the Old Man said absolutely nothing.

The pattern from Jamaica to Gibraltar was the same as on the way down to Chile. We kept on breaking down, almost always because of the tubes leaking. The result was a shortage of water, which was pinched from our domestic supply, leaving the engineers very much out of favour.

We found the ship's position by taking the altitude of a heavenly body (sun, moon, planet or star), but if this was not possible we had to rely on using the compass course and the distance shown by the log. If there was a following sea the log was lifted up and did not turn rapidly enough to register the correct distance.

The captain was assuredly a first-class seaman. He really knew all about ships and had all kinds of ideas of his own. If it rained, he could tell the trim of the ship by observing the puddles on top of the galley. He could also tell how much the ship was sagged by looking at the flanges of the steering rods.

He was, however, a poor navigator. Every morning the officers took a sight of the sun. What they were really doing, as mentioned before, was to calculate the ship's mean time. Since the vessel carried Greenwich Mean Time around in the chronometer, the difference in the two gave an approximate longitude in time. This was easily converted from time to arc as there are 24 hours in the day and also 360 degrees, thus there are 15 degrees to each hour. We now had a position line running roughly north to south, and the ship was then somewhere along that line. At noon the officers kept following the sun's ascent in the sky and noted when it reached its maximum altitude; the latitude was worked out from this. The position line arrived at earlier was carried up to the noon latitude and together they gave the ship's position – latitude and longitude.

Now, it is obvious that if this longitude was taken at 8am and run up to noon by the dead reckoning method, we had a 4-hour period open to inaccuracy. Were we to wait until nearer noon to find our longitude, the position line would not be running north and south and our calculated location would not be accurate.

However, as we travelled further and further to the south, the sun rose higher in the sky each day and the longitude might be found at a later time. If the sun was almost overhead at noon, then it could be bearing due east at 10 minutes to noon, and this would be the ideal time to find the longitude as the position line would be running north to south.

Captain Keir would still take his morning sight at 8am, just out of habit, when he could have taken it at 10 to noon and had only 10 minutes of the inaccurate dead reckoning.

Of course, by using two or three stars a position could be instantly obtainable. The snag here was that the horizon had to be visible at the same time as the stars. This happened only in the morning or the evening dusk, both of which occurred during the Mate's watch. He regularly took sights of stars or planets, but they never seemed to be accurate, and the skipper, Arthur and I finally gave up using them as our approximate latitude when calculating our longitude for our morning sight.

I could never understand why the Mate's sights were so unreliable. In the morning one officer would take an altitude of the sun and, at the exact moment, would shout out 'stop' to the other officer, who duly noted the time on the chronometer. But the Mate, being alone, would have had to count seconds in his head from the time of taking each sight until he reached the chronometer.

This still should have presented no problem. All navigators are used to identifying different lighthouses and buoys by counting the intervals of their flashes, and soon acquire the knack of counting seconds to a very high degree of accuracy.

We were held up by a strong breeze blowing through the Strait of Gibraltar – quite a common occurrence, though it always seemed that, whichever way we were travelling, the wind was sure to come from the opposite direction. We had only 4½ hours there, so had no time to see Major Douglas and Carlos.

Leaving Gibraltar we arrived at Alexandria on 10 August 1947. The passage was good apart from some fog leaving Gibraltar, and we were now told that we were to take salt from Port Said to Sasebo, a small town in the south of Japan.

Alexandria had not changed. What seemed like hundreds of people came on board to sell the most awful junk – bracelets, necklaces, rings, etc – all most likely made in Birmingham. I was of the opinion that half the population lived by theft, and the other half on the illicit earnings of the first lot.

The bosun paid off, suffering from appendicitis, and a drunken Estonian AB took his place. Our cook also took ill and we had to sign on an Egyptian.

The Mate had never been near North or South America in his travels, but now we were in the Middle East he proclaimed that this was his 'stamping ground' and that he knew all there was to know about it.

On the second day there, we were ashore together when he chose for us to take a taxi. There were two men in the cab (I usually do not look favourably on this when alone) but, as there two of us, I had no fears. When the journey was completed the Mate offered to pay and, to my utter astonishment, produced a very high-denomination note – possibly about 100 piastres. I had a gut feeling that we were (or rather, he was) about to be swindled, but, with him being such a know-it-all, I said nothing.

As I expected, the driver said that he had no change but that his 'co-driver' would get some from a nearby shop. The man got out and hurried down the street, repeatedly turning round to reassure us that it was not any of the shops that he had just passed, but was seeking one that was further on. From only one previous visit to Egypt, I could tell exactly what was going to happen. The companion arrived at the corner of a street and, as he rapidly hurried round it, the driver quickly sped off, leaving the Mate and me on the pavement, without the change. I could not understand how a man that had spent years travelling in the Middle and Far East could have fallen for such a simple and obvious trick.

Not long after reaching Egypt I had more trouble with one of my teeth. Together with an AB, I visited a dentist. I recollect sitting in the waiting room, which had all round its walls nerve-racking pictures of teeth being extracted in medieval times – dentists with their feet up on a patient's chin yanking out teeth using crude pliers. I realised how fortunate I was not to be living in those bygone ages. However, as far as the AB was concerned it was counter-productive, for he took one look at them and departed at speed!

We started discharging the nitrate and I was in charge of Nos 1, 2 and 3 holds. My shore counterpart was a Turkish man by the name of Kiazam and we became good friends, corresponding with each other for some time after leaving Egypt.

It was the month of Ramadan, the ninth month in the Muslim year during which strict fasting is observed from sunrise to sunset. Kiazam was of the Islamic faith and ate nothing all day. At sunset he

My last ship: Part 2

rushed into our mess to eat whatever he could lay his hands on.

I remember teasing him a few minutes before sunset by saying that he could begin eating, as, owing to refraction (the bending of light as it passes from a medium of one density to another of different density) the sun was actually below the horizon. He was an educated man who knew what refraction was, but merely smiled and would not be tempted by me.

Neither would he smoke a cigarette during the fasting period. I said that there was no tobacco in Mohammed's time so how could smoking be proscribed. His reply was to quote the Qu'ran, which stated that 'nothing must enter the lips'.

Kiazam gave me my kismet (the Arabic word for destiny or fate), saying that I would not remain at sea, would marry a fairly rich lady and have two children, and that I would live a very happy life until I was 55 years old. Just what would happen after that time left me wondering. He was certainly right about the two children, but not about the rich lady – unless he meant rich in virtue!

I was quite busy when the cargo was being discharged and did not venture ashore much. Alexandria is not my favourite port and I was glad when we set off for Port Said, at the north end of the Suez Canal.

Arthur and I both bought chatties there. These were jars made of a kind of porous clay material, holding around 3 pints. Water leaks through to the outside surface of the jar and, as the heat causes this water to evaporate, the water inside becomes very cold. We used to hang these up on the bridge and they were a godsend in the warm weather. However, some Egyptians were selling chatties with painted surfaces to enhance their appearances. They may have looked more attractive but they were now ordinary vessels, and the whole purpose of cooling water was to no avail.

We arrived at Port Said on a Sunday and were all ready to load a cargo of salt. However, Ramadan had ended on the Saturday and this meant that we could not begin loading until Tuesday – Sunday and Monday being feast days and roughly the equivalent of our Christmas.

Port Said was better than Alexandria. The Egyptians had been protesting about so many British troops in places like Alexandria, but I think that they just moved them into the canal zone where British interests lay.

I was ashore one evening with the 4th Engineer. We were warned that there was to be an anti-British demonstration but, since we were already dressed, we decided to go on. Luckily it took place at the other end of the town. Anyway, there were plenty of British soldiers about.

As usual in such times a big cruiser, HMS *Leander*, arrived the next day – paying a courtesy visit! When we had arrived at Port Said HMS *Glasgow* was there together with a French destroyer, so paying courtesy calls was very much in fashion.

A troop ship passed us loaded with Dutch soldiers bound for Indonesia. Later I heard that she wanted to call in at Port Said for stores, but public opinion was very much against this. First, the Egyptians signalled to the vessel telling her not to bother calling in. When she did drop anchor and stores were sent out in launches, the Egyptians overturned the boats. The ship had finally to get a government order to get her stores. The reason for all this was that many of the Egyptians were Muslims, as were the Indonesians.

One good point there was the lovely warm water. Arthur and I swam about half a mile over to a Glasgow tramp ship, the *Baron Inchcape*, belonging to Hogarth's. Arthur had been relieving 3rd Mate on her some time before and we both hoped to see someone we knew. A couple of the crew knew Arthur, and one of their apprentices was from my part of Glasgow and I knew his sister. We spent a pleasant couple of hours there before swimming back.

It was a treat to be in water of this temperature rather than the cold sea around our home shores. Before I learned to swim many folk said that as soon as I could do so, I would never be out of the water. This proved not to be the case. I recall swimming at Millport in the River Clyde and being very cold indeed. Possibly swimming in the Mediterranean spoiled me, for I did very little swimming at home after this.

During the voyage I kept thinking about my future, and particularly the grant to go to university. It seemed that this was a year out of my life and I felt slightly depressed over it. In Alexandria I had seen a book, *Mathematics for the Million* by Professor Lancelot Hogben, and as this had once been recommended to me, I bought it.

Hogben taught mathematics in a most interesting way. Much of it was based on the history of maths. He explained how they determined the heights of the pyramids by measuring the shadows when the sun was 45 degrees above the horizon. He went on to pose various problems (such as measuring the circumference of the earth) and how these were solved. This was most interesting and was bringing mathematics alive for me.

On 23 August 1947 we completed loading the salt but could not leave Port Said because of engine trouble, the main bearings being the chief cause. The *Celtic Monarch* was insured with the British Corporation (as were most tramp ships), but their surveyor was on holiday and a Lloyd's surveyor was sent in his place. As expected, he was a bit stricter. The white metal on the main bearing had run and the 2nd Engineer reckoned that it was caused by foreign matter. He furthermore suspected that some Egyptians in Alexandria had done it on purpose.

On 8 September, after more than six weeks and many repairs, we went out for engine trials. These being more or less satisfactory, we returned to Port Said to pick up our Suez Canal light, a huge contrivance fitted to each ship for the passage through the canal. In fact, most ships were built with a davit up at the bow especially for this light.

Before entering the canal we had to sweep out some 'tween-deck compartments that usually carried coal; this was to reduce our canal dues. There was plenty of coal dust left as evidence of what we had been doing, but so long as the coal had gone the authorities seemed satisfied.

Talking of dues, at one time these were based on the capacity of the ship above the waterline. This led to some companies that were regular users of the canal designing ships that bulged out below the waterline, thus saving money. They were odd-looking craft (I recall seeing one in my early days at sea) and were known as 'turret ships'.

Compared with the Panama Canal, the Suez had obviously taken a great deal more time in the making. The Panama had locks at Gatun (the Atlantic entrance), then a lake and another set of locks called Pedro Miguel (probably the name of one of the engineers), then another lake and finally the two Miraflores locks at the Pacific end. The lakes were narrow and dredgers had to be used to keep the channels sufficiently deep. Apart from that, the main work at Panama had been the construction and maintenance of the huge locks, which were the last word in efficiency.

The Suez, on the other hand, had no locks, having been made through flat terrain. After leaving Port Said there was a 50-mile stretch to Ishmalia, where the pilots changed over. This section (which is almost as long as the whole Panama Zone) had been blasted through barren desert, and must have taken a colossal amount of labour to make. After Ishmalia came the Bitter Lakes, then another stretch of canal and out you came into the Gulf of Suez.

Like the Panama Canal, its use saved an amazing number of miles. A voyage from England to Bombay took an extra 4,450 miles before the canal was built!

The Panama was also the handier of the two canals. All its pilots were in constant touch with any point in the canal by means of a small portable radio (walkie-talkie), which they all carried. Ships could pass each other in the lakes, and even the locks could accommodate two ships at a time regardless of their direction.

The Suez Canal had such long stretches that it would have almost doubled the cost to have built two canals side by side. If ships of any decent size had to pass each other, one of them had to tie up at the canal bank to allow the other through. Vessels carrying light spirit were given 100% priority, so we had to stop and tie up to allow an Italian tanker to pass. One last word of comparison: the Suez, being longer, ran a night and day service, but if a ship did not reach either end of the Panama by about 11pm (this would vary according to the time of year) she had to anchor until the following day. Both waterways were, in those days, capable of admitting all but the very largest ships.

Ferdinand de Lesseps built the Suez (there is a statue of him at the Port Said entrance) and began on the Panama, but never completed it. His efforts, known as 'the Frenchman's canal', could still be seen at the Atlantic end of the Panama isthmus.

Short haircuts were all the vogue when we entered the Red Sea. The 'sparks' and I went a stage further and shaved each other's heads. I had hoped that my hair would grow back into an even thatch like a Russian soldier's but, to my chagrin, it appeared that the front part was growing at only half the rate of the rest. I now had to shave the back part again to help uniformity. My mother was in tears when she received a photograph. She had some queer notion that the hair might not grow in again!

Our seven-day passage down the Red Sea was very hot, but not quite so bad as we expected. There was a gentle breeze blowing but, since it was behind us, we did not get the full benefit of it. The temperature reached more than 100°F, but fortunately the air was not too humid. The deck officers certainly had the best of it. It was much preferable to walk about on a shady bridge than to work in the engine room. I really felt sorry for the latter as the temperature below topped 115°F!

As usual one of our boiler tubes burst and this delayed us 12 hours. When we got to Aden, rather than wait till the boiler was cool the 2nd Engineer went in as soon as the heat was bearable. He worked for three-quarters of an hour in a temperature of 135°F. It just about did for him and he was laid up for a day or two. I was glad that I did not have any such zealous moods.

As soon as we came out of the Gulf of Aden into the Arabian Sea the temperature dropped to 75°F. We arrived at Colombo, the capital of Ceylon (later Sri Lanka) and anchored, the skipper ringing 'finished with engines' to the Chief Engineer at 11.50pm.

We reckoned that we were due a lot of overtime because it

was a Sunday. However, the captain said that it was 'day of arrival' and accordingly we had to work 10 hours before qualifying for any overtime.

Then we said that we should get an extra day of paid leave because we had spent a Sunday at sea, only to be told that we had not been a whole Sunday at sea, but had spent 10 minutes in port! Now the stupid and loose phraseology agreed to by our Federation was to be our undoing.

A bumboat man came on board with black elephants and all kinds of souvenirs. Traders were setting up stalls on the hatches to sell ebony elephants and other beautifully hand-carved goods as souvenirs. In conversation with one of them I mentioned that I would have liked to have seen the Temple of the Sleeping Buddha at the old capital, Kandy. Immediately his business veneer vanished and he wanted to take me there, as he was a devout Buddhist. Unfortunately Kandy was too far away for a visit.

Again we had problems with leaking tubes and again the 2nd Engineer went into the boiler before it had properly cooled. This time he required medical attention. The skipper was the only one ashore and I was asked at short notice to find him and arrange for a doctor to come out to the ship. I had not expected to be going ashore for some time yet, so picture me helping two Indians row a small boat across Colombo harbour, then wandering around the main street clad in scruffy khaki working clothes with one-eighth of an inch of hair on my head.

After I had caught up with the captain and the matter of the doctor had been settled, the Old Man asked if I would like an iced beer. When I assented he headed straight for the main entrance of the Grand Oriental Hotel, the number one hotel in town.

'Had we not better go in the side door?' I mildly suggested, conscious of my appearance.

'Why the devil should we?' he demanded.

'Well, if you're not ashamed of me, I'm not ashamed of you,' I replied.

The place was full of pukkah sahibs having a morning refreshment. I recall George Bernard Shaw stating that the worst sin against our fellow creatures is not to hate them, but to be indifferent to them. Alas, my appearance must have shocked them so much that they could not show indifference, but frowned at it. I cared not a whit and revelled in the fact that I had jarred them – so I showed indifference to them!

The 2nd Engineer recovered and we set off for Singapore. Going through the Straits of Malacca it became warm again. We were astonished to find that none of the lighthouses was functioning. I did not know whether this was due to Indonesian activity, but it was a predicament.

Another problem was that this area was renowned for junks sailing at night without lights. You would cruise along in the blackness when suddenly you would see the flash of a burning torch. The junk had been sailing along without any lights with one man steering and the rest sleeping, but as soon as a ship's presence was detected the helmsman would jump up and grab a brand from the fire and exhibit it. The trouble was that the 50 or so sleepers would all swear that they were awake and that lights were showing.

We stayed in Singapore only for one day, then departed for Hong Kong. We were only three days out when orders came for us to proceed to Yokosuka (about 10 miles from Yokohama) in Tokyo Bay instead of Sasebo. This was not well received as at Sasebo we would be tied up in a dock, but at Yokosuka we would most likely unload at anchor.

Two days were spent in Hong Kong for repairs. While there we picked up a seaman who was to work his passage home. The Mate immediately pronounced him to be a born sailor, saying that he could always tell. Two days later on the bridge the 'born sailor' put a flag hoist upside down and I fairly rubbed it in to the Mate. It turned out that he had never been a sailor but was a steward coming home as a DBS (Distressed British Seaman).

Three days out from Hong Kong the orders were changed back to Sasebo because Yokosuka could not supply us with coal.

16

My last ship: part 3

On 28 October 1947 we arrived safely in Sasebo. The Japanese began unloading 24 hours a day so that Arthur and I were 8 hours on and 8 hours off. The town was not very big and there was a curfew at 11pm. All Japanese transport and eating-houses were out of bounds and we had to go ashore in pairs in the evening.

Apparently Sasebo had been a naval port during the war and was now declared an open one. We were officially the first merchant vessel to enter after the restriction had been lifted and the mayor and his wife came down with an interpreter to visit us as a sort of welcoming committee. The Old Man was on the gangway talking to the Mate when the party beckoned him over and the mayor's wife handed him a large bouquet of flowers. He looked quite embarrassed and I could see the Mate having a grin from the top of the gangway.

We were also invited to a festival that was taking place the following week to mark the occasion, and given six tickets for it. The captain, the four apprentices and I were to turn up in our No 1 uniforms to represent the ship, but I would really be keeping the seat warm for the Mate, who would take my place as soon as the booze appeared.

However the Mate, as arrogant as ever, ran foul of the US authorities, who confined him to the ship. This meant that his crony, the 2nd Engineer, had no one to go ashore with. Neither Arthur nor I wanted the job so the Mate, overbearing as usual, detailed the junior apprentice to go. The lad did not want to accompany the engineer, so the Mate said that he would not be allowed to attend the festival.

The junior apprentice was inclined to be a bit cheeky and was certainly not my favourite but, as a matter of principle, I would not permit him to be bullied in this way. I went straight to the skipper and got him to confirm that the apprentice could go to the festival and thus the Mate was presented with a *fait accompli*.

It was a beautiful sunny day for the ceremony and we were like guests of honour. The first speaker spoke for 10 minutes and our interpreter gave us the gist of the speech. Apparently he was the head of police in Sasebo. Next was the head of police of the neighbouring town, then the chief of the fire brigade, and so on. Soon both the interpreter and we got tired of the business and did not ask for further information.

Now, Japanese is an ideographic language; that is to say that they do not form words the way westerners do. A drawing done with a brush represents a man, another a woman, and if the two are put together it may mean marriage, family or something like that. Consequently a lot of paper is required for even a 10-minute oration. Each speaker had a very long piece of paper folded zigzag fashion so that it made up many pages of about 8 by 6 inches. As the speech was delivered the length of paper was gradually dropped on to the grass.

Halfway through the ceremony the leading US soldier, Colonel Byng, spoke and we could almost understand what he was saying. He had the reputation of being henpecked, to the extent that the troops in Sasebo were known as 'Mrs Byng's army'. Now, Mrs Byng liked soldiers to have very short hair so my Red Sea effort (now half an inch long) was right in the height of tonsorial fashion.

The Japanese love ceremony and it lasted quite a while. Afterwards we were taken to the Town Hall for lunch. We did not sit down but stood at the table while geisha girls danced and sang on an elevated platform. Lunch was an ordeal. In front of me was a little wooden box with a sliding lid and, on opening it, I found a dead raw fish fixing me with its glassy eye. It was surrounded by a gruesome assortment, the only recognizable item of which was a carrot in pretty poor shape. I grabbed the chopsticks and did my best but was able to manage only a tenth of the contents. These I washed down with plenty of sake.

We then went outside to see some of the festival dances, displays of judo and exhibitions of various sorts, and finished up in a cabaret. When I left, one small Jap toddled after me with the remains of my lunch in the little box – no doubt he thought that I would eat these delicacies later on.

When we had arrived in Japan we had all thought that it would be unsafe to go around at night for fear of a knife in the back. Later we sensed that this was utterly unlikely. The Japanese were very courteous, honest and very hard-working. They were also exceptionally clean.

One day I was watching two of them shovelling coal wearing pure white clothes, and they did not seem to be getting dirty. Seemingly they wore white so that any dirt would show up, and they would then wash the garments; unlike back home, where we would choose a dark colour so that the dirt would not show up. There were

My last ship: Part 3

barges alongside the ship and they scrubbed the decks many times during the day and lay some type of food on the deck to dry it.

This part of Japan was famed for its pottery. At 200 yen to the pound the prices varied from £10 to £30 for a 96-piece dinner set. This rate of exchange was very poor (200 yen was worth about 10 shillings) and we all resorted to using cigarettes as currency. Arthur bought a teaset for the equivalent of 1,500 yen, but was mortified to see the same one later in Yokohama for 1,100 yen.

One little boat fascinated me. In Britain we sometimes put a single oar out at the stern of a boat and twist its blade in a figure-of-eight pattern. This is called sculling and causes the boat to go ahead. The Japanese had a small rowing boat with an outboard bracket amidships, and attached to this was more of a paddle than an oar. It had a broad blade and at the handle end had a small crosspiece like that on a spade. This paddle could manoeuvre the boat forwards, backwards and sideways with amazing control.

Nagasaki was about 20 miles away but, probably owing to the city having had an atomic bomb dropped on it, the Yanks put it out of bounds to us. Anyway, it would have taken 4 hours by rail to get there, I was told.

The people of Sasebo tended to wear the national dress of kimono and obi. On their feet they wore little close-fitting rubber boots with a separate compartment for the big toe. This puzzled me until one very rainy day I heard a clatter on the streets and found that they were all wearing on their feet a kind of raised wooden sandal with cords that engaged between the big toe and the other toes, hence the reason for the separate compartment in the boots.

The *Celtic Monarch* set off round the coast for Yokohama. No sooner had we cast off when four stowaways were discovered. They were four young boys aged between 8 and 12 and we put them to work polishing brass around the bridge. The eldest spoke English quite well and asked if we would show him how to steer the ship. He picked it up very quickly and was obviously an intelligent lad. He told me that they were all orphans and had lost their parents when the bomb fell on Nagasaki.

As soon as we docked a sergeant from the US Medical Corps came on board and explained that no one would be allowed ashore until he had received immunisation against smallpox, typhoid, typhus, yellow fever and cholera. As 3rd Mate I had to identify each member of the crew to this orderly as he jabbed and scraped their arms. It was strange to witness fellows who fancied themselves as tough members staring straight ahead and turning white as the needle went into their arms. In view of this, I could never understand why drug addicts do not seem to mind jabbing themselves with needles.

Arthur always fancied himself as a man of business and had bought a bag of rice in Egypt, intending to sell it at a profit in Japan. He now saw more rice than he had ever seen in his life. What he should have bought was saccharine, but he was not to know this.

Now, the steward we had picked up at Hong Kong had been to Japan before and knew a thing or two. His total wealth on arrival was a few coins he had picked up in Ceylon. He did not exchange these for yen but sold them to US soldiers as souvenirs. He knew that American troops like to tell people back in the USA that they had been to many countries and liked some currency with which to show off. By this means he received $10.

In Japan at that time there were three currencies: the Japanese yen, the USA dollar (a special occupation version), and BAF (British Armed Forces) money. Our entrepreneur took his US dollars to the Yankee PX – a sort of superior NAAFI – and bought soap, toothpaste and various other items he knew were wanted in the Japanese black market. Selling these to the Japs he received yen far in excess of the exchange rate of 50 yen to the dollar. This he took to the PX, where the GIs were now coming out and wanting to visit Japanese night clubs, where they would require yen. So he traded his yen for dollars at a favourable rate to the Yanks – but a much more favourable rate to him!

He repeated this cycle of dealing until he had to hire some of his shipmates to cope with the increase in business. Naturally they enjoyed a share of the spoils. The first wind I got of this was when our drunken Estonian bosun (who would have pawned his oilskin to get money for booze) turned up in a leather fleece-lined jacket.

On 19 November I planned a visit to the capital city, which was not far away. I caught the famous 'Tokyo Express', which whisked me to my destination in just under 40 minutes – and gratis at that – in a beautiful carriage reserved for Allied Personnel. Wandering around for some time I found myself at the Union Jack Club among a mixed crowd of British and Australians; the latter predominated and the main body of the former were there expressly to take part in the festivities for the following day's Royal Wedding between Princess Elizabeth (later to become Queen Elizabeth II) and Philip Mountbatten.

I was fortunate to meet up with an RAF gentleman from Edinburgh who changed a small sum of my sterling into British occupational currency thereby enabling me to have lunch at the club. It was the first I had seen BAF money, since there were no British troops in Sasebo. The meal turned out to be the best I had had since

Making Waves XVII

Maritime Museum
The Royal College of Science & Technology (later Strathclyde

University), where I studied for my 2nd Mate's certificate.

The *Athelregent. Author's collection*
The *Radcombe. National Maritime Museum*

XVIII   Making Waves

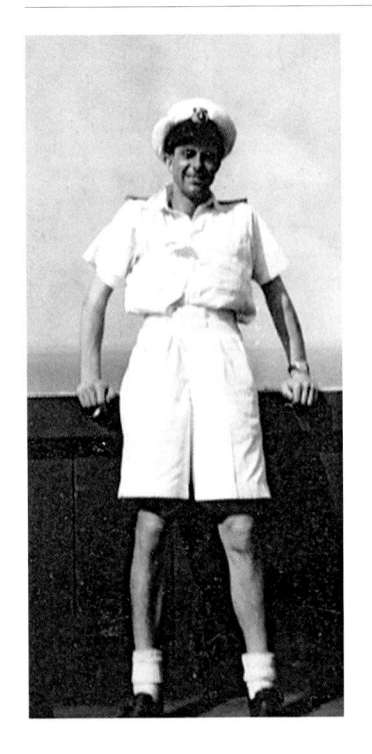

Getting ready for Miami, 1945.   **A studio portrait taken in Port Talbot.**

The Masunda. Ships in Focus

Making Waves   XIX

Taking a meridian sight at noon.

The *Fort Aspin*. *National Maritime Museum*

xx   Making Waves

Having a cuppa while checking lifeboat stores on the *Dentonia Park*. You can see what a state a ship gets into when the stay in port is prolonged – there are ashes all over the deck.

David Robb, myself and the Radio Officer on *Dentonia Park*.

A satisfactory picture of *Celtic Monarch* could not be found, but she was sister ship of, and identical to, *Caledonian Monarch*, seen here. *Reproduced from Nicholls's* Seamanship and Nautical Knowledge *with kind permission of the publishers, Brown, Son & Ferguson Ltd*

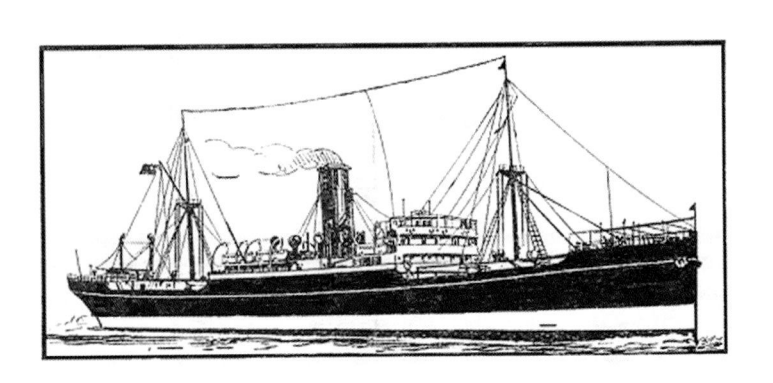

Arthur Fisken (2nd Mate), Eric Thomson (Chief Mate) and me during our first trip on *Celtic Monarch*.

John Steel (Radio Officer) and me on the first trip.

A liner in the Panama Canal. *Reproduced from Nicholls's* Seamanship and Nautical Knowledge *with kind permission of the publishers, Brown, Son & Ferguson Ltd*

A junior apprentice, me and the 4th Engineer on *Celtic Monarch*.

Me and the Radio Officer after our heads had been shaved.

Making Waves   XXIII

Myself with two Japanese children at the festival in Sasebo.

Arthur (2nd Mate) and the skipper taking sights.

An Account of Wages. As can be seen, my total earnings were £400 2s 6d. I must have left an Allotment Note of £10 a month to be sent home, for the total for this item is £120. Income tax is £47 16s 6d, and underneath this entry is all the money that was issued to me at the various ports.

£13 10s 1d was deducted for putting into a pension fund. The company held on to the total money in this fund until I had been three years ashore; presumably they expected I might return to sea.

Just above the £4 that I seem to have drawn at Dundee is the total tobacco bill, amounting to £21 18s 3d, which would work out at about 8s 1d a week.

£5 8s was deducted for Health and Pensions, and £2 5s for Unemployment Insurance, making a total of £7 13s; this caused me a deal of annoyance to think that I was contributing to this every week but still had to pay for dental treatment done abroad.

I was paid £19 3s 6d in advance for the leave I was due, leaving me the sum of £137 14s 4d (about £8,000 at 2000 values).

My last ship: Part 3

leaving home. The club was a goodly size and boasted a small library, so I soon found myself browsing over various books.

My wandering continued but darkness had set in. I toured the shopping centre, beholding some beautiful objects of exquisite craftsmanship. At a dimly lit corner of one street a Japanese sculptor was clay modelling and, as was usual, was thronged by Japanese citizens who displayed a healthy curiosity towards anything of this nature. He was fashioning the clay in the likeness of any chance passer-by and asking 200 yen for this service. The entire operation took about 25 minutes (although he advertised it as 10, to solicit custom) and the results were astonishingly good. I watched patiently as he worked at the life-mask of a young RAF corporal.

One thing that was very noticeable in Japan (especially Tokyo) was the large number of people wearing masks. As soon as anyone got a cold a mask would be worn to prevent spreading infection. I thought this practice most commendable.

Soon we were in dry dock for repairs in Yokohama. We had an immense amount of barnacles on the hull – probably collected during our long stay at Port Said – and this would have seriously reduced our speed.

The Japanese in Yokohama and Tokyo mostly wore western clothing, unlike those in Sasebo. They were an impassive folk and very reticent to give their views on anything. On being asked how he liked the Americans, one of the dry dock workers replied, 'American, rich man – Englishman, gentleman.'

They gave the Americans a great deal of help and cooperation, and their general policy would seem to indicate that, by causing as little trouble as possible to the powers that be, they hoped to hasten the US exodus. This was really a wise plan, but I did not know whether it was born of the old military class, or merely Japanese popular thought. I had heard only one man openly denounce Tojo's creed, and credit him with full responsibility for the Pearl Harbor attack, although it was widely held that Tojo had acted on his own without the Imperial sanction.

Any time we had Japanese lunching on the ship, politics were never broached. In fact, their main contribution to the conversation was a loud sucking noise (especially with soup), a custom in Japan that appears to be the hallmark of very good manners. We had a visit from the local Christian ecclesiastic, who must have been over-endowed with good breeding for he advertised the meal to all and sundry within a radius of nearly 5 yards!

The USA brought over two detachments of black troops and the Japanese did not like this. I had no side on this matter. The Nippons were, after all, a conquered race and colour prejudice is a bad trait at any time: nevertheless, tact is a wonderful asset when dealing with Orientals.

The Yanks put in charge of Yokohama No 1 dry dock a man with six months' sea experience as a marine engineer. The erstwhile Japanese manager had been an executive there for 20 years, as well as having trained for five years in a British shipyard. As the Chinese would have it, 'he had lost face'.

It was really very difficult to associate the delightful Nipponese courtesy with the nefarious conduct of their soldiers. As Hamlet says, 'A man may smile and smile, and be a villain.' But I preferred to believe that any submissive person or race would act in similar manner if a certain doctrine were drilled into them for long enough.

I remember when taking part in *The Mikado* that, near the beginning of Act 2, the Mikado arrives with the chorus singing 'Mija sama, mija sama, on n'n-ma no mayé ni. Pira pira suru no wa nan gia na. Toko tonyaré tonyaré na?' I resolved to try to find out what it meant. Every time I mentioned it, people started to laugh and I began to think it might be somewhat risqué.

Finally someone said the translation was 'My prince, my prince, what is the meaning of the flag that is waving in front of your horse?' Seemingly the 'Toko tonyaré tonyaré na?' is simply expletive and is similar to our 'With a hey nonny no nonny no'.

One day I heard the tune on Japanese radio and it was altogether different from Sullivan's music. Sullivan had put it in 4/4 time as a march, whereas the Japanese version gave the impression that there were no bars, and the music just slithered along without any rhythm.

Shortage of supplies, together with the fact that the American Army doctor condemned some of our meat, forced the skipper to take US Army iron rations on board as we prepared for the voyage across to Canada. Having the same fare every day would be monotonous, but we did not grumble as it would be wholesome.

Our entrepreneurial shipmate was left with about $100 as we were about to sail. A US merchant ship had just arrived and he paid the crew a visit. Offhandedly he asked if they needed money for going ashore and they dismissed his remark, saying that they had plenty of dollars. He produced a wad of the special occupation dollars, which were different from those in common usage in the USA – one had a gold seal and the other a blue one – but I cannot remember which was which. This startled them out of their complacency and he was able to exchange his occupation dollars for the regular ones. When we reached Canada he could readily convert them to Canadian dollars at $1.10 for each US dollar.

My last ship: Part 3

He certainly was quite a character. When we were chatting on watch one evening he told me that the Yanks were the most gullible race in the world. He went on to back up this assertion by telling me stories of when he was a steward on a troop ship carrying Americans to Britain. Many of them had very expensive watches and were showing them off to him. He affected to admire them greatly, but then went on to say that they would be of no use at all in Britain because of the different climate. Many of them believed him and he was able to buy the watches from the Americans very cheaply.

The voyage across the Pacific gave us some bad weather with fierce head winds. One day, when about five days out, we were heading in an east-north-easterly direction and the head wind was particularly strong. The ship wandered off course to starboard and resisted all efforts to get her back on course. The helmsman kept holding the helm hard over to port, but to no avail. On our new course we were heading for Mexico and there was nothing we could do about it.

The trouble was that we had no cargo and no ballast, so we were very high out of the water. As the ship was trimmed down by the stern, this meant that the fore part was much higher above the sea than the after part, and the wind was catching the ship there and forcing her off course.

We sailed towards Mexico for a day then, with the wind just as powerful and coming from the same direction, we thought to balance things up by turning towards the northern part of Alaska. We were, in effect, behaving like a sailing ship and could not sail directly into the wind. If a sailing craft's destination is from where the wind is blowing, she 'tacks' – that is to say, she zigzags from side to side, moving towards her destination in a series of tacks.

Alas we could not tack, so had to do what the sailing vessels did when they could not tack. This was called 'wearing ship' and meant that, instead of going round to port, we put the helm hard a starboard and did almost a complete turn to finish up heading for the north part of Alaska. After two days of this the wind moderated a bit and we were able to sail in the direction of Canada.

You see, Plimsoll had a good idea by forcing vessels not to overload, but, had he been a sailor, he might have introduced a second line to prevent ships going to sea with too little in them and being too high out of the water. On the *Newton Pine*, and also on the *Norvarg*, we loaded rubble for ballast, but I think our owners were too mean to incur the extra expense of loading and discharging this.

Going in an easterly direction one has constantly to advance the clock. On liners they calculate the ship's approximate position for the next day, and alter the clock by a few minutes so that the sun will be on the meridian at the time of the ship's noon. Cargo ships do not bother with this refinement and wait and change their clocks by an hour at a time.

We had been steadily putting our clock forward by an hour every few days until we reached the International Date Line, when we had to compensate by turning it back 24 hours – or one full day. This meant that we had eight days in one week. In our case we had two consecutive days, both being 6 December. Now, as this was my father's anniversary, it occurred to me that, had he been on board, he would have had two birthdays in the same year – and the same week!

At sea the skipper had an easy time. He rose just before 8am and came up to the bridge to take his morning longitude sight and enquire how many miles the log was showing. After a leisurely breakfast he came back to the bridge and worked out his sight. For the rest of the morning he lazed about talking to the Mate and the Chief Engineer, and watched what was going on. At noon he came on to the bridge, took his latitude sight and, together with the 2nd and 3rd Mates, worked out the ship's position, its average speed since the previous noon, and the general average speed since the start of this leg of the voyage.

After lunch he had a nap until the steward brought him a cup of tea and a biscuit at 3pm. He then might go down to the engine room if the Chief was there and have a chat with him, but always he would come to the lower bridge at 4pm to see what was on the log. After tea the Chief Engineer went to his cabin and they played cribbage until almost the end of the first watch, when the Chief departed and the captain waited until midnight and enquired again about the log before turning in for the night.

Nearing the American continent we began to receive US radio stations. Like the Canadians, they were commercial. The famous 'Brown Bomber' Joe Louis was preparing for a title fight with Jersey Joe Walcott and I recall the skipper saying, 'Where are all the young men now, when an old man like Louis has to defend his title?'

What none of us knew at the time was that Jersey Joe was six months older than Louis and had been boxing for just over three years. The fight went the full 15 rounds with Jersey Joe hitting Louis about five times as often as Louis hit him – albeit he was retreating most of the time. The fight was declared a draw and this was an unpopular decision. Seconds after the end, an interviewer approached Louis and asked how he felt. In between bouts of heavy breathing Louis said he thought a draw was a fair verdict, whereupon the interviewer snatched the microphone from him, saying, 'Well, that was a close shave, Joe

– but not as close a shave as you get with Gillette!'

It took us 28 days 2 hours and 25 minutes to do the 4,252 miles across the Pacific, giving an average speed of just 6.3 knots, and resulted in our losing the charter for grain and general cargo. This meant that we now had to take a mixed cargo of wheat and timber. Our first port of call was Nanaimo on Vancouver Island. We spent a day there loading coal for our bunkers before setting off for the town of Vancouver, which is on the mainland.

Approaching Vancouver was an ordeal for me. The 3rd Mate's work when a pilot is on board is to relay his helm orders to the man at the wheel and to respond to the pilot's engine orders (slow ahead, stop her, half astern, etc) by ringing the command down to the engineers.

Now, I had no trouble at all with American pilots; they always gave the helm orders as 'right rudder' or 'left rudder' and such like. Unfortunately the Canadians use port and starboard – but with a transatlantic accent. We suffered from his inability to communicate properly. When he wanted the vessel stopped he would yell 'Stop her', but it sounded like 'Stap her' and, from a distance of about 10 yards away, and with the pilot having a pipe stuck in his mouth, it was indistinguishable from 'Starboard', the accent in both cases being on the first syllable.

Before we had left Middlesbrough all the officers had had to submit to the owners a request for stores. When I found out that we were not going back to Pepel but going round the world, I put in for six red ensigns and a storm ensign (a smaller ensign used if one was obliged to fly an ensign in very breezy weather).

When the stores arrived there was only one ensign. I went to an engineer who had been several trips on the ship and asked what had gone wrong. His answer was that there was a clerk up at head office who thought he would be smart and cut back on everyone's requests, possibly to incur the owner's pleasure. He further recommended that I should do as he did, and put in for three times the quantity required so that, after the reduction, a reasonable amount was sent. I was not prepared to do this and told him so, whereupon he just remarked that I would not get my stores.

So, we sailed with only one new ensign together with two dirty ones from the previous voyage. I suppose had I wanted I could have saved the good one for special occasions and put up the old ones when our funnel was smoking furiously, but out of sheer cussedness I chose not to do so.

Now, the skipper did not normally wear uniform when entering and leaving most ports, but for Vancouver, being a high-prestige port, he was arrayed in his best uniform with the four gold bands glittering in the morning light. His chest was swelling with pride until he happened to look astern and saw the ensign.

'What the hell is that flag flying there?' he demanded to know.

'It's the red ensign,' I replied with a feigned show of meekness.

'Red? It's coal black,' said he, 'and more like the Jolly Roger. Get it down at once and put up a better one.'

'We have no better one. The others are in an even worse state.'

'What sort of bloody 3rd Mate are you, to disgrace us with an ensign like that ... in Vancouver of all places?' he stormed.

I had foreseen this event coming sooner or later and was overjoyed that it had taken place in such a port as Vancouver. Furthermore, I was fully prepared for the encounter.

'If you permit me half a minute to go to my cabin, I will show you what sort of 3rd Mate I am.'

After a very short interval I returned to the bridge with all the documents regarding the ordering of the stores.

'You will see from these forms that I ordered seven ensigns but was cut back to one.'

'Well,' said he, his bluster diminishing a great deal, 'you could have seen me about it and I might…'

'No … either I am in charge of the flags in this ship,' I cut in, 'or an office boy in Glasgow is. We cannot both be.'

This was the end of the matter as far as I was concerned. The Old Man would now have to cable the owners and ask them to send out some ensigns by express air-mail. He obviously would protect his own reputation by giving them the full facts. This would be an expensive business and the owners would take the clerk to task over it and he would think twice before being so presumptuous in future.

17

My last ship: part 4

We spent three days in Vancouver loading wheat. A day was wasted when the Canadian authorities condemned some of our equipment and the items had to be replaced. This was a wonderful city and everyone enjoyed our brief sojourn very much.

Some time before we reached Vancouver two British ships had arrived with immigrants. However, these were immigrants with a difference. Two British shipping companies found themselves in the position of having to return ships to the Canadian Government, and were faced with the expense of having to put up the crews in hotels and pay their fares home. They hit on the idea of advertising for any officers or ratings that wanted to settle around Vancouver and, in due course, signed on two complete crews apart from the skippers and Chief Engineers. There were mutual advantages in this plan. The owners would not have to pay hotel bills and the cost of shipping the crews home, and the ships' complements would not only save passage money but would receive payment for their work on the voyage.

It turned out all right for the shipping companies, but not for the men. The sailors were looking for work as riggers or dockers, but the Canadian unions closed the door on these jobs. The engine room members were faced with similar restrictions. Part of the trouble I suspect was the unwillingness of the officers to roll up their sleeves and do manual work. Driving a lorry at that time did not pay much in Britain, but in Canada it was quite different. Also, had they gone to a lumber camp the lowest-paid job there was the whistle man, who gave the signal when trees were being felled and was paid $50 a week. The end of this sad tale was that by the time we arrived there were only four men left out of two crews!

Once the grain was loaded we set off up the Frazer River to the smaller town of New Westminster and began loading Douglas fir – sometimes known as Oregon pine. New Westminster was reputed to be the oldest city in Western Canada.

Our stay here lasted 15 days and I enjoyed every minute of it. Timber was, of course, abundant here and, with the exception of banks, municipal buildings, etc, all the dwellings were wooden, and quite magnificent.

The climate was similar to that in Britain, save for being a few degrees warmer all the year round. It is on a western seaboard and, like back home, one was never sure whether or not to take a raincoat when going out.

The cargo superintendent became friendly with me and invited the Chief Engineer, the Mate and me to his house in North Vancouver for Christmas dinner. Having heard some of our records he asked if I would bring some to his house as they were keen on classical music. I had misgiving about this, having had experience of folk saying to me that they were fond of opera, then asking if I could play them *Show Boat* or something similar.

The dinner was really something. They produced the biggest turkey I had ever seen – it looked more like an ostrich! Having had a reasonable Christmas lunch on board the *Celtic Monarch*, we were soon at bursting point after this second feast. I had brought only two gramophone records with me and, as soon as they were played, I was subjected to some appalling dance music.

I realised that I would have to look as if I was enjoying it, so put a feigned look of pleasure on my dial. I suffered in silence for the space of 30 minutes when their daughter, of 20 years or so, asked if I would care to meet her uncle who lived only a short distance away. I think the cargo superintendent appreciated that the two of us were in a different age group and would be happier on our own and he raised no objections.

The uncle happened to be the president of the local Gilbert and Sullivan Society and had the complete Savoy operas on records. We had a wonderful evening and I was invited back for a second recital. The cargo superintendent kindly responded by driving me to his house for that evening, putting me up for the night and taking me back to the ship next morning.

The second evening was as good as the first. The uncle had 2,000 records, all in albums in a sort of bookcase, and catalogued with meticulous care. I could not help noticing that there were not many complete operas in the collection. The transatlantics went in more for individual singers; thus we had an album of Gigli singing Puccini, one of Melchior doing arias from Wagner operas, and another of Tibbett giving recitals of Verdi, and so on. I gave him the translation of the passage of Japanese in *The Mikado* and he was overjoyed.

We went for a few evenings to Vancouver, although it was 40 minutes on the train to get there. For one of the dances I took with me the two junior apprentices, dressed in their best uniforms. The ploy

My last ship: Part 4

was highly successful and they were besieged by females, the older ones taking a motherly interest and the younger crowd hoping for some dances with them. Once I was fixed up with someone of my own age, I gave the signal that it was now every man for himself.

As a consequence of this I, together with seven other officers and a steward, had an invitation to go to a house in Vancouver to take in the New Year. This proved to be a most enjoyable occasion. We brought some grub and drink with us and handed it over to the lassies. They supplied us with a drink every hour, on the hour, so that we were constantly in a merry mood but no one was drunk. When it came to midnight they all began banging pots and pans, which appeared to be their way of bringing in the New Year.

We had had a goodly meal so it was a case of off with the navy blue and gold braid, on with an apron and, with rolled-up sleeves, pitching in with the washing-up. I led the merry band to the sink where there were so many dishes that we jokingly suggested to the girls that they had brought in some of their neighbours' crockery.

After a thoroughly good time the girls toasted our health. The steward, who was a bit older than the rest of us and made a little bit maudlin by the booze, proposed a serious toast to the ladies of Vancouver, ending by saying, 'God bless them.' This was greeted without great enthusiasm, so he sheepishly asked if anyone else wanted to make a toast. Recognising that it would be better to restore some of the former levity, I assumed a very grave expression and said, 'To wives and sweethearts' and, just as the company were lifting their glasses, I added, 'May they never meet.' This was received with much hilarity. It was in the very small hours of the morning that I arrived back at the ship.

The hospitality was staggering. One lad on the ship had been telephoning a number when the operator invited him for Christmas dinner. I met up with a charming family with three daughters. Together with two engineers off another ship I regularly visited them and their father and mother, who were splendid types, more like a big brother and sister. Their Dad used to drive me back to the ship.

I received mail from home and was dismayed to learn that their food rations were still very tight and that motoring was banned after 7pm. There was also a big cut in clothing coupons, and just at this time the fashion designers were bringing out something they chose to call the 'new look'. The pre-war skirts were knee length and the new ones stretched down to the middle of the calf. When clothing material was in such limited supply I failed to understand why the Government did not step in and put a stop to this nonsense.

Our magazines were all from the USA and seemed to indicate

that a war with the Soviet Union was inevitable. Ever since the cessation of hostilities, the Americans had been pumping out anti-Soviet propaganda with ever-increasing fervour. This led me to conclude that the USA had a bigger communist element within its own walls than I had hitherto suspected. Of course, communism was always a sort of bogey in the States, a red rag to the American bull. But since communism is a doctrine that commonly has its roots in bad conditions, dissatisfaction among the workers, extremes of wealth, etc, there must have been some cause for its growth apart from external influences sponsored by Moscow.

I could not help but feel that the USA was responsible for much of the present unrest; with her atomic bomb tests coming, as they did, so soon after the armistice. It just did not seem like the actions of a nation desiring a lasting peace.

All this led me to put aside any thought of sitting a Chief Mate's certificate. If I passed the exam and went back to sea and a war broke out, I would be at sea until it ended, or until I had notched up enough sea time to sit for my Master's ticket. But if I stayed on at sea, I could get three months ashore to sit for the Chief Mate's ticket.

Unfortunately all good things come to an end and we sailed down the Frazer River heading for Vancouver Island and a port called Cowichan Bay, which was on its east coast. This was a small village that seemed to be composed entirely of Red Indians and there was a reservation nearby. As well as loading the timber, they tried to sell us hand-made pullovers with moose designs on them. At $20 (£5) a time I thought this was a bit dear and an inflated tourist price. We were four days there and shipped more Douglas fir, hemlock and cedar.

Arthur and I had to make cargo plans as the stuff was being loaded. Canada used the same terms as the USA. Some of the pieces were for railway sleepers, which they termed 'ties'. There were longer ones specially made for where sets of points occur, and for short distances, had to support two lines of rail. We called these 'points sleepers' but they were listed as 'switch ties'.

From Cowichan Bay we sailed to Victoria, which, as well as being the main town on the island, was the capital of the province of British Columbia. The people in Vancouver had painted a gloomy picture of the place, saying that it was full of 'remittance men'. This was a new term to me, and meant that many of the black sheep of British families were posted there to be out of circulation, and sent money (remittance) to stay there. It was certainly quieter that Vancouver but was nevertheless very pleasant and agreeable. It dawned on me that the real reason for folk in Vancouver disliking Victoria was that it had a shortage of beer parlours.

We continued to take on board timber. By now the holds were full and we were having to load it on to the tops of the hatches, which was normal practice. Timber being less dense than other cargoes, we could have a lot of it on deck before the ship was down to the load line.

I took the chance to buy some more food here. There was tinned butter on offer but what happened was that one bought the butter then took it to a different part of the building to have it tinned on the spot at 7 cents a tin. The trouble was that it was not hermetically sealed – merely dumped into a tin and taken to a fancy hand-operated machine (many folks there had machines of their own) so that it would have to be kept reasonably cool on the passage home. The lad that did the 'tinning' told me that if it was not in top condition when I reached home, to wash it in salt water and it would be fully restored to health.

Instead of completing loading at Victoria we had a change of plans and had to proceed to Port Alberni, a small town on the west coast of Vancouver Island. Alberni and Port Alberni were two small towns, the first having one cinema and the other two. Port Alberni was said to be the salmon capital of the world, and boasted all five species of Pacific salmon.

There is a custom on merchant ships, when painting the ship's hull in a foreign port, to finish up by painting the vessel's name on the dock. I noticed that 'Trevaylion' had been freshly painted and, since Robert Cromb was in her crew, I reckoned that I had not missed him by any more than a few days.

I must say I enjoyed my stay in British Columbia. It would no doubt have been better still had we visited one or two ports instead of six. However, I was assured that we were lucky to get off so lightly – one South African vessel had to call at no fewer than 16 ports in as many days, which must surely have been a record.

Just before leaving we took on board a Swede as a steward. He was being deported from Canada for illegal entry, and as a trumpet player he fitted nicely into our music circle.

Before departing from Canada Arthur and I had a conference. We were not at all sure that enough food would be loaded for the voyage home, and decided to take turns at checking all stores coming on board. After doing so, we did some calculations with the quantities and the number in the crew and found that it was very tight generally, but for tea and sugar there was an insufficiency. We resolved to demand, if it should prove necessary, our dry stores of tea and sugar each week from the steward, and look after ourselves.

Leaving Port Alberni on 15 January 1948 we headed for Panama.

We had gone less than 2 miles down the 37-mile canal (known as the Alberni canal) when dense fog set in. After two unsuccessful attempts to continue, we anchored for the night. Next day we left in very good weather and sailed down the west coat of the USA.

By 24 January we were off the coast of Mexico in continuing fine weather. The old tub was knocking up 200 miles a day, which was really good for her.

It was about this time that we received instructions to destroy some of the extra stuff that had been put into the lifeboats for the war period. One was a packet marked 'energy tablets'. Arthur imagined that these would supply him with immense amounts of vim and vigour (possibly enabling him to climb up the forestay hand over hand without using his feet), and consumed quite a few.

Next watch, when someone came to wake him he was completely out to the wide, and had to be literally hauled out of his bunk. What these tablets were meant for was to keep men awake when some vital requirement arose, possibly when they were in a lifeboat. Arthur had stayed awake for hours and had fallen asleep just half an hour before he was due to go on watch.

On 7 February we passed through the Panama Canal for the third time. There was some trouble when the pilot came on board and wanted Captain Keir to sign a paper to the effect that the Panama authorities would not take any responsibility for the safety of the ship, and absolving the pilots from all blame in case of an accident. The skipper refused to do so and demanded to know the whys and wherefores of such a request.

The joke was that we were designated by them to be a 'low-powered vessel with a history of mechanical failure'. I expect that they had got their information from Lloyd's. Anyway, the Old Man and the pilot had quite an argument and it ended up with the Americans agreeing to take us through if we managed up to the first lock without a breakdown or without the aid of a tug. We just managed this.

At the time I considered their description of us very funny but, writing this more than 60 years later, I shudder to think of the *Celtic Monarch* having to battle her way round the tip of South America.

We had had exceptionally fine weather from Canada to Bilbao and averaged nearly 8 knots, but as we were rounding the headland to sail up the Gulf of Panama the shore authorities timed us and we were not making even 6 knots. I could not blame the Americans. After all, it was their canal and no one wanted an old wreck jamming up the works, especially when a lock at Miraflores was undergoing a three-month repair.

We came back to Jamaica for the third time with serious boiler trouble. Orders came through that we were to unload the timber at Dundee and go on to Leith to discharge the grain.

Our usual fixture with the local Jamaican team was arranged and we were beaten 3-0. After licking our wounds we thought of picking the best team from the *Celtic Monarch* and another ship in Jamaica, strangely enough named the *Port Alberni*. The Swede was a very good player, but I cannot recall why I was picked to play.

So, six from the *Celtic Monarch* and five from the *Port Alberni* faced up to the opposition. The first half ended with us down by 0-2. We did a bit better in the second half, and when the 90 minutes was up we were only down by 2-3. This was very good considering that we played a lot of the time with only nine men, the Swede being one of the injured. Oddly enough, the referee decided to add on 10 minutes for stoppage time. This was fatal – we went to pieces and were beaten 2-7. The game ended in darkness and one could hardly see the ball.

Employment was very bad in Jamaica and there was little provision made for those idle. As a result of this there were numerous attempts to stow away. I caught 16 on my watch one night and Arthur had found nine the previous night. Strictly speaking we should have handed them over to the police for a $10 fine or a 30-day sentence, but we did not do so, as we felt sorry for them. They did not seem to understand that taking them off the ship was for their own good. The deck timber was lashed very tightly with wire ropes tightened by a bottle screw. Despite this, we knew that once the vessel was subjected to rolling, the timber would shift and have to be retightened. The intended stowaways jammed themselves into small spaces between the timber and would likely have been crushed to death in a heavy seaway.

The island was then fighting for its independence but I doubted if it would have made much difference to the rank and file. They had some kind of government of their own, and the British Governor left almost everything in its hands.

Leaving Jamaica we went through the Windward Passage between Cuba and Haiti. But how would we go to Dundee? The northerly route through the Pentland Firth was 375 miles shorter than going up the English Channel but there was a good chance of having bad weather. The alternative, though longer, was almost certain to provide better conditions. Captain Keir was all for going north about while his three Mates were united in favouring the southerly course.

The skipper decided to compromise. He planned to pick a spot halfway to the UK, and halfway between the two tracks and make for this. The idea was that, arriving at that place, he could then choose whether to go north or south.

The relative distances may not be apparent on the usual atlas based on a Mercator projection, which tries to present a global world on a flat surface. As the meridians converge on the globe, but run parallel on the flat adaptation, the Mercator map has to make some allowance for this or the land masses will be hopelessly out of shape. Mercator decided to increase the distances between the lines of latitude to compensate for the meridians being parallel and not converging. This keeps all the areas in perfect shape but out of scale. The further north you go the greater the distortion becomes until you reach the poles, when their points are represented by lines the length of the equator! This makes Greenland look a lot larger than Australia, although it is actually much smaller. Also, the shortest routes on the globe are shown on Mercator maps as lines curving towards the poles.

On the third day out the steward refused to give us tea for supper and offered cocoa in its place. This had happened once before, so Arthur and I demanded our Board of Trade rations. We had made a full list of the stores loaded in Canada and calculated that, at 3oz per man per week (perhaps), we had enough to last us until 22 March – so we demanded our legal rights.

Our 3oz allowance was weighed for us out each week, and now we were sure of a decent brew instead of the watery, probably thrice-infused, stuff that was dished out in the saloon. I was all for drawing our quota of sugar, but Arthur disagreed, so we settled on forcing the steward to give the tea ration for the first week, then to see how things were going.

Our campaign began. Arthur, being the senior, dined first and had most of the embarrassment. He brewed up his own tea and poured it out in the saloon. The skipper would not be drawn and said never a word. After the meal Arthur would take the teapot to the galley and add more water and, if necessary, dry tea before going on to the bridge to relieve me. I would then take it from the galley, sit in the saloon and help myself to tea from this pot – with still no response from the Old Man. I suppose there was nothing he could have done, for we were legally entitled to the Board of Trade rations.

We continued on the skipper's compromise course but struck an exceptionally violent storm that lasted 26 hours. It covered a huge area giving strong gales nearly 800 miles from the centre of the depression. The ship refused to steer and would head only in a south-south-westerly direction, and this was the best we could do.

She weathered it passably well, all things considered, and the deck cargo did not behave as badly as I had expected. One of our lifeboats was in a poor state, and the timber on the foredeck shifted and left lovely bends in the two for'ard derricks. The bulkhead outside the Chief Engineer's cabin caved in nearly an inch, while the deckhead rose almost 1½ inches, it must have been some sea that caused that lot.

This particular storm was a bit unorthodox and did not behave according to the laws of storms in the northern hemisphere. We were blown many miles off our track but, when we were able to resume steering, we made for the position that the skipper wanted. Our Radio Officer picked up a broadcast from the *Queen Elizabeth* stating that she was forced to reduce her speed to less than 12 knots.

Just to be awkward, when the storm abated we got rain and fog but no sun, leaving us to wonder where the devil we were. When the sun did appear at last, we got a position that put us 800 miles from Cape Wrath and 700 miles from Land's End. The Chief Engineer reported that we had 380 tons of coal left, some of it Japanese stuff, which was not good for steaming purposes.

The skipper was now on the horns of a dilemma. The north track was still 400 miles shorter and this amount of fuel could take us the remaining 1,030 miles to Dundee quite easily, but only if we did not meet any tough weather. On the other hand, the coal would certainly not be sufficient to reach Dundee via the English Channel, but we could call in at Falmouth for bunkers. The fact that our fresh water had almost disappeared seemed not to enter into the argument.

On 10 March we were back on the northern route. There was a large anticyclone in our area and this gave us a strong breeze behind us. We had to run before it or risk losing steering way, but it took us only 10 degrees off our intended course, and that was not at all bad.

At noon that day we had exactly 700 miles left to Dundee, so the bolder spirits and perennial optimists were reckoning on which tide we would catch on 14 March. I was not so sure because we still had the Pentland Firth to go through. The weather was surprisingly good for the time of year and our temperature stood at 50°F, while 800 miles to the south they were getting barely 45°F.

We sped through the Pentland Firth at 13 knots – about 6 of which were due to the strong flood tide. Just as we were halfway through, the Chief Engineer came on to the bridge to tell the skipper that we had boiler trouble and would have to stop. Of course, the Old Man told him we would need to clear the land first. I do not know how it was managed, for they had been using salt water in the boiler for the past five days, but we did reach Dundee. Since our draught was almost 20 feet we had to wait for a tide to enter the harbour.

A ship that had left Jamaica 12 hours after us, and had taken the southern route, had arrived a few hours before us and was now discharging her cargo. The good news was that we were to unload all our cargo at Dundee and would pay off there.

When we tied up Arthur had the first evening on watch while I made off for the shore. Rumour had it that the women in Dundee outnumbered the men by five to one, and I wanted to check this statistic for myself.

I caught up with another sailor off a neighbouring ship and we were exchanging experiences. He advised me that the Customs were very strict in Dundee but I told him that I had no worries on that account as we had run short of tobacco and I did not even have my 200 duty-free allowance. I went on to say that I had a lot more than the 25lb of food but, since we had been away for a long time, I did not think they would be particularly worried about this. He replied that they were very particular and that their 'flying squad' would be through from Methyl at 8am the next morning and would give the ship a thorough going over.

I was in two minds whether to return to the ship, but the five-to-one ratio of the sexes was too compelling to ignore. Surely the Customs would make us a special case. If we had been on the North Atlantic run we could have made at least nine trips in this time and landed a total of 225lb quite legally.

At the end of the evening I met Arthur, who had been told a similar tale about the Customs. After some discussion we decided to do nothing that night but to order a taxi for 7.15am next morning. I asked who would call us and Arthur said he had fixed it for the shore night watchman to give him a shake.

'Do you think he's reliable?' I asked. Arthur assured me that he was an old sailing-ship man and that was almost a guarantee of trust.

I must have had nearly 80lb of food, while Arthur, though he had less than a quarter of this, had half a Canadian hundredweight (50lb) bag of white flour – then a very scarce commodity at home.

To make assurance doubly sure, as the Bard would say, I went to this worthy watchman and told him, 'Don't wake the 2nd Mate. He doesn't sleep but dies and has to be resurrected. You make sure to wake me.'

Arthur and I then took all the food that was over the allowance and set it aside, ready to take to the railway left-luggage office in suitcases the next morning.

As it turned out, the watchman did not give either of us a call and, at about 7.20am, I woke to hear an irate voice announce that some 'rotten bastard' had ordered a taxi and that he would not wait a moment longer. This put mettle in my heels and, tumbling out of bed, I promised the driver that we would be ready in 5 minutes.

The Mate, who had passed only a moment before, got the shock of his life to see Arthur and me in our No 1 uniforms hurrying down

My last ship: Part 4

the gangway with the surplus grub. Into the taxi we went and, as the bag of flour was dumped in the back, a huge shower of white dust arose.

'Look at the mess you've made,' complained the driver.

'Never mind it,' we answered. 'Drive on and you'll get double fare.'

We reached the dock gates just as the Customs were entering.

By the time we arrived at the left-luggage office, the flour dust was all over us, and our navy blue uniforms looked more like tropical whites. The population of Dundee must have sensed we were up to something judging by the looks we received.

Returning to the *Celtic Monarch*, we met the Customs and showed them what was left of the food. One of them actually added up the weight of each tin.

In our chart room we had several books to help navigation. One of these was Burdwood's *Sun's True Bearing or Azimuth Tables*. It had a claret-coloured cover, but the most interesting point was that, on this cover, in stylish gold lettering, was inscribed the words 'Stolen from S.S. Celtic Monarch'. Now, I had never stolen anything from a ship in all my days at sea, but here I decided to make an exception. When I finally went down the gangway it was in my kitbag. It was not in great condition and it did not seem like stealing; it was more a case of turning a lie into the truth!

Reminiscing over my time at sea I realised that, despite being a maritime nation, we do not hold our merchant seamen in high esteem. If a Dutch or Scandinavian sailor, in his own country, is asked what occupation he follows and replies that he is a 2nd Mate of a cargo ship, he is immediately deemed to be a person worthy of respect. Not so in Britain. Although to become a 2nd Mate takes four years on deck, followed by a successful result in an examination lasting the best part of a week, he is not accorded anything like the status that other nations give to their seafarers.

As for UK ship owners (apart from the few top-class ones), they must be about the worst in the world. I was in a position to compare them with Norwegians, and the British could not hold a candle to Scandinavian companies.

As for field days, the tradition of having to work 10 hours on days of sailing or arrival without overtime, the appalling accommodation for their crews, the inferior food and the habit of classing certain work as 'for the safety of ship' and refusing overtime for it, all this would have been anathema to Norwegian owners.

In addition, the vastly superior life-saving equipment showed just how much the Norwegians valued their seamen. As for the niggardly practice of paying 7s 6d for a single radio bearing (and hoping that the sun would appear next day) when two bearings would have fixed the ship's position for a total of 15 shillings was a combination of frugality and stupidity!

A few months earlier I had designed a type of azimuth mirror. The normal azimuth was used to take compass bearings of heavenly bodies and objects ashore. Going up an estuary one could take what are called transit bearings – these are bearings of two objects in a direct line. Now, the ship is definitely on this line regardless of any compass error and, if one takes a compass bearing at the same time, the difference is the compass error, and by taking another bearing and applying this error, we have a fixed position.

The trouble is that good transit bearings are hard to come by for various reasons, the main one being that if they are too close together they will not give an accurate line. Coming up an estuary it is common to find lighthouses and other landmarks on both sides of the estuary. I used to keep taking bearings of two suitable landmarks until they were exactly 180° apart. The ship would now be on a straight line connecting the two landmarks and this was better than most transit bearings.

This practice was a bit tedious, which is why I thought of creating an azimuth mirror that could line up the objects when they were 180° apart, and save all the effort of taking umpteen bearings. Just as I was thinking of applying for a patent it occurred to me that all the better-class companies were now going on to gyro compasses like the *Athelregent*'s, where there was a constant and fixed error. The other poorer-class ones (that grudged paying a paltry 7s 6d for an extra radio bearing) would be most unlikely to beat a path to my door to buy a new azimuth mirror!

*

So here endeth the tale. The exceptionally cold winter of 1947 had had a profound effect on my life. Had I managed to go home to Glasgow I probably could have got a grant to go to university. As it was, the Government had handed out these grants like confetti and it seemed that the funds were fast running out. I was asked to provide proof that I had sought civil engineering employment in 1939, otherwise my case would be 'very weak'. I immediately produced two letters testifying to this, but their refusal came back almost by return of post, which proved that, had they been waiting on this final piece of evidence to give my case consideration, the consideration given must have been very scant indeed.

My last ship: Part 4

Going back to 1947, if I had then failed to get a grant I could have sat for my Chief Mate's Certificate. So, either way I felt aggrieved.

Yet it was a wonderful sensation to be back in Britain at last. I began looking on the brighter side of the voyage. The year was not entirely wasted. I now realised that I had learned a lot more mathematics, had been one and a half times round the world, crossed the International Date Line, had been three times through the Panama Canal, once through the Suez Canal and had seen many new countries.

Conditions on the *Celtic Monarch* during this voyage had been little short of appalling. Despite this I had a grudging admiration for Captain Keir as a fine seaman – also, he was a man, and you do not see a man every time you open your eyes. To be fair to him, I fancy the real villains of the piece were Raeburn & Verel Ltd or, to be more specific, their superintendent, who, you may recall, shut off our lights in Middlesbrough and tried to blame the Coal Board for it. At any rate I rated the skipper well above the Mate, who was a shallow character.

Failing to get to university, I should have liked to have had another five or six years at sea – but what would I have come ashore to? Jobs as harbour masters or as marine surveyors were most difficult to come by and I was still haunted by the memory of seeing scores of ships anchored in the Clyde Estuary in the 1930s because of the depression.

I gave up the sea ('swallowed the anchor' as the saying goes) and came ashore for good. Later I gave up the notion of becoming a civil engineer and settled instead for being a civil servant. So, in a way, I achieved half of my ambition, the 'civil' part – though I dare say many of my superiors would dispute that!

Appendix: Background to ships and the sea

Ships in my time were measured and registered in gross tons and net tons. Neither of these terms is related in any way to tons or tonnes, but is a throwback to the old days when ships carried tuns of wine, and a gross ton was supposedly the measurement of the space taken up by one tun. This was taken to be 100 cubic feet.

The gross tonnage is the measurement of the total enclosed space in the vessel, and the net tonnage is the gross tonnage less the volume taken up by the 'non-earning' space, such as the crew's quarters, engine room, storage spaces, etc. Thus the *Reina del Pacifico*'s gross tonnage was about 17,700 and her net tonnage was 10,719.

On the other hand, the displacement tonnage is the weight of the quantity of water displaced by the vessel when floating at the load draught. Put simply, it is the total weight of the ship and her cargo when fully loaded.

The deadweight tonnage is the number of imperial tons (2,240lb) of cargo, stores, etc, that a vessel is capable of carrying when she is floating at her load draught.

Another point that seems to cause difficulty is when the ship's speed is referred to in knots. Many people talk about knots per hour. This is a nonsense. A knot is one nautical mile (6,080 feet) per hour. The problem appears to be caused by the phonetic connection between knot and nautical.

Long ago, before patent logs were introduced, the ship's speed was found by the following method. A small piece of wood was weighted at one end so that it would float upright and stay in the one spot. Attached to this was a line with a number of knots on it. A sand-glass was turned upside down and, during the period it took to empty, a sailor counted the number of knots that passed as the line was paid out.

The trick was that the distance between the knots bore the same relation to a nautical mile as the number of seconds for the glass to empty did to an hour. So, if the sand-glass was timed to drain in 28 seconds, the distance between each knot would have to be 47.3 feet. Thus if nine knots passed in the allotted time, the vessel's speed was said to be 9 knots.

Appendix: Background to ships and the sea

There are seven watches when a ship is at sea:

Midnight to 4am	The middle watch
4am to 8am	The morning watch
8am to noon	The forenoon watch
Noon to 4pm	The afternoon watch
4pm to 6pm	The first dog watch
6pm to 8pm	The second dog watch
8pm to midnight	The first watch

The dog watches were originally designed for the days when there were two watches on a ship – port and starboard. Both watches worked 4 hours on, then 4 hours off. By splitting the 4pm to 8pm watch into two separate spells, it meant that neither watch would always be landed with a bad watch such as the midnight to 4am period, commonly referred to as the 'dead man's watch' or the 'graveyard watch'.

When a third watch was introduced, the crew worked 4 hours on and 8 hours off. Obviously one watch would now always have the midnight to 4am stint.

To be fair, the watches were chosen by lot, and changed from time to time. As I write this, those crews on coasting trade still have the old 4 on and 4 off arrangement.

The helmsman would ring the bells every half hour, starting at 30 minutes from the beginning of the watch, when he would strike one bell; 1 hour into the watch he struck two bells; 1½ hours in he struck three bells; and so on until the end of the watch, when he sounded eight bells.

Because the dog watch was at one time split into two, the second dog watch did not sound five bells at 6.30pm, as one would expect, but started again with one bell, then two bells at 7pm and finally eight bells at 8pm.

It is practice to sound one bell 15 minutes before the start of a new watch to give the seamen warning that they are about to go on deck; at midnight on 31 December 16 bells are struck – eight to see out the old year, and another eight to welcome in the new one.

A further complication is that, on merchant ships, seven bells on the morning and the forenoon watches are sounded at 7.20am and 11.20am instead of 7.30am and 11.30am in order to give the watch coming on deck an extra 10 minutes for breakfast and lunch.

The man at the wheel sounds the bells in pairs, so that for five bells he would strike two pairs of strokes followed by a single one.

The bell on the fo'c'sle head is used when weighing anchor. The anchor cable is known as a cable length and is roughly one-tenth of a nautical mile – that is, about 600 feet or 100 fathoms. This is divided into ten short lengths called shackles, because the lengths are joined together with shackles. It would be impossible to make a permanent mark on this cable with paint so, at the first shackle from the anchor, a wire is wound round the first link from the shackle. Similarly a wire is fixed to the second link from the second shackle, and so on. This lets the crew know what length of cable is out. It is usual when taking in the anchor to strike bells denoting what shackle is in the water. Unlike the bells on the bridge, these are sounded singly and not in pairs.

At the bow there are two anchors, each with its own length of chain. They are known as bower anchors. Usually lashed to the deck on the fo'c'sle head is another anchor kept as a spare and known as a 'sheet anchor'. Often at the stern is an anchor called a 'stream anchor', and this is used while anchored in a river when it is essential that the vessel keeps in her position.

Except for during wars, when no lights of any kind were shown, the man on lookout duty would, every half hour on hearing the helmsman strike the bells, look to see if the masthead and navigations lights were satisfactorily lit. He would then turn and call out to the officer on the bridge, 'Lights are bright, sir.' To which the officer would make reply by answering, 'Aye, aye.'

As it was difficult to distinguish words at the distance from the fo'c'sle head (or crow's-nest) to the bridge, there were many variations of this report. One of the most popular was, 'Go and have a shite, sir', and there was much merriment in the crew's quarters at hearing the officer gratefully acknowledge this request.

The fathom as a unit of measure came into use as a quick method of determining length. A sailor picked up a piece of rope and stretched it from fingertip to fingertip, and this length was known as a fathom. Naturally all sailors have different lengths of arms, and the sailor gets to know how much extra or less he needs to allow when measuring.

At sea the word forecastle – used to denote the living quarters of the lower deck members of the crew – was always shortened to fo'c'sle. Similarly the term forward was shortened to for'ard.

On liners the size of the *Reina del Pacifico* there would be about 300 in the crew; some 50 would be on deck, another 50 in the engine room and the remaining 200 in the catering department. Most of the stewards did not act as waiters but carried stores from place to place. Some were termed 'kitchen porters', and among their various duties was the peeling of potatoes, hence their nickname, 'spud barbers'.

As mentioned, the *Reina* had six bakers and six assistant bakers.

They were designated as 'baker/confectioner' and were responsible for providing all the dessert dishes. She had six butchers and, since they had most of the cold storage space, they stored the butter.

As a menu had to be printed out twice a day, as well as various other notices and bulletins, the ship also had a printer. I believe very large liners, where there are many flowers planted in containers, carry a gardener.

On the lower deck of liners there would be a bosun and two carpenters – they were classed as chief petty officers. Other petty officers included three bosun's mates (one in charge of each watch), six quartermasters, who did all the steering, and a lamp-trimmer, who had charge of the paint and other stores and did any splicing as required. Some ships of this size also had a petty officer known as the 'master at arms'.

Liners did not go in much for splicing wire, as they had spare ones, and could leave any splicing to the shore workers in riggers' lofts when the vessel arrived home. In cargo ships any splicing was done right away as necessary, by the crew. In an emergency one could just put a bend in the hawser and make an eye by using two bulldog grips.

It takes three years to become an AB (able seaman), but after two years or so an ordinary seaman can be signed on as a sailor or efficient deckhand. Curiously enough, he is paid the same as an AB but cannot be forced to do work above a certain height from the main deck.

On the *Reina* there were about twenty ABs (or sailors) and three ordinary seamen. This allowed her to have six ABs (or sailors) and one ordinary seaman on each watch; the other two sailors were permanently on day work (8am to 5pm).

In the engine room department on liners there would be a plumber, known as a sanitary engineer, and an electrician, who was called an electrical engineer. If the ship was burning coal, firemen stoked the furnaces. Others, termed trimmers, took the coal from the bunkers to the firemen. There were also greasers who were petty officers and were responsible for seeing that the many bearings were kept lubricated. The top man in the lower engine room department was the donkeyman, so called because one of his duties was to look after the donkey (or auxiliary) engine. This would be used in port when the main one was not required.

Conditions were better on liners. Seamen were given proper mattresses and not the palliasses that tramp steamers supplied. At breakfast on Tuesdays and Thursdays they had an egg, and on Sundays two eggs. Tramps had only two eggs a week, one on Thursday and one on Sunday.

Cigarettes on liners were a lot cheaper, as I understand the company managed the bond, whereas on the tramps the captain took over everything and charged what he liked! When the skipper wanted the Customs to open the bond, the red ensign had a knot tied to the fly (the part furthest from the mast) and was then hoisted as a signal.

Of course, the big advantage was that, on the liners, the watches worked 4 hours on and 8 hours off but, as explained in Chapter 3 regarding the *Newton Pine*, some tramps worked field days of 4 on 8 off, followed by 4 on 4 off.

In the old days the sailors' quarters were always up for'ard of the foremast; hence the term 'before the mast' meant to be a sailor. Later on, many ships provided accommodation under the poop deck at the stern of the vessel, but the phrase 'before the mast' continued to be used to denote someone from the lower deck.

On cargo ships, on the 4 to 8 watch one man will do the first wheel from 4 to 6, then he will work or stand by from 6 until 7 and go on lookout from 7 to 8. Next time on watch he will do 4 to 5 on lookout, 5 to 6 on work or standby, then 6 to 8 on the wheel. Lastly he will do 4 to 5 work or standby, 5 to 7 on lookout, then 7 to 8 back on work or standby. The man who did not take a turn at the wheel was known as the 'farmer'. I was told that this term was a throwback from the days when cattle were carried, and the man with the least to do looked after them, but I always have had doubts about this.

Index

Roman numerals indicate the photograph pages

Able Seaman,
    term explained 247
Acasta 76ff, VIII
Aden 218
Admiral Graf Spee 24, 25, 38, 177
Admiral Scheer 24, 25, 162
Aitchison, Tommy 173
Alexandria 126-130, 205, 213-217
Almeria, Spain 135-136
Altbea 123, 125
Altmark 38
Anchor Line 33
Anchors 246
Antwerp 164
Archibald Russell 203
Armour, Jim and Mae XIV
Arundel Castle 98-99, X
Athel Line 153, 157
Athelregent 145, 146ff, XVII
Atlantic, Battle of the 102
Avonmouth 21, 22, 49, 99

Bahia Blanca, Argentina 177, 182
Banavie 6, 10, II
Bank Line 187
Baron Inchcape 216
Baron Line 83
Beaton, Alec 14, 125
Beecham, Sir Thomas 15-16
Birkenhead 160
Bizerta, Tunisia 168

Blairgowrie 132
Blairspey 132
Boilers, ship's 204
Bonitos, fishing for 175-176
British Tradition 90ff, VIII
Bulk Fuel 154-155
Burntisland 162
Byng, Colonel 222

Caduceus 125ff, 205, XV
Caledonian Canal 6, 10, 13-14, 122, 152
California 93ff, IX;
    bombing and sinking of 95-97, 99-101
CAM (Catapult Armed Merchantman) ships 72-73, 92, VII
Cape Town 32-33
Cardiff 49-50, 61, 62
Carpenter, role at sea 113-114
Casablanca 97-98, 121
Celtic Monarch 196ff, 243, XX, XXII
Censorship 31-32
Chelmar, HMS 117, 119, 120
Chief Mate's certificate 185, 197, 201, 234, 243
Churchill, Winston 39, 54
Coal, as ship's cargo 51-52, 134, 183
Colombo, Ceylon 218-219
Convoys 28, 30, 34, 39-42, 44, 48, 51, 53-54, 59, 60, 72, 79-80, 89, 94, 100, 103, 109, 122, 147, 148;
    convoy 'FAITH' 100-101;

refuelling of escort ships at sea 85-86
Copeland 103, 109, 111, XIV
Cornwell, Captain 146, 151, 171
Cowichan Bay, Canada 234
Crews, sizes of 246-247
Cromb, Robert 32, 33, 99-100, 235
Currie, Sir Donald 122
Customs 35-36, 108-109, 163, 169, 178, 240-241

Deck boy, duties of 20ff, 34-35
DEMS (defensively equipped merchant ships) 20-21
Dentonia Park 189, 191, 183, 195, XX
Depth-charges 53
Deutschland 24, 25
Dive-bombers 44
Dockers 22-23, 165-166, 181
Dolan, Bob 91, 93, 96, 109
Dominion Monarch 23
Douglas, Captain 188
Douglas, HMS 94, 95, 96, IX
Douglas, Major 130-131, 136, 169
Duchess of York 94, 95, 98, 100
Dundee 239-240
Dunotter Castle 98
Durban 31

East London, South Africa 181-182, 184
Eddystone 103
EDH (Efficient Deck Hand) 83
Empire Blackwater 202
Empire Mariner 83, 86
Empire Spey 132, 133, XVI
Empress of Asia 23
Empress of Russia 23
Exchange rates, exploitation of 70, 163, 224, 226

Fastnet 103
Fathom, explanation of 246
Firemen and firing on board ship 38-39, 134
First-aid certificate 142-143
Fisken, Arthur 91, 93, 94, 96, 97, 98, 109, 196-197, 199, 201, 203, 205, 211, 215, 221, 224, 234, 235, 236, 238, 240, XXI, XXIII
F. J. Wolfe 83ff, VIII
Food rationing 35, 39, 62-63, 74
Football matches 179, 190, 206, 209, 211, 237
Fort Aspin 187ff, XIX
Fort Augustus 7, 13, 16, 17, I
Fort William 14-15
Fowler, Captain 43
Freetown, Sierra Leone 29, 184, 200
Fuel oil, as ship's cargo 92

Gaizka 59ff
Garthpool 126
Ghent 170
Gibraltar 130, 211, 213
Glasgow, HMS 216
Gondolier, RMS 6ff, 19, 125, 152, I
Good Hope, Cape of 30
Goodall, HMS 119
Goodwin 103, 104ff, XI, XIV
Gordon, Robert 166
Grain, as ship's cargo 46-47, 55, 179-180
Greenock 39
Gunnery course 57-58

Hair-cutting 30, 126
Halifax, Nova Scotia 52, 89, 105-107, 110, 114-116

Index

Hall Brothers, shipping company 125
Hartley, Capt W. J. DSC 110, 113, 115, 117, 121, XIV;
report of *Goodwin*'s voyage, March-April 1944 117-120
Haxton, Andy 8, 12, 17
Hendry, P. D., shipping company 162
Highland Chieftain 23, 31, V
Hill, Captain 141
Hogarth, H., shipping company 83, 173, 216
Hogben, Prof Lancelot 216
Hong Kong 220
Hood, HMS 25
Hot weather at sea, effect of 28, 29, 129, 178, 218
Huelva, Spain 163
Humby, Betty 16

Illness at sea 184-185
In Which We Serve (film) 115-116
Ingeniero White, Argentina 177, 181
Inverness 11
Iolaire, steam yacht 122ff, 132, XV
Iroquois, HMCS 94, 97

Jamaica 206, 211, 236-237

Keir, Capt John 198, 212, 213, 236, 237, 243
Kelly, HMS 116
Kenilworth Castle, HMS 119
Kingsborough Line 162
Kitbag, how to make 28
Knives, usefulness of 28-29
Knots (speed), explained 244
Knots, tying 114

Latta, Captain 141
Leander, HMS 216
Liberty Ships 74-76, VII
Lifeboats 96-97, 158, 174, 236, XX
Life jackets 64-65
Lisbon 134-135
Liverpool Docks 22-23
Loch Eil 12
Loch Ewe 56, 122, 123
Loch Fyne 6, 11, 12
Loch Garry 59, 133
Loch Ness 11, 16
Loch Lomond 57, VI
Log, ship's 43, 61, 244
Louis, Joe 228
Lourenço Marques, Mozambique 184
Lynch, Benny 17

MacBrayne's 6, 9, 10, 11, 17, 59, 124
Mackintosh, John 130, XVI
MacLay & MacIntyre, shipping company 173
MacQuarrie, Donald and Lachie 29-30, 35, 107
Manganese ore, as ship's cargo 129-130
Masunda 173ff, XVIII
Merchant navy, role in war 40, 58, 161, 241
'Mersigs' (merchant ship signals) 139, 148
Miami 157-158, XVIII
Middlesbrough 187, 201
Milford Haven 90
Mindelo, St Vincent 183
Mines, magnetic 21
Molasses, as ship's cargo 160-161
Montevideo 177
Montreal 52, 188ff

Morse code 139-140, 156-157
Moville, Ireland 82
Moyola, HMS 94, 97
Muir, Robert 107, 111, 112, 165
Muirton Wharf, Inverness 13, I

Nautical College, University of
    Southampton 59, 131, 138
Nea Hellas 33, 98
New Westminster, Canada 231
New York 44-47, 65-66,
    76-77, 81, 86-89, 154
Newcastle-upon-Tyne 56
Newton Beech 38
Newton Pine 37ff, 227, V; sunk 56
Nisbet, G. & Co,
    shipping line 132, 133
Normandie 47
North Shields 171
Norvarg 64ff, 227, VII
Norwegian
    merchant navy 64ff, 73, 241

Oldham 117, 120
Ordinary seaman, life as 37ff, 64
Orontes 21

Pacific Steam
    Navigation Co 20, 173
Panama Canal 206-207, 217,
    236, XXI
Pantry boy, duties of 6ff
Parker, Lt-Cdr 58
Pay, of seamen 11, 12, 35, 36,
    37, 55, 60, 62,
    153, 196, XXIV
Peninsular & Oriental,
    shipping line 202, 203, 204
Pepel, Sierra Leone 184, 201, 202
Philadelphia 66-69, 92, 156

Phosphate (fertiliser),
    as ship's cargo 168
Pinto 104
Plimsoll Line 201, 227
Point Fortin, Trinidad 77
Poolewe 56
Porchester Castle, HMS 117, 120
Port Alberni 237
Port Alberni, Canada 235-236
Port Elizabeth, South Africa 32
Port Everglades 157
Port Fairy 94, 97
Port of Spain, Trinidad 78-81
Port Said 215-216
Port Talbot 168
Prohibition 68

Queenstown, Ireland 61-62

Radcombe 162ff, XVII
Raeburn & Verel Ltd, shipping
    company 196, 204, 205,
    211-212, 243
Rathlin 103, 104
Reina del Pacifico 19ff, 42, 114,
    123, IV
Renown, HMS 25
Repulse, HMS 24, 25, 26,
    29, 30, IV
Rescue Ships 102ff, XI-XIII
Richards, Anne 69, 92
Robb, David 187, 190-193, XX
Rosa, Jack 49
Rothesay 65
Royal College of Science &
    Technology 138, XVII
Royal Naval Reserves (RNR) 58
Royal Navy Volunteer
    Reserves (RNVR) 58
Royal Oak, HMS 152
Ruth 117, 119, 120

Saint Columba 6

Index

St Johns,
   Newfoundland 166-167
St Sunniva 104
Sasebo, Japan 220, 221-223, XXIII
2nd Mate's certificate 59, 131, 137, 138ff
Secondi, Gold Coast 129
Sfax, Tunisia 168
Shaw Saville & Albion,
   shipping company 173
Signalling 139, 148
Sinclair, Captain 175, 178, 181
Singapore 220
Smuggling 109-110
Sobieski 24
South Africa 182
South America 117, 118, 121, XV
Splicing rope and wire 16, 247
Stankeld 179
Steel, John XXI
Steering ships 42
Stirling Castle 24
Stockport 104
Strathaird 23
Stratheden 24
Suez Canal 217-218
Sunburn, dangers of 25
Swale, HMS 94, 97
Sydney Cape Breton 47-48, 53

Takoradi, Gold Coast 129-130
Tankers, safety of 93
Terneusen, Netherlands 170
Thomson, Eric XXI
Timber, as ship's cargo 235
Tocopilla, Chile 208-210
Tokyo 224-225
Tonnage, ships', explained 244
Torpedoes 79-80
Toward 103, 104
Tuscania 33

U-boats 40-41, 53, 65-66, 79, 82, 85, 98-99, 102, 121, 152; *Das Boot* (film) 153
Uniform, naval 58, 123-124, 229-230;
   dungarees 27
Unions, seamen's 202, 211-212
United States,
   wartime life in 44-47, 67, 70-73, 87-89, 156
USSR, in WWII 36, 234

V weapons ('doodle-bugs') 127, 132, 136
Vancouver 229-233
Victoria, British Columbia 234

Wabana, Newfoundland 166
Walmer Castle 104
War, declaration of 17;
   air raids 21, 22;
   USA joins 66;
   end of 152
Watches, at sea 20, 42-43, 54, 147, 149, 163, 196-197, 245, 248
Waterguards *see* Customs
Watt, David 14-15, III
Weir, Andrew,
   shipping company 187
Wishart, Jack 114
'Woolworth' aircraft carriers 92
Workington 136-137

Yokohama, Japan 223, 225-226

Zaafaran 104

Further reading from Silver Link...

Horton's Guide to Britain's Railways in Feature Films
Updated 2nd edition
Glyn Horton

The first movie guide for the British railway enthusiast!

Railways and the cinema have a long association, from early silent films to Harry Potter. This enlarged second edition lists almost 1,000 feature films that have British railway content, and gives details of where the sequences were filmed, whether on the contemporary railway or more recently using the facilities of today's preserved lines.

The first film to use a railway as part of the storyline was the saucy A Kiss in the Tunnel in 1900. Since then hundreds of feature films have used railways as a backdrop or as an important plot ingredient, including Train of Events, The Titfield Thunderbolt, The Ladykillers, Oh Mr Porter, The Railway Children and, more recently, several of the 'James Bond' and 'Harry Potter' films, as well as many where the railway – steam, diesel or electric – makes a brief and tantalising appearance, unwittingly providing a living archive of railway footage.

- Enlarged and updated second edition
- The railway element of almost 1,000 films described, from 1900 to the present day
- Steam, diesel and electric – contemporary scenes and preserved railways
- Includes trams, the London Underground and Irish railway scenes
- Filming locations identified
- Howlers, continuity errors and fascinating trivia

Glyn Horton is a lifelong railway enthusiast with a degree in Film Studies. He contributes to film websites, and lives and works in South Wales. His book is the result of 10 years' research.

234 x 153mm   208 pages   40 b&w illustrations 24 pages plates
978 1 85794 334 4   Paperback   £17.99

An Illustrated History of Cardiff Docks

Volume 3: The Cardiff Railway Company and the docks at war

John Hutton

The concluding volume of this trilogy concentrates on two main aspects of the history of Cardiff Docks. The first is the ill-fated Cardiff Railway, built under considerable difficulty to tap the South Wales coalfield but blocked by its rival the Taff Vale Railway. The second main focus is a vivid depiction of the docks during the air raids of the Second World War, when considerable damage was caused to track, stock, buildings and shipping. Also included are portraits of the directors and staff of the railway and docks, and descriptions of the various locomotive sheds that served the docks.

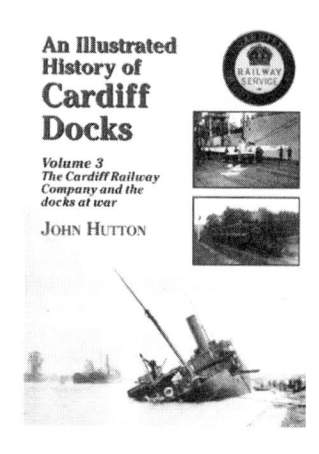

Covering a century of industrial history with more than 360 photographs, maps and items of ephemera, many from the extensive archive of Associated British Ports, this comprehensive volume vividly portrays the vastly complex dockland and railway operations in an area of little more than a square mile that nonetheless contained some 120 miles of track – almost unimaginable when one compares it with today's glittering Cardiff Bay waterfront development.

John Hutton was brought up in a mining community in the North East before joining the Army and serving for three years in the Royal Corps of Transport. Moving to Cardiff, he worked in the prison service there for 15 years, and it was during that time that his deep interest in the area's railways and docks was born, together with a strong desire to reveal their history to younger generations. For the past 18 years he has worked as a prison officer in Portland, Dorset.

238 x 172mm   160 pages   Approx 360 photographs
978 1 85794 309 2   **Paperback**   £19.99

THE RECOLLECTIONS SERIES

The aim of this series is to appeal to readers of all ages, perhaps for different reasons...
For the younger reader there are wonderful pictures of trains, real trains. There will, for example, be tank engines, steam engines, electric trains and multiple units and many more varieties besides! Some will be recognised from train sets, model railways and books, while others will be seen for the first time. For the older reader the books are designed to build into a collection placing the railway in the context of key events thus providing an historical perspective of travel in times past. For those old enough to remember the years depicted, the series will, we hope, provide reminders for many of school days, time perhaps spent train-spotting, shed bashing and generally gricing! The books also make ideal theme gifts for the year of birth, marriage, retirement, starting work and other such events in life. Many volumes in the series include happenings away from the railway in the particular year, including political events, sporting events, the hit records of the year and arrivals and departures.

RAILWAYS

VOLUME 1: 1956
978 1 85794 274 3 Paperback RPND

VOLUME 2: 1964
978 1 85794 275 0 Paperback RPND

VOLUME 3: 1973
978 1 85794 276 7 Paperback RPND

VOLUME 4: 1981
978 1 85794 277 4 Paperback £4.99

VOLUME 5: 1964 ISLE OF MAN
978 1 85794 278 1 Paperback £4.99

VOLUME 8: 1957
978 1 85794 291 0 Paperback £4.99

VOLUME 9: 1961
978 1 85794 292 7 Paperback £4.99

VOLUME 10: 1963
978 1 85794 296 5 Paperback £4.99

VOLUME 11: 1975
978 1 85794 294 1 Paperback £4.99

VOLUME 13: 1967 *Farewell to Southern Steam*
978 1 85794 336 8 Paperback £4.99

VOLUME 14: 1955
978 1 85794 337 5 Paperback £4.99

VOLUME 15: 1961 Part 2
978 1 85794 338 2 Paperback £4.99

VOLUME (13) 1967
978 1 85794 336 8 Paperback £4.99

VOLUME (14) 1955
978 1 85794 337 5 Paperback £4.99

VOLUME (15) 1961 (Part 2)
978 1 85794 333 7 Paperback £4.99

VOLUME 16: Severn Valley Railway
978 1 85794 353 5 Paperback £5.99 (Colour)

VOLUME 17: West Somerset Railway
978 1 85794 360 3 Paperback £5.99 (Colour)

TRAMS

VOLUME 6: 1971 BLACKPOOL
978 1 85794 280 4 Paperback £4.99

COACHES AND BUSES

VOLUME 7: 1959 MIDLAND RED
978 1 85794 301 6 Paperback £4.99

VOLUME 12: 1958 BIRMINGHAM BUSES
978 1 85794 325 2 Paperback RPND

AVIATION

AQUILA TO MADEIRA
978 1 85794 351 1 Paperback RPND

RPND *Reprint no date*